COMMERCIAL TELEVISION AND EUROP

The editors wish to thank the Wharton School, University of Pennsylvania and the Children's Committee of the European Advertising Agencies Association for their support.

Commercial Television and European Children

An International Research Digest

Edited by

SCOTT WARD
Professor of Marketing, Wharton School,
University of Pennsylvania and
Senior Research Associate,
Marketing Science Institute

TOM ROBERTSON
Associate Dean and Professor of Marketing,
Wharton School, University of Pennsylvania

RAY BROWN
Media Consultant, London

Gower

Published by
Gower Publishing Company Limited,
Gower House,
Croft Road,
Aldershot,
Hants GU11 3HR,
England

Gower Publishing Company,
Old Post Road,
Brookfield,
Vermont 05036,
U.S.A.

SB 29173 /18.50 .2.86.

British Library Cataloguing in Publication Data

Commercial television and European children : an
   international research digest.
   1. Television advertising and children
   I. Ward, Scott   II. Robertson, Tom
   III. Brown, Ray
   305.2'3   HQ784.T4

ISBN 0 566 05073 0

Printed in Great Britain

Contents

PART I

Introduction and conference agenda

This publication contains the proceedings of the research conference, "International Perspectives on Television Advertising and Children: The Role of Research for Policy Issues in Europe" held in Provence, France, July 1st-3rd 1984.

The conference was organized as a result of the spread of transborder advertising by satellite and growth of private broadcasting and mass media services generally. These had given rise to concern in Europe about the possible effects of advertising on children - and television advertising in particular. Sponsorship was obtained from: The Lauder Institute of the Wharton Business School at the The University of Pennsylvania, and the Children's Committee of the European Advertising Agencies Association.

The objective of the conference was to provide leading academics in Europe with an opportunity to exchange knowledge about advertising and children and identify appropriate avenues for future research. It was felt that the wealth of research-based expertise which had accumulated in Europe would both prove invaluable in future discussions on the subject, and provide a framework to improve understanding of the complex issues involved.

It was further believed that empirical research would provide a sounder foundation for decision-making than polemic or one-sided arguments - which are frequently based on anecdotal evidence and personal perceptions.

Finally, when considering the need for the conference two further observations emerged: although a large quantity of existing research has been done outside Europe, some of the results are trans-cultural and of relevance to the European child; secondly, as Europe and the rest of the world converge through the increased use of electronic communications systems, so too must research perspectives and theories.

Taking these observations altogether, the following conference objectives emerged:

1. To summarize existing research in Europe relevant to policy issues concerning television advertising and children;

2. To establish the relevance of worldwide research to the European child;

3. To identify areas where further information is required in Europe.

In identifying researchers in Western European countries who have interests in children and television, it was considered vital that the conference include those who could support their empirical research with theoretical models. Possible invitees were obtained by reviewing academic journals in Western Europe, and from individuals with extensive contacts in the European academic community.*

The call for papers requested contributions in two areas:

1. Conceptual or empirical "macro-level" studies which focus broadly on the role of television advertising in children's lives, and

2. "Micro-level" conceptual or empirical studies examining the processes and mechanisms by which children process information in television advertising.

These two perspectives reflected the desire to invite individuals whose backgrounds and interests lay in the "macro-level" disciplines of sociology, anthropology, economics and cultural studies, and other individuals who specialise in the "micro-level" disciplines of psychology, child development and communications research.

The key elements which speakers were requested to address for the conference, were decided in advance. However, it soon became clear from the keen, informed, response to the call for papers, that discussion of these key elements would be further enhanced by additional input from a wider range of viewpoints. It was therefore decided, to invite selected

_____

* In particular, Aimee Dorr (University of California, Los Angeles) and Gerry Lesser (Harvard) were helpful and research directors of relevant industry bodies within Europe.

individuals to present short papers in the role of "discussants", as well as requesting full papers from principal speakers.

The drafts which were received concentrated on four major, relevant, areas: (1) those focusing on age-related differences among children in responding to television advertising; (2) micro-processes of children's processing of information in television advertising; (3) parent-child relationships relating to children's reactions to television advertising and (4) consumer socialization - that is, patterns by which children develop knowledge, attitudes and skills relevant to consumer behaviour.

Given the time constraints of a two-day seminar, 11 principle papers were selected which best fitted the seminar's objectives and which also represented a cross-section of European countries and disciplines. The only regret was being unable to invite all those who had submitted relevant drafts to the meeting.

The conference was finally composed of 20 participants from eight European countries and two speakers from the United States: the participants represented a variety of disciplines - from economics to psychology and child psychiatry to media education.

It is to be noted that this particular conference was unique in several ways - and not just in the quality of research presented or depth of discussion stimulated. Its "uniqueness" perhaps, lay in the fact, that for the first time, a small group of academics came together from a wide variety of disciplines and cultures, to discuss a common theme and shared interest with international implications. It is the sincere hope of the participants, the organizers and the sponsors that the conclusions drawn from this meeting will receive the attention, discussion and status they merit.

AGE-RELATED DIFFERENCES IN CHILDREN'S REACTIONS TO TELEVISION ADVERTISING

Speakers	Subject
Prof. Scott Ward (United States)	"How children understand with age"
Dr. Theo Poeisz (Holland)	"Children's relationships between repetition and affect; theory, research & policy implications"
Dr. Brian Young (United Kingdom)	"New approaches to old problems; the growth of advertising literacy"

Discussant

Prof. Kaj Wickbom (Sweden)	"Media education and critical awareness of television advertising"

MICRO-PROCESSES OF CHILDREN'S RESPONSE TO ADVERTISING

Speakers	Subject
Prof. Liisa Uusitalo (Finland)	"The symbolic dynamics of television viewing"
Prof. F. van Raaij (Holland)	"Cognitive & affective effects of TV advertising on children"

Discussants

Dr. P. Vitouch (Austria)	"The influence of word-picture relationships of TV films on the emotional reactions and retention performance of children"
Prof. Hertha Sturm (Germany)	"Children's perception processing of TV advertising - the missing half - second"
Dr. M. Grewe-Partsch	"Emotional aspects of television"

PARENT—CHILD RELATIONSHIPS RELATING TO TV ADVERTISING

Speakers	Subject
Prof. J.N. Kapferer (France)	"A comparison of TV advertising and mother's influence on children's attitudes and values"
Prof. T. Robertson (United States)	"Intra-family processes - the American experience"
Prof. P. Graham (United Kingdom)	"Relevance of parent—child interactions"

Discussants

Madame D. Lassarre (France)	"The child consumer in the French family"
Mr. C. Cullingford (United Kingdom)	"Children and advertising - a recent experience"

CONSUMER—SOCIALISATION AND TV ADVERTISING

Speakers	Subject
Mr. R.A. Sander (Germany)	'The role of Mass—Media in modern society"
Dr. K. Grunert (Germany)	"Television advertising, product preferences and consumer socialisation: A German perspective".
Dr. Asle Dahl (Norway)	"The role for TV advertising in consumer socialisation in Norway".

Discussants

Dr. B. Tufte (Denmark)	"TV advertising as a future socialising, factor in Denmark's children".
Mr. E. Williams (United Kingdom)	"Consumer socialisation".

We were pleased also to call upon the expertise of Professors J. Halloran (U.K.) and Hilda Himmelweit (U.K.) for the duration of the Seminar.

PART II

Summary and overview

The central purpose of the seminar was to exchange information and ideas about policy-related research on advertising and children among European researchers with demonstrated interests in the area.

OVERALL CONCLUSIONS

Given the relatively recent emergence of concerns about advertising and children in Europe, and the resulting surge of interest among academic researchers in this area, it is not surprising that the seminar's overall conclusions dealt more with specifying areas for needed research, and research approaches, than with summarising existing research. There seemed to be some general agreement on the following conclusions:

Effects of television advertising on children

While television advertising has a variety of effects on children,

- these effects are no more or less pronounced and significant than effects of other influences on children;

- TV advertising effects are strongly mediated by the child's environment, especially the family unit;

- empirical research can present ways of viewing the interaction of children and television advertising, and data concerning the incidence; it cannot specify "good" and "bad" effects of television advertising, which is dependent on the value-position of individuals.

The variables and processes involved in television advertising's effects on children are relatively universal. However, the degree of influence of some variables and the magnitude of their effects may vary, depending on the environment in different cultures. For example, the family plays a crucial role in mediating effects of television advertising on children, but the magnitude of family influences may vary due to differences in cultural norms governing parent-child relationships, incidence of television advertising, and so forth.

Relevance of North American research to European children

Existing North American research which is most relevant to European children concerns age-related differences in children's responses to advertising. This is because such age-related differences are relatively universal. However, North American research has focused largely on Piagetian and information-processing frameworks for understanding effects of television advertising on children. It has generally not proceeded from a more integrated and complete view of the child's world, and this lack of breadth in American research has two consequences: first, the role of television in children's lives is not put into perspective, and second, American research has focused on effects of television without examining the broader context of children's uses of television, the gratifications they obtain from the medium and the even broader context of television's role in the family and cultural environment. Research in Europe should seek to extend our knowledge of these broader contexts for television.

Approaches to Research

- There is no, one, "best" theoretical framework for structuring research in this area;

- Studies of television advertising and children must take environmental characteristics into account -- especially the role of the family;

- Research should focus on basic processes of children across cultures, rather than pursue differences which may occur as a function of structural characteristics of specific countries or cultures;

- Research should be oriented toward process models for understanding the role of advertising in children's lives, rather than simple input-output "effects" models which measure effects of some independent variables on depended variables. That is, we should seek to understand the processes by which some effects develop, rather than just document the incidence of such effects.

OVERVIEW OF PRESENTATIONS

The seminar consisted of four sessions, each devoted to a particular content area: age-related differences, microprocesses, parent-child relationships, and consumer socialisation. These four areas seem to represent the most important streams of research in previous work in this field, and they are highly relevant for many of the issues concerning advertising and children which are being raised in Europe.

In his opening paper, Prof. Scott Ward (Wharton School, University of Pennsylvania, USA) suggested a framework for structuring many of the issues concerning advertising and children, and attempted to summarise the existing North American research relevant to these issues. While nine specific issues were identified in an earlier study, [1] Ward attempted to conceptualise these issues in terms of their underlying dimensions. One conceptualisation encompasses two underlying dimensions: the duration of effects (long-versus short-term), and the type of effect (cognitive vs. behavioural). Another conceptualisation includes the bases and the focus of specific concerns. For example, some people base their concerns about advertising's effects on children on their percep- tions of age-related differences in children's abilities to properly evaluate advertising. Their focus of concern might be on the effects of particular message characteristics on children at different ages.

Ward then identified the major theoretical streams which have guided North American research in the area. These streams are [1] social- isation theory, [2] modeling theory, [3] learning theory, and [4] cog- nitive development theory. The latter theoretical area -- identified with the Swiss psychologist, Jean Piaget -- has dominated studies of age-related differences in children's responses to advertising, since the theory is useful in describing age-related differences in children's perceptual and cognitive abilities to process environmental stimuli. The major concepts of this theory are reviewed, and empirical findings are presented concerning empirical issues which underlie concerns about age-related differences in children's abilities vis-a-vis television advertising. Based on previous research, Ward presents the following conclusions:

---

[1] Nine issues were identified in a study funded by the National Science Foundation in the United States. These were: [1] children's ability to distinguish television commercials from program materials' [2] the influence of format and audio-visual techniques on childrens' perception of commercial messages; [3] source effects and self-concept appeals in children's television advertising; [4] the effects of premium offers in children's television advertising; [5] the impact on children of Proprietary medicine advertising; [6] the effects on children of television food advertising; [7] the effects of volume and repetition of television commercials; [8] the impact of television advertising on consumer socialisation; and [9] television advertising and parent-child relations. Also, a useful review of issues posed in various countries by J.J. Boddewyn, "Advertising to Children: An International Survey" (New York: International Advertising Association, 1979).

[1] Children are not necessarily confused by advertising but are, rather, cognitively limited in their ability to gather and efficiently analyse information from a variety of relevant sources, a "limitation" which rapidly decreases with age and experience; nor have particular message characteristics been shown to significantly contribute to this hypothesised "confusion effect".

[2] Even very young children have been shown to be able to differentiate programming and commercials, although the basis on which they do so (frequently perceptual or affective cues) is not likely to be as sophisticated (or as readily articulated) as the conceptual grounds on which older children make this distinction.

[3] Heavy television viewers at all age levels are more "vulnerable" to advertising persuasion because of their greater aggregate exposure to commercial messages; children's attitudinal defenses to advertising increase with age; the behavioural effects of advertising on children (manifested by expressed desire for advertised products and purchase requests made to parents) is mediated by family structures and processes.

[4] By the age of 8, the vast majority of children do understand advertising's selling intent; research indicates that about 50% of 5-6 year-olds are aware of the purpose of commercials, although they have some difficulty verbalising this awareness.

[5] Studies show that recall, comprehension, and learning of both advertising and programming content may actually be inhibited by "blocking" of advertising, since research has found patterns of fatigue and loss of attention to unbroken programming stimuli.

Ward argues that age-related differences in children's perceptual and cognitive abilities have been demonstrated to be relatively insensitive to cultural differences. Therefore, research on age-related differences in children's responses to advertising may be less important than research in other areas, since existing research is applicable to issues in all countries.

Theo Poiesz Department of Economic Psychology, Tilburg University, Holland) and J.W.J.M. Van Gerwen (Institute for Residential Family Treatment, Rotterdam, Holland) present results of two experiments testing the relationship between children's liking of stimuli -- such as advertised products, or brand names -- and frequency of exposure to the stimuli. Psychologists have long noted that when subjects are exposed to unfamiliar stimuli, such as Chinese language characters or nonsense syllables, they come to express liking (positive affect) for stimuli to which they are most frequently exposed, compared to less frequently encountered stimuli. This is known as the "mere exposure" hypothesis, or, simply, "familiarity breeds liking". Reinterpreting this hypothesis Poiesz and Van Gerwen speculate that positive affects may result from what they call "functional exposure". By this they mean that frequently exposed stimuli are functional in that they reduce the uncertainty of the task with which a subject is faced in an experimental situation. Extrapolating to the real world, the "functional exposure" hypothesis suggests that repetition of a commercial or brand name becomes functional for an individual in that uncertainty is reduced, at least under moderate conditions of risk.

If the "functional exposure" hypothesis is correct, then we might expect the counter-intuitive result that older children would express greater liking of frequently appearing stimuli than younger children. This might be because younger children find frequent exposure confusing and distracting, while older children perceive that frequently encountered stimuli may be useful in reducing task-related uncertainty. This is precisely what Poiesz and Van Gerwen find in their two experiments. While the authors caution that the stimuli used were not commercials or brand names, and the research was conducted in a laboratory setting instead of in the natural television viewing environment, they suggest two hypotheses based on their findings:

[1] Exposure frequency of brand names does have an influence on positive affect under conditions of a moderate degree of perceived risk;

[2] Age plays a mediating role in the frequency-affect relationship, such that, counter-intuitively, older children may be more responsive to frequently appearing stimuli compared to younger children because they are more able to use the information.

Brian Young (Department of Sociological and Anthropological Science, University of Salford, UK) presented a theoretical paper in which he examines how children develop what he calls "advertising literacy". Young's training as a linguist, with special interest in language development, leads him to severely question research which attempts to assess children's comprehension of television advertising by verbal questioning. He notes that when very young children are asked questions about advertising, their limited answers lead many to conclude that they are confused and perhaps misled by advertising. However, their responses may be due to verbal production deficiencies, rather than to actual miscomprehension. Studies which have used other, non-verbal measures, suggest that children may know more than they can say. Young observes that children seem to "sort" television into two categories -- commercials and all other content -- by the time they are 2½. The root problem, in Young's view, is that true comprehension of television advertising, and children's verbalisations of their comprehension, depends on their making several conceptual and linguistic associations -- for example, between advertising, the product, buying, and so forth. Nonetheless, true comprehension of any stimuli, including advertising, depends upon cognitive processing abilities, in a Piagetian sense, or the ability to "stand back" from language or communication events, in the linguistic sense, in order to understand them. For example, this kind of skill is required for adults and children to appreciate metaphors, puns, and other linguistic conventions.

Young states that his notion of advertising literacy is related to the work of Dorr et al in the more general area of television literacy. Young's objective would be to encourage the development of children's understanding of "forms and conventions used in programmes, comprehension of television narrative, distinguishing between fantasy, role-playing and reality, as well as appreciation of the process underlying television production." He suggests that the notion of advertising literacy is relatively value-free, in that the approach is not aligned with any special interest groups. Moreover, Young concludes that a central advantage of the advertising literacy approach is that: it focuses attention on issues of curriculum development if placed in an educational context whereas an "effects" model suggests to the concerned parent or educationalist the need to put a protective shield around the child against the onslaught of commercial advertising, an approach that has regulatory consequences as opposed to the more positive consequences of the former.

We posed four questions to structure our discussion of the papers in the session:

[1] What specific measurement approaches should be used in research on children's relations to advertising?

[2] What are the most important dependant variables to focus on in assessing age-related research: e.g., awareness, attention, retention, comprehension, patterns of information use?

[3] What means can serve to augment the development of children's abilities to understand commercials?

[4] Is there any real need for further research in Europe on age-related differences?

Regarding the first question, it seems clear that one must be exceedingly careful in using verbal measures exclusively in research on age-related differences in children's reactions to television advertising. Non-verbal measures are often preferable, but have the difficulty of being limited to elementary aspects of children's responses to advertising. That is, non-verbal measures are seemingly most useful in assessing children's recall, and recognition, but are less useful in gauging more complex dimensions of their reactions, such as comprehension and patterns of information use. It may be more useful to consider using a variety of verbal and non-verbal measures, particularly in research with young children.

Regarding the second question, concerning the relative utility of research on various aspects of children's responses to commercials, there was no unanimous verdict on which variables are most important. While most previous research has focused on the more elementary variables -- attention, awareness of what commercials are, understanding their persuasive intent, etc., it was felt that these variables need to be included in studies of the more complex reactions, such as comprehension and patterns of information use. There was some feeling that research should focus on the entire process of different-aged children's responses to commercials, rather than on any single part of their reactions. This feeling reflects the participants' interest in process-oriented research, as opposed to studies which merely focus on particular effects of advertising as noted earlier.

There was some consensus that it is quite possible to instruct children to augment their abilities to develop understanding of commercials --

along the lines, perhaps, of the provocative "advertising literacy" ideas expressed by Brian Young. In addition to the extensive media education project in Sweden described by Kaj Wickbom, it was noted that some curriculum development toward these goals has been carried out in the U.S. and Canada.

Finally, it was concluded that the research in the area of age-related differences in children's responses may be somewhat less important than research in the other areas, because much, if not most, of the North American research has focused on this area, and results are relatively insensitive to cultural and national differences.

MICRO-PROCESSES

The session on micro-processes aimed to examine the individual mechanisms and processes which constitute children's cognitive responses to television advertising. Stated differently: given exposure to a television commercial, and some degree of attention to it, what processes go on "inside the head" of a child which can be said to constitute some cognitive response to the commercial?

Liisa Uusitalo (Helsinki School of Economics, Finland) provides a comprehensive review and assessment of important theoretical paradigms which could be used to study micro-processes of children's responses to television advertising. She begins by noting the various interests and points of view which shape what she calls "discourses" or approaches to analysis in this area. The "Consumer Policy" discourse is based on a normative model of rational decision-making, and aims to restrict advertising. Its major deficiency is its normative emphasis: consumer behaviour may not always be "rational" in the economist's sense of the word. That is, consumers may not always maximise their behaviour —they may simply seek solutions -- and they may not absorb all relevant information -- they may selectively choose and use information relevant to a purchase.

The "Creative Advertising" discourse is of most concern to creators of advertising, who use copy tests, experience, and intuition to guide their efforts to produce effective commercials on a case-by-case basis. The major problem with this discourse is that advertisers do not seek systematic understanding of the processes underlying desirable effects of advertising. Consequently, there is no theory or model to provide a basis for testing various hypotheses, or a basis to accumulate and transmit understanding.

The "scientific" discourse is employed by academic researchers, and focuses on measurable effects of communications. It is limited because it ignores the larger context of television viewing, such as cultural codes and symbols affecting both what is communicated and how communication is processed by individuals.

These "discourses" or approaches to studying television, form separate contexts for various theoretical paradigms used to carry out television research. Uusitalo reviews paradigms which have been little used in television research but which could be useful in studies of television advertising and children. For example, she notes that psychoanalytic concepts are useful, since they emphasise the "passive transference" processes by which individuals relate unconscious processes and feelings to the flow of television events; the theory of film could focus research on product-specific characteristics (e.g. codes), type-characteristics (drama, dialogue, etc.) and narrative characteristic (visualisation, sound) which comprise television commercials.

Uusitalo provides an extended discussion of another paradigm which she believes could be particularly useful. This is the "uses and gratifications" approach or the "functional" approach to understanding media affects. In contrast to the "passive" model provided by psychoanalytic theory, the "uses and gratifications" approach emphasises an active television viewer who uses television to provide certain gratifications or functions — to provide information, social integration, and/or emotional gratification. In Uusitalo's view, little has been done to explore children's emotional gratifications resulting from exposure to television advertising, although studies in this area could reveal much about children's abilities to understand social and stylistic codes (what she calls "cultural competencies"). Moreover, Uusitalo argues that studying children's emotional gratifications from television could give new insight into their cognitive processing of commercials -- in particular, how they come to establish what is relevant and what is not, and how they conceptualise products and services from what they see.

W. Fred van Raaij (Erasmus University, Rotterdam, The Netherlands) presents a model of cognitive and affective effects of advertising on children. He applies important concepts and variables from studies of information-processing among adults, and offers hypotheses about the applicability of these variables and concepts to questions of children's processing of television advertising.

For van Raaij, processing a television commercial involves four complex sets of variables: [1] commercial variables, such as information content in the commercial, its repetition, etc: [2] environmental or antecedent variables, such as how "involved" with the product or with viewing the commercial an individual is, and how much distraction is in the viewing environment; [3] processing variables, such as whether viewers counter-argue when they see a commercial, derogate or react positively to the commercial source, and so on; and [4] consequences, such as formation and change of attitudes, preferences, and the like.

In his paper, van Raaij also presents a model which portrays each of the "micro" processes which may occur when individuals are exposed to a television commercial, and he posits a set of hypotheses pertaining to children's commercial processing. These hypotheses refer to cognitive elaboration processes (internal arguments for or against what is being said in the commercial), social elaboration (learning social codes and skills as a function of commercial portrayals), and affective reactions (liking and disliking) as a function of children's age and product involvement.

Discussion papers for the "micro-processes" session were presented by Peter Vitouch (Institute of Psychology, University of Vienna) and by Prof. Dr. Hertha Sturm and Dr. Marianne Grewe-Partsch (both of the

Erziehungswissenschaftliche Hochschule Landau, Germany). Drs. Sturm and Grewe-Partsch examine the processes by which children classify and label what they see on television. In reviewing various studies, Grewe-Partsch notes that children forget television content, but recall emotional states generated by television viewing for as long as three weeks. Moreover, very young children show difficulties in directing their attention to television materials, but they are significantly aided by verbal cues to direct their attention. Greater learning from television results from programming which is paced, in that children have a moment to label what they see on television -- that is to differentiate and code what they see in terms of personal reactions, such as liking or disliking, happiness, and so forth. This is what the German authors call "the missing half-second", to refer to this time for reaction, differentiation, and coding.

Peter Vitouch explores children's reactions in detail. He uses physiological measures, such as changes in galvanic skin resistance, heart rate, and respiratory rate, as objective measures of children's reactions to television. In his experiment, children were shown one of three versions of a program broadcast on Austrian television. The program was broadcast without words -- only background music, to describe how a child attempts to prevent his snowman from melting as Spring approaches. In a second version, the program includes "matter of fact" text, which merely labels in objective fashion, what is shown on the television screen. In the third version, emotions are added, to convey the portrayed child's feelings about his odyssey with the snowman.

Vitouch's results show that the "matter of fact" version was experienced very aversively by children, as gauged by physiological measures; moreover, this version resulted in less recall, and was rated as less pleasant than the other versions. The emotional version resulted in much greater recall of program elements. Moreover, when examining cognitive and physiological reactions at 10 points in time during viewing of the film, the children show greater variation over the period of watching; they also recall those scenes rated as pleasant more than those rated as less pleasant.

The papers by Vitouch and by Sturm and Grewe-Partsch demonstrate that microscopic aspects of children's responses to television can be gauged. More importantly, they show that children can utilise paced materials in order to categorise what they see on television, and relate it to their emotions and experiences.

They also show that children are highly selective in their viewing, showing variations in emotional reactions, and showing differences in recall depending on their emotional reactions. Stated quite simply: the notion of a passive child in front of the television set is simply not appropriate. Children respond to what they see on television, and properly paced materials can aid them in categorising, recalling, and understanding what they see.

Taken together, the papers in this session provide some tentative answers as well as some interesting hypotheses pertaining to the questions we posed:

1. What micro-processes do children bring to TV viewing?
    What particular micro-processes should be studied to better under-
    stand children's reactions to television?

2. How do children develop cognitive mechanisms to select, evaluate,
    and use information in advertising?

3. What are the significant differences in the cognitive processes
    underlying children's responses to TV advertising?

4. What are the relationships between exposure, affect, and behaviour?

5. What is the role of the particular advertising message in children's
    abilities to understand, evaluate, and use information in that
    message?

Regarding the micro-processes children "bring to" television viewing,
van Raaij presents an extremely useful review and synthesis; Vitouch,
Grewe-Partsch, and Sturm provide a microscopic view, and Uusitalo
approaches the first question from a broader point of view. Her remarks
suggest that the micro-processes posed by the others could be taken in a
more holistic context -- that is, by considering reactions to television
viewing, and by considering a broader set of message and processing
variables to include cultural codes and symbols.

Regarding the formation of cognitive mechanism, van Raaij suggests that
it is still an open question whether children's information processing
is qualitatively different from that of adults, or whether their processing is simply a more constrained model compared to adults. He does
suggest that children first develop enactive (motor) codes -- for
example, rehearsing jingles they hear in commercials. They also develop
imagery codes, which represent the products they see. These become
active when the situation calls for it -- for example, when they see
products in the store, or when their parents ask them about their
product desires. These types of codes may be the genesis of the cognitive processes van Raaij describes.

These codes may also be developed as children respond and categorise
what they see, as Vitouch, Grewe-Partsch and Sturm demonstrate.

Regarding the other questions, van Raaij suggests that the variables
which comprise cognitive processing may be similar across media, but the
precise operations may vary depending on the media.

For example, print media allow for "self-pacing" while broadcast media
provide an opportunity for attention and immediate processing only as
long as commercials appear on the screen. The relationships between
variables -- exposure, affect, and behaviour -- are well discussed by
van Raaij. In particular, his paper provides a useful and complete view
of the complex processing which individuals undergo as they see a
television commercial. The relationship between viewing a commercial
and behaviour is surely not a simple "stimulus-response" one; van Raaij
documents the powerful mediating processes whch intervene between
exposure and behaviour, and Vitouch, Sturm and Grewe-Partsch present
data concerning physiological, cognitive and emotional mediators of
television context.

Parent-child relationships relating to TV advertising

The second day of the conference was devoted to "macro-level" effects of television advertising. This term refers to effects which extend beyond individual cognitive reactions. For example, the relationship of advertising and parent-child relationships, and the effects of advertising on consumer socialisation processes.

It is important to study how parents mediate the effects of television advertising. For example, they may set rules about how much television a child watches, and they may routinely agree to buy -- or not buy -- products or services which children want, if these are seen as engendered by television advertising. Children may ask parents to buy things they see advertised on television, which may be desirable and encouraged by parents in some cases (for example, when parents ask their children to watch television in order to construct a list of Christmas gifts), or undesirable in other cases (such as when children may nag their parents to buy things).

Prof. Thomas S. Robertson (Wharton School, University of Pennsylvania, U.S.A.) summarised findings from research in this area done in North America. Parents generally express negative attitudes about advertising in spite of the fact that it provides financial support for television programming in the US commercial broadcasting system. Parental mediation has been studied primarily in the context of how often parents and children watch television together. Such co-viewing does not happen often, and occurs only rarely during children's programming times. Research has found that children ask their parents to buy things for them an average of 13 times per month. The frequency of asking behaviour decreases with age, perhaps owing to the fact that older children have more money to spend and they enjoy greater independence in buying behaviour. Also, parents know children's favorite products and brands, so asking behaviour is no longer necessary.

The kinds of products and services children request track their age-related interests: younger children ask for snack foods and toys, and older children are more likely to ask for clothing, records, and the like. Parents are more likely to agree to buy things children ask for as their children grow older; intra-family conflict about purchase requests is quite rare, and parents most often simply agree to buy inexpensive things their children request, and report discussing more expensive purchase requests.

A limited amount of research has been done about processes by which parents "instruct" their children to evaluate commercials, engage in buying activity, with children and so on. It has been found that purposive discussions about commercials with younger children (under 7 years of age) are effective in encouraging the development of some consumer skills, while older children learn more effectively from observing their parents' behaviour, than from directed discussions.

Jean-Noel M. Kapferer (CESA, France) presented findings from an empirical study comparing television advertising and mothers' influence on childrens attitudes and values. Kapferer is critical of previous research which has examined the influence of television on children who

21

are "heavy" vs. "light" TV viewers. Such research has reported that heavy viewers become more "materialistic" in their attitudes and outlook than do children who watch less television. Kapferer argues that one must control for the influence of parental attitudes, and this is precisely what he did in a study of 2500 French children between eight and fifteen years of age, and their parents.

He found that heavy viewers of television differed little from light viewers, and when differences were found, they were most often attributable to parental attitudes and values. Interestingly, Kapferer reports that heavy viewers of television report less dissatisfacton with advertised products that do light viewers -- a finding which contradicts previous research conducted in North America. Kapferer's explanation of this finding echoes the notion expressed earlier by Theo Poiesz that frequent exposure to commercials may result in the information becoming more functional, or useful, for the viewer.

Professor Philip Graham (Institute of Child Health, London, U.K.), a child psychiatrist, presented a paper from the vantage point of his experiences in dealing with disturbed children. He suggests that the impact of requests for products which may or may not be generated by television advertising may seem trivial in comparison with other intra-family stresses which characterise disturbed families. In any case, conflict and stress in parent-child relationships is an unavoidable and normal aspect of family life. The issue is whether advertising - engendered requests produces abnormal and dysfunctional stress.

There was general consensus that the family unit plays a primary role in mediating advertising's influences on children, but research has not penetrated the key questions of exactly what parental mediation does and how it does it. This was identified as an important area for future research.

In discussion papers, Cedric Cullingford (Faculty of Educational Studies, Oxford Polytechnic, England), and Madame Dominique Lassarre, (Laboratory de Psychologie Sociale, France), presented other views of television advertising in the context of family processes. Cedric Cullingford presented data from extensive personal interviews with a large sample of young children concerning advertising. He noted that children's reactions to advertising can be analysed at several levels, from information about products, effects on buying habits, reactions to particular themes, and so forth. Children's attitudes toward advertising are highly complex, particularly as they respond to fantasy versus other content and form in advertising in making distinctions about what is true and what is fantasy. Their responses to advertising, as well as broader sets of preferences are to some extent conditioned by the family, but the precise mechanisms by which families condition children's reactions to commercials are not yet known.

Madame Lassarre speculated on the nature of these mechanisms in her discussion of the child consumer in the French family. She notes that the attitudes and habits of parents are strong influences on emerging patterns of product preferences and buying behaviour among children.

We structured the following questions to guide our discussion in this area:

1. What aspects of children's reactions to TV advertising are affected by particular parental attitudes?

2. What particular cultural values are most important in studying the role of advertising in parent-child relationships?

3. What conclusions can be drawn concerning the strength of the parent-child relationship and its effects on mediating the impact of television on children?

4. What kinds of parental activity can usefully serve to develop children's abilities to evaluate and use advertising information?

5. What conclusions can be drawn about children's requests for products in the family?

Regarding the first question, it was agreed that differences in cultural values may affect patterns of parent-child relationships, and, therefore, the ways in which parents mediate television's influences. Such cultural values may also shape the kinds of parental activities which shapes children's abilities to evaluate and use advertising information. The age-related effects of parent-child discussions and observational learning may vary by culture: moreover, the frequency and nature of children's purchase requests may vary from the U.S. finding of 13 per month, and parental responses to children's requests may also vary between cultures.

Regarding the cultural values which are important in studying the role of advertising in parent-child relationships, there may be some values which transcend cultures, and form a universal influence. For example, traditions of thrift, the wisdom of carefully considering purchases, as well as more specific values which govern aspects of parent child relationships ("respect for elders") may exist in many cultures. Nevertheless, we do not have extensive data concerning the extent to which the strength of the parent-child relationship mediates advertising's impact. We do know, from American research, that children in families characterised by a high amount of direct interaction (discussions) about buying, show greater levels of consumer skills. This finding is relevant to the 3rd and 4th questions. Research in Europe might test this finding from American research, and delve more specifically into the nature of parent-child relationships which fosters consumer skills and other aspects of children's reactions to advertising.

Finally, there were no data concerning children's requests for products in the European family. Graham notes that children's requests for products may be one source of stress in some family relationships.

However, it is important to note that stress occurs in all family relationships, and it is questionable whether children's requests for products produce some sort of abnormal stress.

Consumer socialisation

Our final session dealt with the role of television advertising in "consumer socialisation" processes. This term refers to children's acquisition of knowledge, skills, and attitudes which are relevant to consumption behaviour.

Klaus G. Grunert (Institut fur Haushalts and Konsumokonomik, West Germany) presented a model of information processing which could be used to structure research in several areas of consumer socialisation. Prof. Grunert noted that most research in socialisation proceeds from one of three perspectives: social learning theory, cognitive development theory, or attitude theory. Problems with each of these approaches are discussed, as well as problems with more recent conceptualisations of consumer socialisation processes. For example, Ward's information-processing model attempts to relate family and media influences on aspects of children's consumption-related knowledge, attitudes, and skills, but Grunert notes that the model does not clearly account for the impact of incoming stimuli and its impact on cognitive structures, nor does it make a clear distinction between children's knowledge and skills.

Grunert's model draws heavily on information-processing concepts, particularly in the area of memory processes. He begins by distin- guishing between "factual knowledge" and "procedural knowledge' which children come to store in long-term memory. Factual knowledge is stored in a semantic network, such as that portrayed in Figure 2. Procedural knowledge, which is more difficult to verbalise than factual knowledge, is conceptualised as a system of productions. For example, we may know how to go about building a cabinet, but it would be hard to list and verbalise all the steps, in spite of the fact that we could quite readily call upon our procedural knowlege to go about building a cabinet.

Grunert integrates these networks into what he calls the SNPS model, for Semantic Network/Production System. The model is further divided into substantial and formal criteria. The former are categorisation criteria (e.g. which products are associated with which products and attributes are important), while the latter are more elaborate criteria which distinguish degrees of difference betwen criteria, brands, and so forth.

In a socialisation framework, the SNPS model is related to two major normative criteria: how children come to the point at which they develop autonomy in their consumer behaviour. While Grunert indicates that considerably more research in terms of variables in the model is needed, a tentative conclusion is that television advertising is a positive social agent for children's knowledge of the functioning of markets, measured by variables such as their abilities to develop differentiated consumption knowledge.

Grunert concludes: "these effects must be regarded as positive in the sense that they further cognitive states which enable the consumer to behave in a way that is in accordance with the principles of marked economy." On the other hand, television advertising may not contribute to consumer autonomy, primarily because advertising does not help children to develop skills to define what are "good" or "bad" criteria across product categories.

Reinhard A.M. Sander (Institut for Sozialwissenschaften der Technischen Universitat Munchen, West Germany) presents a "macro-sociological perspective on the configuration of television, children, and advertising in advanced societies".

His central thesis is that television must be considered as an integral part of industrial society. He draws on classic sociological perspectives to trace the simultaneous and interacting advances in industrialisation and communications in advanced nations. Television's impacts are discussed in terms of the medium's abilities to integrate heterogeneous population groups, and aspects of industrialisation are discussed in terms of their effects on how people use television -- for example, in redefining aspects of the nature of play, increased urbanisation and smaller living spaces have resulted in different kinds of play for children, but television has also played a role in redefining types of play activity.

Industrialisation and television has interacted to supplement and sometimes substitute for interpersonal relationships — a notion relating to the "uses and gratifications" or "functional" view of mass media discussed earlier by Liisa Uusitalo. Sander's review of various theories and studies also leads him to speculate that television viewing contributes to children's cognitive organisation abilities, and he reinforces the strong sentiment of the seminar concerning the primary role of the family in shaping children's reactions to television generally, and to television advertising specifically.

Our final paper was delivered by Asle Gire Dahl (Norwegian Council of Research, Tyristrand, Norway). Dahl reports that there is considerable interest in effects of advertising on children in Norway, since satellite communications will enable children to view commercial television in addition to the state-owned network in Norway. Dahl articulates many of the concerns and hopes for commercial television in Norway, and the possibilities for research to trace the emergence of effects of television advertising among children not previously exposed to such advertising. He points out that the introduction of commercial television poses interesting research questions in three areas :[1] the educational relevance of commercial television, [2] relevance for consumer socialisation, and [3] relevance for media consciousness.

Dahl concludes with a proposal for a pilot project in Norway, and three general hypotheses to be tested following the introduction of commercial television.

1. Children gradually acquire scattered isolated pieces of information about single products from television commercials;

25

2. Television advertising does not represent any stronger influence on children than other types of program content;

3. The introduction of commercial broadcasts will strengthen teaching in consumer questions as well as in mass media.

We posed the following questions to structure our discussion:

1. What particular aspects of children's knowledge, attitudes, and skills comprise "consumer socialisation?"

2. What is the role of television advertising in developing consumer socialisation in the child?

3. What actions are necessary to encourage and reinforce television advertising's role in consumer socialisation?

4. Are there aspects of consumer socialisation which encourage age-related abilities to evaluate television advertising?

Regarding these questions, the relatively straightforward definition of consumer socialisation as comprising consumption-related "knowledge, attitudes, and skills" was broadened considerably. As Grunert illustrated, consumer socialisation might well be considered as having to do with types of cognitions beyond those required for specific consumption tasks. He would argue that consumer socialisation also involves knowledge of how markets work, and how to plan and proceed within market economies. Clearly, television advertising does contribute to children's consumer socialisation, but it also contributes to particular aspects of knowledge and behaviour that can be defined as "consumption-related".

There was some discussion of the possible role of media education and formal education to develop children's consumer socialisation processes -- in particular, to help children to evaluate and use information in advertising in ways which maximise their consumption experiences and their learning processes related to consumption.

PART III
AGE-RELATED
DIFFERENCES

Session summary

The three papers in this session address various aspects of the question of how children at different ages respond to advertising on television.

Scott Ward suggests a framework for research in the area of advertising and children which is particularly useful in orienting research to important policy issues. He argues that concerns about children's responses to advertising stem from more basic concerns with: (1) age-related differences in the effects of television advertising; (2) the underlying processes by which children perceive and evaluate advertising, and (3) message characteristics which some feel may be more or less "effective" depending on the age of the child. He summarizes empirical research findings on specific issues within each of these three areas.

Ward notes that most of the research on age-related differences in children's responses to television advertising has been based on concepts from cognitive development theories. These concepts and theories are explained. Overall, research suggests that, with age, children become more focused and efficient at utilizing information in advertising, and they become more aware of advertising's selling intent, so that, by the age of 8, the vast majority of children are aware of the persuasive intent of advertising.

Ward also argues that, since developmental processes have been shown to apply to children at different ages across cultures, the American research in this area should apply to European children, making this a less-important area for research in Europe than research in areas which are relatively more sensitive to cultural differences.

Brian Young explores the question of advertising literacy, defined in terms of children's abilities to understand both the audio-visual features of television advertising, and their abilities to inter-relate the basic concepts of buying, selling, and advertising. He argues that research approaches to date have focused on age-related differences in children's comprehension of television advertising messages, resulting in two important problems: (1) research is overly-dependent on children's verbal abilities to respond to an interviewer, and these limited abilities may jeopardise valid assessment of children's comprehension, and (2) the focus is on comprehension of messages, rather than on the broader relationship of advertising and consumption activities.

Young argues that children's comprehension is the result of a long developmental process, reflected in the Piagetian emphasis in research to date, but it is also the result of a more defined developmental shift in middle childhood having to do with children's abilities to understand and use language. These metalinguistic abilities are discussed in terms of linguistic theories, which focus on children's developing abilities "to attach meaning to utterances and messages that take into account the message and intent of the communicator".

Young concludes with suggestions about how understanding the development of these metalinguistic processes in children represents an advance beyond simplistic "stimulus-response" models of television advertising's effects on children. Moreover, study in this area should help to develop pro-active programs to foster children's advertising literacy.

Theo Poiesz and J.W.J.M. Van Gerwen present empirical results bearing on the question of advertising's persuasive effects. They view persuasion as an interaction between receiver and message characteristics. The latter include message format, context, and content, and repetition. Their study focuses on the effects of repetition. If much repetition of a message leads to greater liking, this is one dimension of persuasion. However, the important question is why repetition should lead to heightened liking of a stimulus, such as a television ad. One explanation may be what the authors call the "functional exposure" hypothesis.

This hypothesis holds that people like frequently-appearing stimuli because such stimuli come to be regarded as providing more information which may be useful than stimuli which appear less frequently. The authors present empirical results which support this hypothesis. Interestingly, older children showed a stronger relationship between frequency of exposure and liking than did younger children. This may be because younger children were bored with high-repetition stimuli, while older children believed it to be more useful.

While the study did not use advertising stimuli, the authors suggest that the results could be tested with advertising stimuli. Such research could bring a new perspective on the question of effects of advertising repetition.

In the final paper, Kaj Wickbom describes a media education program in Sweden, which includes curriculum materials designed to heighten adolescent's understanding of the institution and nature of advertising. After students receive basic grounding in theories of communication, they learn about the considerations involved in different communication media. A second course then affords students an opportunity to apply their knowledge in practical exercises, such as making a film, or designing an advertisement.

The course Professor Wickbom describes, demonstrates that young people can learn about the nature of communication media and messages, including advertising. While the course he describes has focused on adolescents, similar courses have been designed for younger children in pilot media education projects in the United States and Canada.

Taken together, the papers by Ward, Young, and by Poiesz and Van Gerwen explore mechanisms underlying age-related differences in children's responses to television advertising, while the papers by Young and Wickbom suggest pro-active kinds of activities which could augment children's skills to evaluate and use properly information in advertising. The papers make it clear that one must be exceedingly careful to define and investigate, accurately, age-related phenomena. For example, "persuasion," as defined by Poiesz and Van Gerwen is not necessarily a negative effect, and repetition is not in itself "harmful", if repetition increases not only liking but the utility of information in advertising. Moreover, as Young points out, great care must be taken in assessing children's comprehension, since verbal measures may not tap children's true understanding: their verbal skills may not develop as rapidly as their cognitive skills which maybe used in evaluative advertising messages.

How children understand with age

PROFESSOR SCOTT WARD

It seems clear that issues concerning the effects of television advertising on children are emerging in Europe, despite considerable differences among Western European countries in the nature of broadcasting systems and the incidence and nature of regulations in this area. The central purpose of this conference is to foster a climate for an effective role for empirical research in the emerging policy deliberations. Empirical research alone cannot resolve the complex issues in this area; however, it can be a useful guide to policy decision-making. Policy decisions which have been informed by research results are vastly preferable to those which result simply from political polemics and special-interest debates.

Our work here should characterize the emerging European research in important areas, set an agenda for important research needs, and establish a basis for the role of dispassionate, empirical research in policy formulations concerning advertising and children in Europe.

In this overview, I will first discuss my view of a common framework for the issues. That is, despite differences in specific issues and regulations in various Western European countries, what are the fundamental issues that are being raised, and how can we understand them in a way which points to the most useful avenues for research?

My second purpose is to provide an overview for our opening session on age-related differences in children's responses to television advertising.

A FRAMEWORK FOR THE ISSUES

Just what are the specific issues concerning the effects of television advertising on children? At first glance, it would seem appropriate to list the issues by country, as they are reflected in various regulations; or, one could enumerate the issues which are being raised by various individuals or groups in various countries.* The problem with such approaches is that such listings are likely to be transient as well as incomplete. It is more useful to conceptualize the issues in terms of braoder underlying concerns. Such conceptually-driven frameworks bring theories, concepts and studies to bear and they orient us to examine the mechanisms underlying specific issues.

The framework in Exhibit 1 attempts to conceptualize the issues in terms of two dimensions: duration of effects (long-term vs. short term) and type of effect (cognitive vs. behavioral). Exhibit 2 attempts to visually locate four areas of concern in terms of two other criteria: existing research base, and sensitivity to cultural differences. For example, there is a great deal of research on short-term cognitive effects of advertising, and cognitive development theory suggests that such differences are relatively insensitive to cultural differences. On the other hand, there is relatively little research on long-term cognitive effects of advertising, and such effects should be sensitive to cultural differences, since many indigenous influences influence cognitions over time. There are differences in the amount of existing research on behavioral effects, but long-term behavioral effects should be more sensitive to cultural differences, owing, again, to the heterogeneity of influences in various cultures which shape behavioral patterns over time.

Another framework reflects two different dimensions which seem to underlie the issues reflected in many countries (Exhibit 3). The first dimension is the basis of concern, and the second is the focus of conern. With regard to the basis of concern, there appear to be four discrete areas:

---

* For example, nine issues were identified in a study funded by the National Science Foundation in the United States. These issues were (1) Children's ability to distinguish television commercials from program materials; (2) The influence of format and audiovisual techniques on children's perceptions of commercial messages; (3) Source effects and self-concept appeals in children's television advertising; (4) The effects of premium offers in children's television advertising; (5) The impact on children of proprietary medicine advertising; (6) The effects on children of television food advertising; (7) The effects of volume and repitition of television commercials; (8) The impact of television advertising on consumer socialization; and (9) Television advertising and parent-child relations. Also a useful review of issues posed in various countries is provided by J. J. Boddewyn, "Advertising to Children: An International Survey" (New York: International Advertising Association, 1979).

Exhibit 1

**CONCEPTUALIZING ADVERTISING'S EFFECTS ON CHILDREN
IN TERMS OF DURATION AND TYPE OF EFFECT**

Effect Duration

		Short-term	Long-Term
Type of Effect	Cognitive	Cognitive responses to advertising, such as understanding intent, program-commercial discrimination	Development of materialistic values; poor decision-making skills.
	Behavioural	Indiscriminant desires to buy advertised products; dysfunctional parent-child relations.	Poor budgeting, shopping skills; propensity to spend vs. save.

Exhibit 2

**PERCEPTUAL MAP OF BASES OF CONCERN RELATED TO
AMOUNT OF EXISTING RESEARCH AND SENSITIVITY TO
CULTURAL/NATIONAL DIFFERENCES**

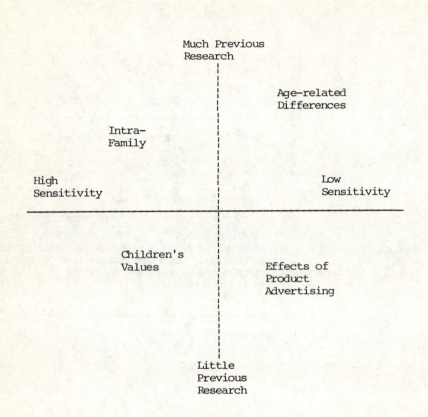

EXHIBIT 3

CLASSIFICATION OF ISSUES REGARDING ADVERTISING TO CHILDREN

Focus of Concern	Basis of Concern		
	Age-related differences	Children's values and skills	Intra-family issues
Effects	Disappointment, frustration. Attitudes.	Materialism; instant gratification Social.	Nagging; Anger
Process	Distinguishing programs and advertising; "unfairness"; selling intent	Heavy viewing; Amount of exposure.	Frequency and nature of children's purchase requests, and reactions
Message Characteristics	Host selling, premium advertising	Pro-social themes.	Urging

1. Age-related differences. Almost all specific issues regarding advertising to children are related to concerns about age-related differences in children's abilities to properly select, evaluate, and use advertising information.

2. Advertising's long-term effects on children's values. Many issues reflect concern that advertising somehow inculcates values which are viewed by some as highly negative. For example, there is expressed concern that advertising causes children to acquire materialistic values, or that advertising leads children to believe that needs can be instantly gratified, or problems can be quickly and easily solved by use of advertised products.

3. Advertising's effects on parent-child relations (intra-family processes). There seems to be widespread concern that, since children most often acquire products by requesting that their parents buy them, such advertising-generated requests lead to dysfunctional parent-child relations. A related concern is that such effects are particularly acute in low-income households.

With regard to the focus of concern, there appear to be three related areas:

1. Advertising's effects on children. The focus of concern here is on ultimate effects of advertising on children, either in the short or long term. For example, some issues refer to children's confusion between programs, and commercials, a program host's role as commercial spokesperson, and so forth. The major research need regarding issues which focus on effects is whether such effects in fact occur, and with what frequency or magnitude.

2. The processes by which advertising affects children. Some critics of advertising to children seem most concerned with the processes which occur as children are exposed to television advertising. Such processes may concern age-related differences in children's cognitive abilities, such as younger children's difficulties in using multiple dimensions to evaluate advertising and products; other process concerns are more long-term in nature e.g. the allegation that heavy viewing of televsion advertising is detrimental.

   While many issues concerning processes are linked with specific alleged effects (e.g. heavy viewing leads to materialistic values), the type of evidence needed to evaluate issues concerning advertising processes, focuses on general theories of child development, family behavior, and so forth. Also needed are empirical evaluations which permit explicit evaluation of alleged processes, e.g. studies of intra-family dynamics relating to children's purchase request behavior.

3. Message Characteristics. The final focus of concern is on message characteristics themselves. Included here are concerns with practices such as host selling, premium advertising, portrayals which might be associated with "dangerous' behavior, inducements for children to make explicit purchase requests, and

so forth. Needed research for this focus of concern are content analyses of advertising messages, as well as advertising which examines casual relationships between message characteristics and attitudinal or behavioral outcomes among children.

The resulting cross-classification is presented in Exhibit 3. Some examples will hopefully serve to clarify. Perhaps the majority of issues regarding advertising's effects on children center around their age-related abilities. The focus of concern within this area varies, depending on whether the issue is about specific effects (for example, whether different-aged children are more or less confused by advertising), or about processes by which advertisements are evaluated (for example, age-related diffferences in children's abilities to distinguish programs from advertising) or about specific message characteristics (for example, whether different-aged children can adequately evaluate advertising with hero presenters, or advertising containing premium offers).

As another example, many people are concerned with advertising effects on intra-family relationships. Specific alleged <u>effects</u> include nagging parents to buy; other concerns are with alleged negative <u>processes</u> in families, such as children's frustration and disappointment, and other dysfunctional parent-child interaction processes which may result from advertising-engendered requests; other concerns are with the propriety of <u>messages</u> which are felt to implicitly or explicity urge children to ask their parents to buy things for them, with messages which portray idealized or unrealistic family interrelationships.

The papers submitted for this conference suggest yet another framework, but one which is related to those I have presented. The first day's sessions reflect concerns with specific intra-individual processes—those related to age-related differences, and what we term "micro" processes to refer to cognitive processes underlying children's selection, evaluation, and use of information in television advertising (what might be called "information-processing"). The second day's sessions deal with broader issues. First, the role of television advertising in "consumer socialization," which has been defined as the processes by which children acquire consumption-related knowledge, attitudes and skills. The last session examines television advertising and inter-individual processes -- namely, parent-child interaction in relation to television advertising.

OVERVIEW: age-related differences in Children's reactions to television advertising

In the past 14 years, a great deal of research has focused on age-related differences in American children's responses to television advertising. While there may be significant differences in the ways children of different ages are treated across countries and cultures, a great deal of the variation in children's cognitive responses to advertising stimuli are mediated by their stage in cognitive development. Since such stages have been shown to be relatively invariate across cultures, this area of research would seem to be less sensitive to inter-cultural variations than, say, TV advertising's role in parent–child relationships, which may be highly dependent on cultural differences.

I intend to briefly overview the theoretical perspectives, important empirical research findings, and the cross–cultural implications of research and theory in the area of age–related differences. However, it is first necessary to overview the issues related to age–related differences in children's responses to television advertising. The most prevalent issues seem to be that:

1. children are confused by advertising

2. children are unable to distinguish between advertising and programming content

3. advertising to children is basically unfair (children are especially vulnerable to advertising because it takes advantage of their lack of development, experience, and limited ability to withstand persuasion)

4. Children do not understand advertising's selling intent.

Theoretical perspectives

Four main theoretical perspectives have been useful in guiding empirical research on advertising's effects on children. These are:

1. Socialisation theory, referring to a body of theories and concepts in which "socialisation" refers to processes by which individuals acquire skills, knowledge, and attitudes which are useful in various areas of social behavior. Consumer socialization refers to the processes by which children (and adults) acquire consumption-related sets of skills, knowledge, and attitudes.

2. Modeling Theory, sometimes referred to as Imitation Learning. Theory and research in this area is based on the notion that children learn by imitation -- in this case, observing and imitating parental consumer behaviours, or observing actions portrayed in advertising, and imitating them.

3. Learning Theory, referring to conceptual notions that exposure to rewards and punishments shape behaviour. Research in this area focuses on topics such as effects of advertising recall, etc. Learning theory-orientated research views behaviour as a function of forces applied to the child; in other words, it focuses on the relationship of children's observed responses to exposure to advertising stimuli.

4. Cognitive development theory, referring primarily to the theories and research of Swiss psychologist Jean Piaget. Researchers who have drawn upon cognitive development concepts have typically been interested in age-related differences in children's processing of advertising information.

The cognitive development concepts advanced by Piaget are of most relevance to the following discussion, first because they help to explain the results of studies which have found age-related differences in children's responses to television advertising, and second because cognitive development theory underlies the majority of the empirical research in this area.

COGNITIVE DEVELOPMENT THEORY

In brief, cognitive development theory focuses on the interaction of personal and situational factors in the child's developing abilities to perceive and organize aspects of his/her environment which influence thought and behavior. Such development is theorized to occur in broadly-defined stages which characterize children's cognition at various ages. These stages are labeled: 1) the sensorimotor stage (up to about 2 years old); 2) the pre-operational stage (from 2 to about 7); 3) the concrete operational stage (7 to about 11); and 4) the formal operations stage (age 11 to adulthood).

According to Piaget, each stage is differentiated by particular psychological or cognitive structures which form the basis for intellectual activity, and which thus shape a child's attitudes, knowledge and behavior. Certain structures have been held by reseachers to be most important in the study of children's response to advertising. Foremost among these is centration, a structural characteristic of young children in the pre-operational stage.

Centration refers to the tendency of children to concentrate on only one feature or aspect of an object; as a child grows older, the tendency is towards decentration, or the ability to take into account multiple dimensions of an object in making judgements about it. In terms of advertising's effects on children, this concept leads to the hypothesis that older children (ages 8 and up) will be more likely to recall and use more of the content of commercials than younger children due to uni-dimensional focusing. The pre-operational stage is also characterised by perceptual boundedness, or a child's tendency to focus on the perceptual characteristics of stimuli. As children develop more efficient conceptual skills (i.e., learn to rely upon and manipulate abstract concepts), they are less dependent upon the immediate perceived environment for information to direct their behavior.

Several other structures which are intimately related to perceptual boundedness and centration are also used by Piaget to differentiate the pre-operational and concrete operational stages. These other structures include the following: (1) egocentric communication. i.e., the inability to take the role of others in communicating to them; (2) syncretism, i.e. a tendency to link ideas and images into a confused whole; and (3) juxtaposition, i.e. a tendency to link events, one after the other, without seeing clear relationships among them. The thought of the pre-operational child is characterized by each of these structures, but the concrete-operational child has developed beyond them.

Piaget's assumptions of cognitive development imply several important consequences for children's processing of information, particularly advertising information. First, the child is presumed to be an <u>active</u> agent rather than the passive recipient of information. Second-stage theory posits that children's ability to process information is <u>structurally</u> limited, and that these cognitive levels or structures mediate between what has all too commonly been assumed the direct "cause-effect" relationship of advertising and children's behavior. Since age may be regarded as a surrogate measure for stage of cognitive development, this theoretical perspective suggests that television advertising's effects on children are due to age-related differences in children's cognitive abilities to process and employ information rather than to the characteristics or function of advertising messages themselves.

SUMMARY OF EMPIRICAL RESEARCH

Study findings may be generally categorized according to whether they focus on advertising's presumed effects, the processes by which such effects occur or are facilitated, or the message characteristics or formats which influence these effects.

A. TV ADVERTISING'S EFFECTS ON CHILDREN

A useful summary of research in the area of advertising's effects on children is the 1977 National Science Foundation Report (U.S.), a synthesis of the extensive body of available empirical research on the subject. According to the NSF Report, there appear to be four empirical issues which underlie concerns about amounts of children's exposure to television advertising:

1. Long-term exposure effects;
2. Heavy viewing effects;
3. Clustering effects;
4. Repetition effects.

The question of <u>long-term exposure effects</u> and the attendant implications for the fostering of material values and the learning of consumer skills will largely be addressed in the following sections of this report. Here, long-term exposure effects refer primarily to children's age-related abilities to evaluate advertising and the greater susceptibility to persuasion that is often alleged to occur with cumulative exposure to commercial messages over a period of years. <u>Heavy viewing effects</u> refer to presumed enhanced effect of television advertising on those members of various age groups that would be classified as "heavy" (as opposed to "medium" or "light") viewers or users of televsion. <u>Clustering effects</u> refer to children's reactions to different forms of advertisement aggregation (clustering or blocking commercials at the beginning or end of programs, or dispersing them throughout programming). <u>Repetition effects</u> are alleged to occur from the multiple exposures to a single advertisement, and are thought by some to cause increased susceptibility to persuasion.

<u>Long-term exposure effects</u>. It has been estimated that American children are exposed to an average of over 20,000 commercial messages each year, or about 3½ hours of television advertising per week. The

fact that European children are exposed to considerably less television advertising does not negate the potential issue of advertising's long-term cumulative effects. Discussions of children's exposure to advertising must be carefully framed. First, such figures refer only to potential rather than actual exposure. Several studies have documented the fact that children often engage in other (and therefore distracting) activities while watching, and that attention levels vary even when television viewing is their only activity.

Studies have found that children's visual attention to commercials varies by age. For example, the younger the child, the greater the likelihood that attention directed at a television program will continue during the commercial. Also, older children (8-11) tend to talk more during commercials, with full attention to commercials during prime-time viewing decreasing with age. Research has also found that regardless of commercial length, older children pay less attention to commercials than younger children. Thus while younger children seem to display higher levels and more stable patterns of attention to both commercials and programs, older children show more variation in attention to programming and advertising, i.e. older children show a marked drop in attention when commercials come on.

Researchers have commonly interpreted the tendency of children to change their level of attention during the shift between program and commercial as an indication of the children's awareness of the difference between these stimuli. The lower attention levels and the greater differentiation on older children's attention to commercials are often interpreted to indicate their greater awareness of an "immunity" to television advertising. However, it is not clear whether such age related differences mean anything beyond the observed differences in attention.

Moreover, whether or not attention is a valid measure of children's ability to discriminate between programs and commercials is itself an important issue.

Research also reveals that as children at all age levels watch television for sustained periods of time, their general levels of attention (usually measured by observations of eye and body movements) decline in linear fashion. This overall decrease in attention occurs both within series or blocks of commercials, and also over the course of the program.

Auditory as well as visual measures of attention are relevant to the study of children's long-term exposure to television advertising. In fact, research has shown (in contrast to the findings for visual attention) that brand-name recall, a response that can be learned entirely through auditory attention to commercial content, increases about 100% with age. In more general terms, it has also been found that recall of message elements in commercials increases significantly as children become older (by about 50%), as does the complexity of images recalled from commercials. With reference to cognitive development theory, it seems likely that older children are capable of "processing" commercials faster and consequently have less need to pay much attention during subsequent exposures.

Attention, however, is merely a necessary condition for long-term effects, such as whether children say they like and trust television advertising. These affective or attitudinal responses to commercials are also subject to age-related differences. For example, children report that they trust commercials less as they see more of them. One study found that the percentage of children who trust all commercials declined from 65% at the 1st-grade level to 7% by 5th grade. The proportion of children who said that they liked all commercials exhibited a similar decrease (from 69% of 1st graders to 25% of 8th graders). The decline in belief of, and liking for, commercials with age seems to apply to specific commercials as well as to advertising in general. Several studies corroborate the age-related increase in children's negative feelings toward commercials. Older children become "critics" of advertising messages and perceived techniques, while younger children are far less critical, and most often base their positive attitudes on commercials that are viewed as "funny". Interestingly, what young pre-school and early school-aged children find funny in commercials reflects their very great variances in attending to different elements in commercials. Many children, for example, find relatively minor, irrelevant parts or portions of commercials "funny".

Whether or not intended behavior is seen as a function of age depends on the research measure employed. One study asked a sample of children whether they wanted all products they saw advertised on television. Responses indicated the expected age-related decline (53% of 1st graders said "yes", as compared to only 6% of 5th graders). When another study utilized a more moderate version of this question, however, 66% of kindergarten-aged children said that they wanted most things shown in television commercials. Furthermore, when asked whether commercials made them "want to have things," the children in this study exhibited an apparent increase in perceived motivation with age: affirmative answers increased from 67% of kindergarteners to 84% of 6th graders.

Consequently, the evidence for a decline in advertising-induced intentions with age and cumulative exposure is slight at best.

As for the effects of television advertising on request behavior research has found that young children (3-4 years) make more product requests of their parents than do older children. Of course, younger children have less disposable income and opportunities for independent buying than older children, so they must ask their parents to buy things for them. Moreover, parents of older children come to know their brand preferences, so they do not have to ask as often as younger children. Study findings also indicate that the kind of things requested strongly refect children's age-related interests in products and services. For example, while children most often request food products regardless of age, younger children are far more likely to request toys, while older children are much more likely to request clothing purchases.

In addition, examination of children's request behavior requires the consideration of factors unrelated to advertising-induced intent. One such factor is the extent to which parents comply with children's requests for advertised products and thus reinforce this type of behavior. Research has shown that parental acquiescence increases with the child's age. Thus while older children are likely to make fewer product requests than younger children, they are more likely to get parents to agree to the requested purchases.

The implications of these findings for advertising's long term effects upon children's behavior are complex rather than clearcut. On the one hand, evidence from empirical research indicates that children's expressed negative attitudes towards commercials increase with age. On the other hand, the available evidence suggests that there is only a slight decrease in behavioral effects when both children's intentions /desires and requests are taken into account.

In other words, study results show that the cumulative-exposure effect of commercials is to reduce children's desires for advertised products only slightly and to produce a similarly slight reduction in the frequency of advertising-induced product requests to parents. What these results entail is <u>not</u> that children who understand commercials better and like them less will be less affected by them. This is a contradictory notion only if it is assumed that commercials are in some way "bad or harmful, that they are not supposed to persuade children to want the advertised products, or that children become poorer judges of advertised products as they grow older - all questionable assumptions.

In contrast, these findings imply that children do not become more susceptible to persuasion as they accumulate experience with commercials. Indeed, research on long-term exposure effects suggests quite the contrary: that television advertising is one input to consumer socialization processes, and serves to educate children about the existence of products and brands, their attributes and use, thus contributing to the development of necessary consumer skills and knowledge.

While family interaction strongly mediates such consumer socialization effects of advertising, research shows that consumer skills increase with age; e.g. children exhibit more brand familiarity, they learn to use more sources of information in evaluating products, and they use more attributes in product selection. Socialization research also finds that exposure to commercials does not appear to consistently motivate children towards increased spending or product requests to parents. In general, the available literature in this area asserts that children do gain information from commercials, that the relative importance of commercials in consumer decision-making decreases with age, and that exposure does not tend to foster children's increased purchase or request behavior.

<u>Heavy viewing effects</u>. The research on long-term exposure effects specifically examines the responses of the average child at each age level. In contrast, research on heavy viewing effects involves holding age constant in order to determine whether heavy viewers differ from other viewers in terms of their responsiveness to television commercials. Since the focus here is on children who view more than the average, research in this area has only marginal relevance for age-related difference per se.

Briefly, heavy viewing of television is likely to result in greater aggregate volume of attention to commercials. Heavy child viewers tend to place more trust in commercials than do light viewers. In addition, heavy viewers tend to "like" commercials more than light viewers, and although children's attitudes toward commercials become more negative with age, heavy television viewing within all age groups hold more positive attitudes toward advertising than do their lighter-viewing peers. Heavy-viewing children in all age groups also tend to want more advertised products than other children, and are likely to make more product requests of their parents. The research on the consumer socialization effects of heavy viewing indicates that heavy viewing has little effect on children's acquisition of consumer skills.

In sum, studies of heavy viewing show that children who are heavy television viewers, while not different (neither more nor less sophisticated) in their cognitive understanding and processing of commercials than their lighter-viewing peers, respond on the whole more favourably to television advertising. This greater responsiveness of heavy viewers to commercials does not mean that heavy viewers are more susceptible to persuasion, but only that they see more commercials to be persuaded by because of their great overall exposure.

Clustering Effects. Research in this area has focused on the question of whether "clustering" or "blocking" commercials between television programs aids children in distinguishing advertising from program material. In fact, however, studies have shown that the clustered commercial format is not superior to spaced or dispersed advertising in aiding children's comprehension or recall of commercial message elements, nor in promoting positive attitudes toward television advertising in general.

In terms of age-related differences in children's responses to clustered advertising, there is evidence for a decline in children's attention to clustered commercials, particularly on the part of older children. While younger children's attention may temporarily increase at the onset of a block of commercials; probably in response to the change in audio-visual conditions, their attention declines as a block of advertising proceeds, though not as significantly and rapidly as the decrease in older children's attention.

A frequent contention by opponents of advertising to children is that children's programming should not be interrupted by commercials (i.e that advertising should at least be blocked or clustered between programs). However, research indicates that not only may clustered advertising inhibit recall of commercial content, but also program recall. In addition, research (particularly that on Sesame Street) has examined children's attention patterns to various audio visual presentations and duration times, and related these patterns to learning. The essential finding is that variations in the television "menu" are essential to maintain interest, attention, and learning. Other studies have examined children's abilities to process information varying on content and presentational formats. The basic finding is that "blocking" of audio-visual information can result in what has been called "information overload," i.e. there is so much information being communicated in such a concentrated manner that confusion and misinterpretation result.

Children's fatigue and lowering attention levels to long stretches of programming have been noted, but it can been seen that comprehension of both advertising and programming may be inhibited by a blocked as opposed to a spaced format.

Repetition effects. As defined by the 1977 National Science Foundation Report, the issue of repetition effects concerns whether increased exposure to particular commercials leads to magnified effects. The major question here is whether an increased rate of exposure to a particular advertising message produces a greater intention to purchase or higher rates of purchase requests on the part of children.

The available research in their area yields no evidence that the number of commercial repetions has differential effects upon different -aged children. Indeed, what findings exist indicate that the number of repetitions of commercials has little effect on the rate of learning that occurs, and that the most likely effect of repetition of individual commercials is to prevent forgetting. Also, additional exposures to the same commercial have little effect in changing the attitudes or preferences of children, and it appears that a child's attitude toward the advertised product occurs after the first exposure and exposure to the same commercial thereafter may have only an "irritation effect."

In general, then, there seems to be little evidence that repetitive exposures tend to produce a greater susceptibility to persuasion on the part of child viewers.

B. **PROCESSES UNDERLYING CHILDREN'S RESPONSES TO TELEVISION ADVERTISING**

One argument frequently used by participants in the controversy over children and television is that advertising to children is unfair, that children are especially vulnerable to advertising because (1) they are confused by advertising (i.e. they don't understand what a commercial is or the meaning of specific message elements); (2) children cannot distinguish between programming and commercial content; and (3) they do not understand advertising's selling intent.

Empirical research has addressed each of these issues, particularly with reference to children's age-related cognitive abilities to process information. In this section, each of the assertions above will be examined with reference to study findings, and certain related issues -- particularly those of children's recall and use of advertising information - will also be addressed.

The previous section dealt with the long-term exposure effects of advertising on children, with reference to cognitive, affective, and behavioral effects. Perhaps the most important cognitive effect of long-term exposure is children's ability to understand commercials as a function of cumulative experience. A series of classic studies examined children's understanding of the conceptual basis of television commercials in terms of several variables which measured children's ability to:

1. define the difference between television programs and commercials;

2. comprehend the existence of an external source or advertising sponsor;

3. comprehend the existence of intended audiences for commercials;

4. identify persuasive intent in commercials;

5. identify informative intent in commercials; and

6. understand their symbolic representational characteristics.

Research has consistently found significant correlations between children's age and ability to make these cognitive distinctions.

While studies have shown that children in all age groups can identify the term "commercial," the real test of a child's understanding of the concept is the ability to distinguish between programs and commercials. While early studies found that older children (ages 9 - 12) demonstrated a real understanding of the differences (e.g. "programs are supposed to entertain," "commercials try to sell things"), younger children (5-8) exhibited some confusion about the meaning of "commercial" and tended to judge the relationship between advertising and programming on the basis of either affective ("commercials are more funny") or superficial perceptual cues ("commercials are shorter than programs").

However, these early studies relied solely on children's verbal responses to abstract questions (e.g. "What is the difference between a TV program and a TV commercial?") and their results therefore reflected an unsurprising difference in older and younger children's abilities to verbalize the distinction between programs and commercials. Later research employed other measures of children's ability to differentiate between program and commercial material, often in actual viewing situations.

Recent studies using nonverbal measures of pre-school (preoperational) children's ability to identify commercials, (e.g. "Show me when the commercial comes on") have found that young children can discriminate between programs and commercials -- and often at an earlier age than previously thought -- but the majority still do not understand and cannot express the selling intent behind advertising. One study, for example, showed a group of pre-schoolers an animated cartoon into which a 30-second program segment from a nonanimated children's show had been inserted; most children in the sample responded to this segment as if it were a commercial, although the ability to distingush between this stimuli and an actual commercial increased with age.

The results of this study point up the tendency of younger, pre-operational children to respond to commercials on the basis of perceptual rather than conceptual awareness. Thus the bulk of research in this area indicates that while even very young children can distinguish between programs and commercials, the grounds on which this distinction is most often made are a function of the child's stage of cognitive development and consequently exhibit distinct age-related differences in patterning.

Researchers have hypothesized that the ability to recognize the persuasive intent of commercials is dependent not only upon a cognitive distinction between programming and commercials, but also upon a child's recognition of an external source for the advertising message (a sponsor), perception of an intended audience as the target of the advertiser's message, awareness of the symbolic (as opposed to realistic) nature of commercials, and recall of personal experience with advertised products. Studies have indeed found that development of persuasive-intent awareness on the part of children involves most or all of these criteria. In addition, the evidence is again overwhelming that the ability to identify selling intent is age-related. Studies have consistently shown that older children are more likely to comprehend and attribute persuasive intent to commercials. Researchers in this area conclude that younger children have difficulty "taking the role of the other," in this case the advertiser, and accordingly are unable to attribute purpose to the commercials they see.

Some recent studies claim that recognition of selling intent is a characteristic of many preschool as well as older school-aged children. The ability of preschool children to make elementary forms of discriminations by correctly pointing to "program characters" and "commercial characters" has been documented. Yet a few researchers have employed non-verbal measures rather than a reliance on children's ability to articulate awareness of persuasive intent, and some have claimed that children as young as 3 or 4 can indeed "take another's perspective." One study, for example, had children choose pictures depicting what the character in an animated cartoon "wanted them to do"; the researchers here concluded that children can understand advertising intent and the even more complex notion of market segmentation at a younger age than had previously been reported.

However, the most reasonable assumption that can be drawn from the body of studies in this area is that it is likely that about half of kindergartners do understand persuasive intent and about half do not. Below this age (5-6 years), it is probable that a majority of children do not understand the persuasive intent of commercials; above this age, it is likely that the majority of children do.

It is clear that, for the average child, cumulative exposure to commercials has a definite positive relationship to her/his cognitive understanding of what commercials are and what they are supposed to do. This effect might be due, of course, not only to experimental learning, but also, on Piaget's framework, to age-related increases in children's cognitive abilities. Indeed, it is possible to regard these congitive measurement results as evidence for the proposition that children are less likely to be susceptible to deceptive advertising practices as they grow older, a hypothesis which seems to be borne out by later research.

In fact, children's cognitive understanding of commercials and their purpose has definite implications for both the attitudinal and behavioral effects of advertising. There is consistent evidence that younger children who do not understand the persuasive intent of

49

commercials are more likely to perceive them as truthful messages, while older children who can discern selling intent tend to express sceptical, less accepting attitudes toward commercials. In addition, researchers have found that even young children (ages 5-6) who have developed an understanding of the persuasive nature of commercials request products from parents less frequently than children who do not have this understanding. Furthermore, in comparing brands of a product, children with an awareness of advertising's selling intent are more likely to compare brands on the basis of functional or performance characteristics than on the basis of concrete, physical features of products. These results suggest that an understanding of the purpose of commercials may serve to "filter" their impact and thus allow the child to build up defenses against potentially misleading advertising.

One related extension of the findings of age-related differences in the processes by which advertising affects children concerns the "information use processes" employed by children with regard to the evaluation of advertised products. One group of studies of children's consumer behavior found that children of different age groups (kinder-garten and 3rd graders, falling at important transition points in the development from preoperational to concrete-operational thinking) exhibited the use of different developmental principles in consumer decision-making. Third graders both retained more information from the commercial messages they viewed and used more information -- and more abstract types of information -- in making product choices than younger children. But while most kindergarteners based their product decisions on concrete features of the advertised products, this research showed that younger children do remember information about both product features and elements of the commercial at levels well above chance. The researchers concluded that young children can and do use information, including abstract (conceptual) kinds of information, in a variety of product choice situations. As a result, they theorized, younger children utilize relevant information about products when the situation calls for it, although they typically do not use much information in making product choices as older children. Obviously, then, the specific information a child has retained, and the child's typical strategy for using -- or failing to use -- this information in choice situations has a major effect on the child's response to a commercial. In all likelihood, then, the child's response to an advertisement is probably more dependent on his/her own characteristics of the commercial.

However, certain message characteristics of televised commercials have been examined in terms of their potential impact of children's responses to television advertising. The following section discusses the age-related differences found to exist in the effects of particular commercial content elements on children, specifically, host-selling and premium offers.

C. AGE-RELATED EFFECTS OF ADVERTISING MESSAGE CHARACTERISTICS ON CHILDREN

Issues concerning age-related effects of message characteristics have largely centered on the issues of "host selling" and "premium offers" -- issues of concern primarily in the United States. Consequently, I will only highlight the issues and relevant findings here. The idea of host selling refers to the practice of a program personality also endorsing a product in a commercial. The limited research in this area does not indicate that host selling significantly affects children's abilities to comprehend commercials, nor does it indicate that children are more "susceptible" to such commercials.

"Premium offers" refers to advertisements which feature a small toy "prize" which may be obtained if a particular brand is purchased. Often, these premiums are contained within the package. The issues concern whether such offers confuse children about what is actually being offered for sale. Research in this area is inconclusive, since children like such premiums, and there is a mild "halo" effect in the sense that the more children like the premium, the more favorable they are toward the product.

Summary of research findings on age-related differences and implications for cross-cultural study of children's responses to advertising.

It can be seen from the foregoing discussion that many specific issues regarding advertising to children are related to or can be reduced to underlying fundamental questions and concerns about age-related differences in children's abilities to properly select, evaluate, and use advertising information. Researchers in this area have found maturational development to be the most significant determinant of children's cognitive and attitudinal responses to television advertising. This means, of course, that children exhibit progressively greater understanding of and more "defensive" attitudes toward television commercials as they grow older.

The empirical research results presented in preceding sections of this report have shown that children's comprehension of advertising content and the persuasive intent of commercials increases with age, as do negative attitudes toward advertising in general. Children's progressively greater abilities to process and use advertising information are not significantly mediated (or impeded) by particular message characteristics, but occur as a function of cognitive processes and structures which shape the way in which children perceive and manipulate aspects of their wider environment. Cognitive development theory thus provides a framework within which certain common allegations concerning advertising's effects on children can be examined. These assertions include:

1. that advertising confuses children;

2. that children cannot distinguish between advertising and programming;

3. that advertising to children is basically unfair because children are especially susceptible to persuasion;

4. that children do not understand advertising's persuasive intent; and, as a consequence of all the above,

51

5. that children's programs should not be interrupted by advertising.

To the extent that the available research regarding age-related differences is applicable to these value-based assertions, it may be countered that:

1. children are not necessarily confused by advertising but are, rather, cognitively limited in their ability to gather and efficiently analyze information from a variety of relevant sources, a "limitation" which rapidly decreases with age and experience; nor have particular message characteristics been shown to significantly contribute to this hypothesized "confusion effect";

2. even very young children have been shown to be able to differentiate programming and commercials, although the basis on which they do so (frequently perceptual or affective cues) is not likely to be as sophisticated (or readily articulated) as the conceptual grounds on which older children make this distinction;

3. heavy television viewers at all age levels are more "vulnerable" to advertising persuasion because of their greater aggregate exposure to commercial messages; children's attitudinal defenses to advertising increase with age; the behavioral effect of advertising on children (manifested by expressed desire for advertised products and purchase requests made to parents) is mediated by family structures and processes;

4. by the age of 8, the vast majority of children do understand advertising's selling intent; research indicates that about 50% of 5 - 6 year olds are aware of the purpose of commercialsim although they have some difficulty verbalizing this awareness;

5. studies show that recall, comprehension, and learning of both advertising and programming content may actually be inhibited by "blocking" of advertising since research has found patterns of fatigue and loss of attention to unbroken programming stimuli.

The age-related differences found in children's responses to television advertising provide support for and are most readily explained by Piaget's principles of cognitive development. This theory concerns basic and fundamental processes among children, and its applicability across cultural or national boundaries has been demonstrated. This does not, however, presuppose that research is not needed in particular areas relevant to children's cognitive abilities to process and use advertising information. To the extent that relatively unexplored factors such as race, sex, "intelligence," and socio-economic background may intereact with age-related patterns of response to advertising, gaps in research do exist.

Thus, to the extent that complex social and psychological factors play significant roles in cultures other than the United States, there exists a need for supplementary research in these identifiable areas:

1. How age interacts with basic social and demographic variables (such as race, socioeconomic status, etc.) to mediate children's responses to television advertising;

2. The effects upon different-aged children of advertising message characteristics or formats specific to particular countries or cultures (e.g. whether and in what way age-related differences may be apparent in children's responses to varying types of portrayals and appeals presented in advertising of different cultures);

3. How and in what way important culture-specific factors such as family structure, norms, and processes influence the development of children's values and consumer skills with relation to television advertising. Although the processes by which children learn to evaluate and use advertising information vary little across cultures, these other factors may significantly contribute to differential effects in children's responses to advertising messages.

Children's relationships between repetition and affect; theory, research and policy implications

DR. THEO POIESZ

Behavioural research plays a critical and multiple role in the triangle formed by the relationships among policy-makers, advertisers and children. In the context delineated by the title of the seminar, the basic functions of behavioural research are to increase our understanding of how children react to television advertising, and to suggest and evaluate policy measures aimed at reducing children's potential vulnerability. Obviously, these two functions are closely related.

This paper will concentrate on the first function primarily. It focuses upon a relatively uncultivated area of research that may concern a considerable persuasive effect of children's exposure to television advertising.

When dealing with the impact of television advertising, persuasion is one of the central empirical issues and a phenomenon of concern for both advertisers and policymakers. Persuasion is conceived here as a change in affect towards a person, object, or idea as the result of exposure to (an) external message(s). Persuasion may be viewed as the result of an interaction between receiver and message characteristics. The latter may be classified into a limited number of categories, relating to message content, message format, message context and message exposure in time (rate or number of repetitions). Here, we want to deal with message frequency or repetition as one of the determinants belonging to the latter category.

Rossiter (1980), reviewing the evidence of research on the effects of children's repeated exposure to television commercials, presents the following two conclusions:

- there seems to be little basis for concern that repetition leads to greater persuasion - unless by persuasion we mean no more than the ability to remember the brand name mentioned in the commercial (p. 198); and
- a persuasive effect of brand name repetition within a children's commercial is unlikely (see p.177).

Let us briefly elaborate upon these conclusions. In the first place, they point at the distinction between the repetition of an advertisement and the repetition of its elements, i.e. the advertised product's brand name. Second, they neglect brand name exposure repetition as the mathematical product of message repetition on the one hand and brandname repetition within the message on the other. This product, or the total number of brand name exposures, could have an effect which is not described by the mere combination of conclusions on the separate repetition effects. Therefore, if Rossiter (1980) observes that 'repetition as a phenomenon "within" commercials has not, to our knowledge, been a really controversial issue (...)' (p.177), one can argue that the absence of a controversy may very well be related to a gap in our understanding of the effect of the total number of brand name exposures on children's affect.

In the remainder of this paper we will make an attempt to (partially) close this gap. We will do so in two steps. First, we will summarize the available general literature on stimulus repetition-affect relationships. We will present an empirically based explanation that seems capable of accounting for inconsistencies found in the literature. Second, this explanation is related to children's developmental characteristics. Empirical evidence is presented suggesting that age is a mediating variable in the relationship between exposure frequency and affect. This second step is associated with the question of what behavioural phenomena to consider in relation to policy matters. After the two steps, we will consider the legitimacy of Rossiter's (1980) conclusions.

THE RELATIONSHIP BETWEEN BRANDNAME EXPOSURE FREQUENCY AND AFFECT.

Even if we limit ourselves to television advertising, the total number of volume of brand name exposures is impressive. In 1977, Atkin and Heald calculated the brand name repetition per children's commercial to be 3.65 times on the average.

About a quarter of the commercials exposed the brand name 5 or more times. Of course, we should realize that these numbers related to 1977, to the American media situation and to the average American child's potential number of exposures. At the same time, we may note that commercials themselves are bound to be exposed repeatedly. Together, the two types of repetition result in large total number of exposures of at least a number of brand names. Exact figures for the United States and for European countries are likely to differ. However, it seems fair to assume that differences are found at an invariably high exposure level.

Given this assumption, it is legitimate to ask whether brand name repetition as an autonomous variable does have an effect upon consumer behaviour in general and children's (consumer) behaviour in particular. The influence of repetition seems especially relevant for information processing, and affect - or attitudes - formation. Since we intend to react primarily to Rossiter's (1980) conclusions which refer to the affective aspect of persuasion, we will emphasize this aspect in the discussion below.

In the literature on the relationship between stimulus repetition and affective change, one particular hypothesis emerges as the precursor of a large number of hypotheses concerning the how and why of the phenomenon that it describes. This hypothesis is Zajonc's (1968) 'mere exposure' hypothesis.

The 'mere exposure' hypothesis states that the mere repeated exposure of an individual to a stimulus object enhances his/her attitude towards it. By 'mere exposure' is meant: a condition which just makes the stimulus accessible to the individual's perception. At its introduction, the hypothesis was supported by both correlational and experimental evidence (as in exposure-affect relationships causality may be in either direction, the former type of evidence will not be taken here as corroborating the mere exposure interpretation).

The experimental evidence reviewed by Zajonc (1968) does suggest a positive autonomous influence of exposure frequency upon affect.

Following the presentation of the mere exposure hypothesis, a variety of hypotheses was presented on the influence of factors by which the predicted linear log frequency-affect relationship might be affected. The ones receiving most of the attention in the literature were the response competition hypothesis (Harrison, 1968; Matlin, 1970), the arousal hypothesis (e.g. Berlyne, 1960), the two-factor theories on inverted U-type relationships (Berlyne, 1970; Stang, 1973) and hypotheses on exposure effects as experimental artefacts (Stang, 1974). The evidence obtained did not unequivocally support either one of these hypotheses. Reviewing the evidence, Van Beselaere (1983) concludes that '... the exposure phenomenon remains a phenomenon in search for an explanation'. Similar conclusions have been made by others (see for example, Harrison, 1977; Grush, 1976). Additionally, there is ample evidence on a phenomenon of a quite different nature: the preference for novel as opposed to familiar stimuli (see for example, Berlyne, 1960).

Recently, yet another explanation for frequency-affect relationships has been proposed next to the already suggested ones (Poiesz, 1983): the 'functional exposure' hypothesis. This hypothesis claims to be capable of consistently explaining the available inconsistent evidence. The hypothesis is based upon a reinterpretation of the experimental evidence, departing from the specific interaction of person, object, and situational variables in an experimental setting. We will briefly elaborate upon this.

Subjects in experiments on exposure-affect relationships are usually not informed as to the nature of the study prior to participation. (Sometimes, they are told that some memory task is at issue). Then, subjects are confronted with a series of stimuli of which the respective exposure frequencies are different.

The stimuli tend to be affectively neutral (as assessed prior to the experiment) and not previously exposed to subjects e.g. ideographs, Chinese characters and paralogs). Not knowing the length nor the structure of these series, the subjects may be assumed to become somewhat confused or uncertain as to what will be expected of them. They feel uncertain about the quality of their performance at the anticipated task, which is either vaguely announced or implicitly suggested by the nature of the experimental procedure. In such a situation frequently exposed stimuli are considered to be helpful, useful or instrumental in the attempts to reach the desired level of task performance. In addition, even if familiar stimuli do not give the subject the expectation of success at the task, they may still relieve the experimental stress resulting from uncertainty or confusion. In other words, higher exposure frequencies are functional in that they reduce task-related uncertainty. Functionality of higher exposure frequency-levels is positively related to and expressed in positive affect toward the concerning stimuli, that is, in positive frequency-affect relationships.

Testing the validity of this interpretation in a series of experiments, Poiesz (1983) obtained the following experimental evidence for the functional exposure hypothesis.

GENERAL SOCIAL PSYCHOLOGICAL EVIDENCE ON 'FUNCTIONAL EXPOSURE'

- In a typical 'mere exposure' experimental situation such as the ones described above, the vast majority of subjects do in fact expect a task, at the end of which they expect to receive some personal performance-score (task-anticipation).

- In a situation in which some unidentified task is explicitly announced, frequency-affect relationships are significantly more positive than in a situation in which subjects are made to believe that quality of task performance is irrelevant. In the latter situation, the average frequency affect relationship is nonpositive.

- If the amplitude of the Galvanic Skin Response (GSR) may be taken as an indicator of subject uncertainty: less uncertainty in a task situation, that is, a smaller GSR amplitude - is associated with the more frequently exposed stimuli.

Consumer psychological evidence on functional exposure

In a consumer choice situation, uncertainty may be said to exist if the consumer perceives a moderate degree of risk (operationalized as the midpoint on a rating-scale ranging from very low risk to very high risk). In the concept of perceived risk, subjective uncertainty is combined with the seriousness of the possible detrimental consequences. These consequences may be stated in terms of financial, physical, social, psychological, etc. effects (see,for example, Jacoby & Kaplan, 1972). It was predicted that under conditions of very low and very high levels of perceived risk no positive frequency-affect relationships would be observed. In the former, higher exposure frequency levels are not functional as no uncertainty exists, and nothing is at stake; in the latter, the seriousness of possible detrimental consequences will prevent subjects from basing their (risky) choice on exposure frequency alone. The reduced functionality of high exposure frequencies will be expressed in relatively low affect scores (as compared to the corresponding affect scores under conditions of moderate risk. On the other hand, in moderately risky conditions, higher exposure levels will acquire their uncertainty-reducing effect and positive frequency-affect relationship can be expected).

Hypotheses of this nature were confirmed: in several experiments, nonpositive frequency-affect relationships were observed at both extremes of the perceived risk axis, and a positive relationship was found if perceived risk was at a moderate level. In addition, the slope of frequency-affect relationship was found to depend upon the subjects' (in)tolerance of ambiguity, as measured by an adapted version of the Budner (1962) scale.

The reduction of situational ambiguity of the more frequently exposed stimuli will be experienced and evaluated more positively by intolerant as compared to tolerant subjects. As a result, the former show more positive frequency-affect relationships.

In conclusion, there is evidence of several types suggesting that the "functional exposure" hypothesis is a valid one: functionally familiar stimuli are affectively more positive as compared to unfamiliar or less (functionally) familiar stimuli. Functionality of familiarity, then, may be defined as the extent to which a person perceives familiarity as making it possible for him/her to acquire or maintain a preferred psychological state or to avoid or reduce a nonpreferred state, i.e. uncertainty.

AGE AS A MEDIATOR IN FREQUENCY-AFFECT RELATIONSHIPS

Since there is no obvious a priori subjective link between exposure frequency and (the reduction of) task uncertainty, such a link must be cognitively established. For this, some (sub or preconscious?) subjective theorizing must take place. As the result of this theorizing, a person may perceive familarity as making it possible for him/her to eliminate or reduce the negative experience of subjective uncertainty.

Two points seem worth noting, now. The first point is that, in the literature, a cognitive effect or process such as the one mentioned above has been shown to be dependent upon the stage of cognitive development. The second point is that virtually all theorizing on frequency-affect relationships is based upon studies with adult subjects.

The combination of the two points raises the question whether younger children are cognitively different from older children and adults in experiments on frequency-affect relationships and, if so, whether and how this affects the nature of their respective frequency-affect relationships. In the following, we will consider this briefly.

The increasing ability to think in terms of self-generated hypothetical propositions as a demonstration of cognitive development is well supported in the literature. For example, according to Piagetian theory, we can make a distinction between children at or beyond the stage of formal operations (age 12 on) and children before this stage. Generally, the former are better capable of theorising about new relationships. (Here, we merely want to point at a developmental trend, without departing from a strict stage theory of cognitive development. For a critique on the use of the Piagetian theory in relation to television advertising effects, see Chestnut, 1979).

Thus, we may expect children of, say, 13 or 14 years of age to differ from younger children (age 12) in their capacity to theorise about the function or the significance of events observed in an experimental setting in which stimuli are being exposed at different frequency-levels. Extending upon conclusions presented earlier, we may expect that older children are more likely to interpret the more frequently exposed stimuli as functional in a task-situation than younger children. Consequently, older children are likely to show more positive affect towards the frequently exposed stimuli than younger children. On top of this expected effect, there may be two additional effects that can strengthen or support it.

First, older children have been reported to be more capable of selecting useful information from stimulus components and to tailor attention to task demands (e.g. Hale, 1979; Flavell & Wellman, 1977; Ross, 1976 Stevenson, 1972), and, second, the adaptive (functional) significance of the information-to-be-recalled seems to play a major role in the bases for organisation and memory (Cairns & Valsiner, 1984). In conclusion, there is indirect evidence of several types suggesting that in task-setting, higher exposure frequencies become more functional with age, and that, therefore, frequency-affect relationships become more positive with age.

This provisional conclusion calls for an empirical test, however, in which we can confront children of two age-levels with an experimental procedure of the type usually employed in exposure-affect studies.

In order not to confound capability of theorizing with capability of adequately identifying and differentiating exposure frequency levels, children of age 9 or 10 will be selected as the younger children. At this age, children may be expected to have the ability to arrange objects or events on a quantified dimension according to Piagetian theory and research. This ability is critical in relation to the perception of exposure frequency differences.

Experiment I: The effect of age-level on the frequency-affect relationships: an initial test.

Method

Subjects: 70 children of 9/10 years of age and 76 children of 13/14 years of age (resp. primary and secondary school) participated in the present experiment.

Stimulus-material: The stimuli were 6 slides, each showing the set of eyes of 12 year old children. This type of stimulus was chosen to exclude the possibility that the nature of the stimulus, as, for example, its complexity, would interact with age level. The 6 stimuli were selected out of a large set of eye-pairs on the basis of their relative affective neutrality (which was established by a small group of children at the two age-levels. These children did not participate in the experiment). Slides had a standard format, eye-pairs were shown (no hair, etc). The concerning children all looked straight at the camera and had a "neutral" facial expression on being photographed.

Equipment: the equipment consisted of a Kodak carousel slide projector, a projection-screen placed in front of the subjects, a white instruction-board with text in brown. The instruction could be easily read by all subjects.

Design and procedure: The design involved two experimental groups of subjects distinguished on the basis of age, and a control-group for each of the age levels.

Each of the two experimental groups was confronted with the procedure typically employed in exposure-affect studies. That is, no explicit task-related instructions prior to the exposure frequency manipulation, and in affect rating of all stimuli following this manipulation. For the two control-groups, there was no exposure frequency manipulation and subjects in these groups rated affect associated with the various stimuli on the basis of a single exposure of each stimulus only.

Procedure: The experiment was carried out at the schools of the subject groups, in the respective classrooms. Per condition, subjects participated collectively. Basically, the procedure consisted of three phases: the instruction, the exposure, and the rating-phase, each immediately following each other.

Instructions: "In a few moments I will show you a number of slides of the eyes of children. Later on I will explain to you the reason why. The eyes are those of children of a ...school in Eindhoven. These children are in the same grade and your age. Please look at the screen now!". Subjects in all conditions received these instructions. A particular stimulus was shown 0, 1, 2, 5, 10 cr 20 times. Subjects in the control conditions saw each stimulus once only. Frequencies were intermixed, so that each stimulus did not follow itself. Stimuli were exposed for 2 seconds each. Interstimulus intervals were 4 seconds. Because of practical constraints, the stimulus presentation and the affect rating had to take place for all the subjects per condition simultaneously.

As a result, the order of the frequency-levels in the rating-phase was fixed: 5, 0, 20, 1, 10 and 2 (exposure time: 2 seconds each). Stimuli were rated on the 7-point "smiling-faces" scale (Jolibert & Baumgartner, 1979), after the request to 'indicate how nice you think the child is whose eyes you have just seen'. Subjects were instructed how to interpret the affect scale.

Results and discussion

Assuming psychologically equal intervals at the exposure-frequency continuum, linear trend scores were calculated per condition (see Winer, 1971). This was also done for the two control-conditions, although, in fact, the equal exposure frequencies in these conditions do not allow a trend interpretation. However, for reason of comparison, trendscores could be calculated without violating analytical rules. A linear trend analysis shows an unexpected significant interaction between the base lines of the two control groups ($F_{1,87}$ = 15.95, p < .01), implying that, apparently, stimuli were not equal in affective neutrality. Consequently, a direct comparison between the two age groups is not possible. The only prudent comparison that can be made is, per condition, the one between the experimental frequency affect relationship and the respective baseline. Then, for children of both age-groups, we observe that frequency-affect relationships differ significantly from the baselines. However, for the younger children the trend of the experimental group is negative relative to the baseline ($F_{1.68}$ = 7.04, p < .01), while for the group of older children, this trend is positive relative to its baseline ($F_{1.74}$ = 5.08, p < .05). Even though these results confirm the hypothesis - children in the concrete operational phase (9/10 years of age) show relatively less positive frequency affect relationships as compared to children in the formal operational phase (12/14 years of age) - interpretation is hampered by the significant difference between the control-groups for both age-levels.

The results do suggest that relative to the younger children, the older children appreciated the more frequently exposed stimuli more than the infrequent stimuli. In our interpretation, given the unclear task situation, familiarity bolsters subjective certainty. On the other hand, the younger children possibly may have been annoyed by the (useless?) frequent exposure of some stimuli. We assume here that these children did not regard frequency-differences as the critical aspect of the experimental procedure. Instead, it is assumed that frequency differences were considered to be not basically different from, for example, other differences between the stimuli.

The obtained result requires an additional experimental test on influence of age on frequency-affect relationships. The set-up of the present experiment did not allow counterbalancing of stimuli over frequency levels, nor could the order of stimuli in the rating-phase be varied. Therefore, a second experiment was set up, in which procedural flaws of Experiment I were eliminated.

Experiment II: The effect of age-level on the frequency-affect relation-ship; a second attempt.

Basically,the theoretical background of Experiment II was identical to the one of the Experiment I. Again, we will confront two age-groups with a manipulation of exposure frequency, and hypothesize the frequency-affect relationship of children 13/14 years of age to be more positive than the relationship of children 9/10 years of age.

Method

Subjects: 60 children participated in this experimental study. 30 children of about 9/10 years of age, and 30 children of about 13/14 years of age (primary and secondary school respectively).

Stimulus material: Stimuli were 6 nonsence words, formed by four consonants and one vowel. These words had been selected out of a set of 33 words on the basis of their affective neutrality for both age levels. This was done in a study, prior to the actual experiment, with a group of 13 children per age-group. These children evaluated stimuli on the "smiling faces" scale referred to earlier. The selected words were DONJW, VINCB, RETBG, SBETB, SGLIB, and FUPKZ. The stimuli were presented on slides, all in the same format.

Equipment. Employed were a KODAK carousel slide projector and a projection screen, placed at a distance of about 15 ft. from the subject.

Procedure

In this experiment, subjects participated individually. After entering the experimental room, the subject was requested to sit in front of the screen.

The standard instruction was: 'In a few moments, I will show you a few slides. Later, I will explain why. Each slide shows the name of a child. The names are all unknown to you - you probably never saw them before. Now, look at the screen and I will show you the slides. Please watch them closely'!

During the stimulus-presentation, each stimulus was exposed for two seconds. Interstimulus intervals were 4 seconds. The stimuli were presented in random order, but so that each stimulus did not follow itself. A particular stimulus was shown 0, 1, 3, 5, 10 or 15 times. The exposure phase was followed immediately by the rating phase, in which stimuli had to be rated one by one on the 7-point "smiling faces" scale.

Subjects were instructed how to interpret the scale. In the rating-phase, frequency-levels were rotated over the exposure positions 1 through 6.

Results

Table 1 and Figure 1 show the average affect score per frequency-level and per age group.

		Frequency-Level					
		0	1	3	5	10	15
Age	9/10	4.57	5.47	4.67	5.07	3.93	4.23
	13/14	3.10	4.37	4.50	4.03	4.40	5.17

Table 1:
mean affect scores per age-level and per frequency-level (n=30 per age-level)

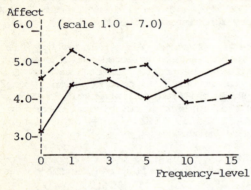

Figure 1:
mean affect scores per age-level and per frequency-level

The results indicate that there is a difference between the age groups with regard to the slope of the frequency-affect relationship. The tendency for the older children is positive, and for the younger children negative. The difference is significant ($F_{1, 58}$ = 10.28, p < .005), confirming the hypothesis.

GENERAL DISCUSSION

The results of the two experiments combined provide indirect support for the argument that cognitive development differences co-determine differences between frequency-affect relationships.

The results seem worthwhile in at least two respects: in the first place, to our knowledge, it has not been suggested before that age, taken here in terms of cognitive development, can have an autonomous influence on the slope of the frequency-affect relationship. Second, the outcome seems to provide indirect support for the "functional exposure" - interpretation of frequency-affect phenomena.

The question remains of how to interpret the slopes of the observed relationships. We note that the average relationship of the older children is more positive than the average relationship of the younger children, as expected. We also observe, however, that for the latter group, the tendency is negative. No explicit hypotheses were formulated on the slope of the relationship of each of the groups (only on the nature of the difference between the two). The a posteriori explanation that seems plausible is that the negative relationship of the younger children is due to the dysfunctionality of the more frequently exposed stimuli: for these subjects frequent exposure of the same stimuli leads to tedium or boredom.

Let us now return to the objective of this paper: to increase our understanding of how children react to brand name repetition as an aspect of television advertising. We realize that we have arrived at a sidetrack. In the first place, the evidence does not relate specifically to brand names; in the second place, subjects were placed in an (implied) <u>task</u>-setting; and, in the third, the evidence was obtained in the laboratory of which the rather artificial conditions can hardly be compared to actual, 'real-life' circumstances.

In spite of these and other possible limitations, we want to argue that, in a particular way, the evidence does relate to this paper's objective. On the basis of the presently reported and earlier research, we can propose several hypotheses. Their respective empirical tests should provide an insight into how children react to brand name repetition under different, specified circumstances.

However, before going into these hypotheses, we want to briefly reconsider the three limitations indicated above.

- Even though stimuli were no brand names (what is the difference between nonsense words and brand names, anyway?), in adult research on frequency-affect relationships, no fundamental difference was found between outcomes of studies with nonsense words and those of studies with so-called brand names. There does not seem to be a reason why this should be different for children.

- Subjects were placed in a task-setting. However, if buying may be seen as problem-solving behaviour, a buying situation may be directly compared to a task situation.

- Finally, we must acknowledge that the evidence is strictly laboratory-bound. However, for the initial identification and explanation of some behavioural phenomena, one can only rely upon laboratory research before these phenomena can be tested in actual circumstances. Affect-formation seems to be one of these phenomena. (See, in this respect, Mook, 1983).

Converging the general evidence on adult frequency-affect relationships and the (limited) evidence on children's frequency-affect relationships, we hypothesize that:

1) Children of age 13/14 on (including adults) will show positive affect towards frequently exposed brand names in buying situations with a moderate degree of perceived risk.

2) Children of age 9/10 and less will show <u>no</u> positive affect towards frequently exposed brand names in buying situations with a moderate degree of perceived risk.

3) Children (and adults) of all ages will show no positive affect towards frequently exposed brand names in buying situations with either a very high or a very low degree of perceived risk.

if in these hypotheses, perceived risk is interpreted as a function of consumer, product and situational variables.

65

In conclusion, referring back to Rossiter's (1980) propositions on the absence of persuasive effects of brand name repetition, we suggest, on the contrary:

1) that exposure frequency of brand names does have a persuasive effect under conditions of a moderate degree of perceived risk; and

2) that age plays a mediating role in the frequency-affect relationship, such that, counter-intuitively, older children may be more vulnerable than younger children with regard to persuasive effect of mere repetition.

The first suggestion is supported by empirical evidence. The evidence relating to the second one is limited. Of course, both suggestions cannot be translated in direct policy implications, yet. However, to the extent that they contribute to the understanding of children's reactions to brand name repetition, they are useful for policy purposes at a general level. At a more specific level, the available evidence implies the necessity of additional research on the hypotheses presented in this paper.

New approaches to old problems – the growth of advertising literacy

DR. BRIAN YOUNG

The rather cryptic title of this paper hides several meanings, and in order to illuminate them it is necessary to provide some background to my present research and interests in the area of children and television advertising. In 1983 the Health Education Council in Britain was prepared to support research into television advertising of sugared products for children, this involvement originating in a concern with the unknown incidence of such advertising to children in Britain and the influence or effect this advertising has on young children. Frequent intake of sugar in the form of snacks is a variable of considerable importance in the complex aetiology of dental caries and caries in young children is a disease that is extremely costly and largely preventable. Consequently the Health Education Council felt that an investigation into television advertising and children with particular reference to the advertising of sugared products for children in the British situation would be worthwhile in that results could contribute to the debate on ways of tackling the problem of child tooth decay. My job is to carry out this research and report to the Health Education in due course which at the time of writing will be early 1985.

The first task was to define a manageable brief that would constitute a workable programme of research over 18 months and that would also avoid some of the problems inherent in this type of investigation. It soon became quite apparent that there were many problems inherent in this type of research and that one in particular was concerned with the scope of the research question. Advertising is shown on British television and children watch it; this defines a workable research issue concerned with content analysis of food advertising and "children's advertising", statistical data on the incidence and viewing audience of such advertising as well as interesting definitional problems, such as the meaning of "children's advertising". This constitutes a sizeable part of the current research but I will not discuss it here apart from mentioning its existence. The next question would be: what _effect_ has this advertising on children who watch?

This question can have many different interpretations ranging from how the child comprehends and makes sense of advertising to the effect advertising has on purchase behaviour, either of the child or of the household. Deciding how far to go in this investigation proved to be extremely important in the formulation of the alternative approach that I have called 'advertising literacy' and I have no doubt that a programme centred round children's consumer behaviour or laboratory simulations of children's consumer behaviour would have not touched on this issue at all. The decision to stop at the point where the child understands to some limited extent and leave future investigators to explore down the line was motivated by several reasons, not least by the intellectual discomfort I felt in adopting some sort of 'effects' model of media influence as well as the notorious gulf that exists in social psychology between perceptions, thoughts, attitudes and subsequent behaviour.

As one reviews research concerning television advertising and children, it appears that much of the focus is on the interaction of the medium and children's developing cognitive abilities which may mediate the impact of television.

The old problem, then, is concerned with the child's comprehension of advertising, and in particular with the developing understanding of the commercial and persuasive intent of advertising.

The new approach is drawn from recent developments in developmental psychology over the last five to ten years. The growth of advertising literacy is a pointer to the future and a description of an alternative way of viewing the relationship between the child and advertising that is independent of the policy interests of either advertisers or consumer groups. The remainder of this paper will deal with these three points in turn.

THE OLD PROBLEM

During the 1970s, in the United States there was a surge of research conducted in the general area of television advertising and children. It is not the purpose of this paper to review all the work in this field as several publications have already produced state-of-the-art assessments and discussions of the policy issues involved (Adler 1980; Adler _et al_ 1980; Barry 1977; Federal Trade Commission 1978; Federal Trade Commission 1981; Rossiter 1980; Shaw 1983). The fact that this phase existed and that there are origins, a period of intense activity and a gradual decline in interest is important in that I shall attempt to characterise this research, what drove it and what conclusions were derived from it. I am entering dangerous ground here as some members of this seminar will certainly be familiar with this work and will themselves have contributed to the output of research. Nevertheless it seems to me that the following generalisations can be made.

Firstly, the question of the child's comprehension or lack of comprehension of commercial or persuasive intent that is inherent in commercial advertising is a central one in past research. Many of the papers published in the 1970s and into the 1980s focus on this issue and the Federal Trade Commission writes the following conclusion into a 1981 summary of research:

> "The overwhelming weight of evidence presented shows simply that young children are unable to evaluate the persuasive bias in television advertising".
> (Federal Trade Commission 1981; p.25)

The age at which young children can be said to be able to evaluate this persuasive bias has not been established with certainty and is dependent, among other factors, upon the methodology used to diagnose awareness or persuasive intent of television advertising. However the consensus would be some age between seven or eight years, a period I shall designate middle childhood. Recently there have been some claims (e.g. Esserman 1981, Donohue et al 1980), that an awareness of the intent of advertising can be detected in the pre-school period and I shall return to this dispute later in the paper.

Secondly, the model of child development that is frequently used in this literature is cognitive developmental based largely on the theories of Jean Piaget. This not not unusual in developmental psychology and the tendency to explain the comprehension of advertising by children in Piagetian terms is not uniform (see, for example, Robertson and Rossiter 1974 and Roedder 1981). The adoption of a Piagetian framework is unusual in that it is noticeable in contrast to associated areas in television research with children where alternative formulations based on social learning theory are frequently found. Where Piagetian based theory is useful is in its prediction of a radical change in cognitive development about six or seven years of age, a change from thought which deals with the appearance of situations as the criterion of reality, to a deeper understanding that the appearance of situations may not correspond to the underlying reality. So, for example, in the classic conservation of amount task the young child asserts that the amount of liquid changes when the liquid is poured from one container to another because it looks as if there is more in the other container. The older child is not deceived by the appearance of things and knows that it is necessarily the case that liquids do not alter their amounts when transferred from one vessel to another vessel unless something is added or taken away from the original amount. Other structural changes occur at this stage in development such as the ability to mentally reverse a sequence of changes and to take the viewpoint of another person; these changes are significant for the older child's problem-solving skills.

These two observations; that the literature on this area deals extensively with the child"s comprehension of persuasive intent or bias in advertising and that the theoretical framework adopted is frequently based on a cognitive developmental or Piagetian model of child development, if taken together with the policy context within which much if not most of the research has been conducted can be integrated as follows. The image of childhood that is conveyed by the Piagetian point of view is one where the young child is characterised more by his or her exotic inadequacies than by real capabilities. The period from early to middle childhood is characterised by Piaget as a preparatory stage before the onset of the stage of concrete operations. Similarly the inability of the young child to recognise persuasive intent in advertising is an image of inadequacy but more an inadequacy in need of protection. Protection from what? From the advertiser as seducer. This relationship between child-as-innocent and advertiser-as-seducer is a relationship which is heavily loaded with emotion and is one which easily fits into a policy context. Consequently, concerned consumers should be on the side of the child who is in need of protection. Advertisers are cast in the role of seducer and their defence would be that children are not as innocent or ignorant as psychologists have assumed. This is precisely one of the themes of Esserman's (1981) collection of articles, that we have underestimated children's ability to comprehend advertising intent largely because of the language-based methodology used in the studies. I read this with a feeling of deja vu because similar criticisms had been expressed in British developmental psychology several years before concerning Piaget's findings (see Donaldson 1978 for criticism and an alternative approach). The advertiser-as-seducer and child-as-innocent roles are longstanding ones and appeared in Packard (1957; ch 15).

In summary, an examination of the literature on children and advertising in the last 15 years reveals that there is an emphasis on a particular change in development from one state to another; from the child as cognitively immature, unable to detect persuasive bias in advertising and consequently defend against it and in need of protection, to an older state of maturity-in-childhood with a corresponding ability to comprehend persuasive bias and erect defences against it and in less need of protection.

I am not suggesting that the validity of the reported findings is threatened by interpreting them as a consequence of a particular social context of research. What is being suggested with the benefit of hindsight is that research that was planned, conducted and published in the 1970s was constrained in its outlook and that the constraints were partly imposed by the image of childhood adopted and the model of child development used. In the next section I shall outline an alternative approach to the problem of the child's understanding of persuasive intent in advertising.

THE NEW APPROACH

An example of the extent to which a Piagetian theoretical framework is presumed to underly the development of comprehension of advertising can be found in one of the relatively recent studies that still appear in journals from time to time and which can be regarded as a relatively straightforward study in this area. Soldow (1983) was interested in comparing the child's processing of information in television, radio and print advertising and chose the child's performance on a Piagetian conservation task as an indicator of level of cognitive development whereby children were classified. On the other hand, as a reaction against Piagetian methodology and in line with the conventional criticism that Piaget uses language a lot in his methods but talks little about language in his theories, there have been studies using non-verbal methods claiming that an understanding of the commercial intent of advertisements emerges at a very early age. For example, Donohue et al (1980) presented a TV commercial to children and asked them to point to one of a set of pictures that best indicated "What Toucan Sam wants you to do". Toucan Sam is the fantasy spokesman of the commercial in question and the three pictures consisted of two distractor items (a close up of an expressionless face with a television screen featured; a picture of a child watching a television screen) and the correct item (a mother and child in a supermarket, the mother holding the product as if she had just picked it off the shelf). 75% of 2 to 3 year olds tested chose the correct item in this task.

It is beyond the purpose of the paper to critically review and analyse the shortcomings of this and other studies. It would appear, however, that the latest research in this area demonstrates some muddled thinking about what is actually being measured or assessed. Before going on to argue for an alternative approach that could unify this now rather desparate research area, it is useful to draw up a set of distinctions that should be made in any study.

i) The development of an understanding of what advertising is all about is a long developmental process commencing in the early pre-school period and continuing into adolescence and beyond. Within this developmental span, there is an important change in middle childhood that coincides with an awareness of the persuasive intent of advertising. I shall discuss the former in the last section on advertising literacy, and I shall talk about the latter in this section.

ii) There is a fundamental difference between being aware of an association or relationship between the processes of buying and selling or the contexts of buying and selling and advertising and being aware that advertising and persuasive intent are intrinsically and necessarily related. Certainly, the observations of Donohue et al (op cit) would seem to show that the former awareness can be diagnosed early in the pre-school period whereas an awareness that advertising is a particular form of communication that necessarily has this function will only emerge in middle childhood and will coincide with other important changes that occur in middle childhood that have been mentioned in (i).

iii) Methodologies that involve asking the child open-ended questions such as "What is a TV commercial?" or "What do TV commercials try to do?" should distinguish between responses that are available and responses that are both available and salient.

71

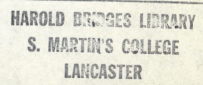

This point is related to (ii) in that available responses such as 'television commercials try to get you to buy things' may not be particularly salient for the respondent and consequently are not elicited whereas 'television commercials are there to entertain us' might be the preferred response. An understanding of the necessity of the link between buying, selling and television advertising would mean that responses of the type 'television commercials try to get you to buy things' would be available and highly salient because of the necessary connection between advertising and such economic activity.

Non-verbal methodologies that involve the child selecting between a set of alternatives by pointing or otherwise indicating one of them suffer from the disadvantage that there is often no indication from the child of the processes utilised in choosing the right (or wrong) answer. Right answers can be obtained using wrong procedures or at least procedures that are not the same as those assumed by the investigator. Donohue et al's (op cit) remarkable result could have been achieved by very young children associating the product in the picture with the vague notion that 'advertisements involve products' and indeed one would expect that this relationship would be present early in the development of advertising literacy. These need not correspond with the strategies assumed by the authors where the mediator between stimuli and correct response is assumed to be an understanding of commercial intent. What is required is to locate the comprehension of persuasive intent firmly in a theoretical framework where it has a natural affinity rather than anchoring it operationally in a set of non-verbal procedures or placing it in the more general context of Piagetian theory. What theoretical framework is suitable?

A partial answer to this question is as follows. Comprehension of the intent of an utterance is an issue that is treated extensively in contemporary linguistics (Austin 1962; Searle 1969; Levinson 1983 - ch 5). In linguistic terms one unit of verbal communication would be the speech act.

Speech acts come in different types. For example there are orders where the speaker attempts to get the hearer to do something, there are wishes which express a psychological state of the speaker and so on. Speech acts have propositional content and they also have illocutionary force. For example a billboard exhorting the consumer to "Drink X's best bitter!" has a propositional content consisting of say the action of drinking, the object called 'X's best bitter' and an implicit subject 'You'. There are various ways of describing propositional content and linguists discuss these in detail as part of their profession. The illocutionary force of this speech act is best described as persuade although one can imagine unlikely situations where the same propositional content can have the illocutionary force of an order, if shouted to a soldier for example. I have chosen this example deliberately not only because its content is appropriate in this seminar but also because it illustrates how illocutionary force will differ depending on the situational definition of the speech act. Such a difference is important when media communication is being discussed where an understanding of the source of the communication is frequently required.

The study of speech acts can be regarded as a branch of pragmatics, a field of linguistic inquiry that has enjoyed a recent and continuing popularity. Although there are different definitions of pragmatics (see Levinson op cit; sect 1.2) the subject can be said to consist of investigations of the meaning of utterances and messages that take into account the context of the message and the intent of the communicator. Pateman (1980) has attempted to apply a pragmatic analysis to advertising and claims that advertisements can be classified as a version of a directive in Searle's (1969) typology. Geis (1982) discusses the pragmatic aspects of the language of television advertising. There are indications that scholars who are interested in advertising either from a critical point of view or from a linguistic viewpoint are tending toward a pragmatic view of the subject.

If social scientists, and psychologists in particular, were to adopt a similar position we may see a convergence of two intellectual traditions which have been so different in their approaches until now.

There are many studies in developmental psychology that deal with the development of a pragmatic competence in language and communication and I shall mention some of them that have been particularly important to me in pinning down just what changes occur when the child becomes capable of understanding persuasive intent. Hakes (1980) argues that an important developmental change occurs in middle childhood (about 7 or 8 years) which is marked by the onset or emergence of a particular set of metalinguistic abilities. These abilities consist of being able to 'stand back' from language and make judgements on the language itself.

For example, judging ambiguity and synonymy, appreciating puns and dealing with non-literal or figurative uses of language such as metaphor and simile would seem to require a common prerequisite ability to 'distance' oneself from the language or to report the language as 'opaque' rather than 'transparent'. The ability to examine the message itself may be related to other cognitive abilities as described in Piaget's developmental theories, and indeed Hakes proposes that performance on conversation tasks and metalinguistic tasks may involve a common fundamental ability that relates to controlled cognitive processing and mental reflection although he states that it "remains an open ended question" (op cit p 100) at the moment. Now understanding persuasive intent in advertising requires just this detachment and assessment of the message that Hakes describes, whether it be an assessment of the form and content of the message or an evaluation of the source of the message.

The growth of an understanding of non-literal uses of language is another area within developmental psychology that is relevant to the problem of what it is to understand persuasive intent.

For example, British television advertising frequently uses indirect forms such as hyperbole, unreal fantasy situations, as well as linguistic devices such as ambiguity, puns and so on, and there is no reason to suppose advertising in other countries does not employ similar forms where you do not say directly what you mean, where some 'reading between the lines' is necessary and where the illocutionary force is not immediately reflected in the propositional content.

73

Advertising that simply states "buy me" is not effective unless it is used in a context where all other advertising is indirect and the form is consequently memorable just because it is novel. An examination of the literature reveals that there is no one transition period before which children are literal and after which children are able to interpret utterances figuratively. This adds weight to the point made earlier in this paper, that understanding advertising is a developing process from early childhood to adolescence (and beyond) and is best described as the development or growth of a process that I have called advertising literacy. For example, the development of an understanding of metaphor has a small literature associated with it (a useful review will be found in Gardner et al (1978). Children in the preschool period frequently produce creative, metaphorical usages spontaneously. Children in late childhood (10 or 11 and older) can comprehend metaphor and also use metaphor creatively in written and spoken discourse. In between there is a period of literalness when children comprehend utterances and messages at their face value. The developmental sequence here does not correspond to the development of metalinguistic ability but metaphorical interpretation would appear to be useful when understanding certain types of advertising. For example, much television advertising of children's food products in Britain can be interpreted metaphorically. The structure of metaphor consists of a topic, a vehicle and a ground. For example in the Shakespearean line "Juliet is the sun" from Romeo and Juliet, Juliet is the topic, the sun is the vehicle and the ground is the set of inferred characteristics that connect the two. Juliet is carried across by the sun and renamed with the ground thus enhancing the literal meaning of the topic.

In television advertisements the product can be taken to be the topic and the setting (for example a fantasy scenario) is the vehicle. Interestingly, in discourse that is intended to clarify or inform, the direction of the metaphor is from abstract to concrete. Abstract concepts in economics are transported into the realm of steam engines or balloons and renamed accordingly as 'overheated' or 'inflated' systems. Often the metaphorical direction in advertising is the opposite of this where the concrete product (a perfume, a chocolate bar or a packet of cigarettes) is renamed with a vehicle of visual allusion as sexual awakening, aesthetic appreciation or romantic attachment. An analysis of metaphorical usage in messages from different sources of communication cannot be separated from the purpose of the communication whether it is to persuade, to inform or to simplify.

Yet another developmental sequence that is important in understanding the comprehension of advertising by the child is found in situations where statements are made about states of affairs which are literally untrue but figuratively interpretable and meaningful. For example, in sarcasm and irony the discrepancy between utterance and state-of-affairs that the utterance refers to should flag the hearer that some inferential work as to the speaker's intent on his or her part is required, assuming that there is no reason to suppose the speaker is lying. Hyperbole similarly provides a discrepancy between what-is-said and what-is-the-case that should warn the hearer that a literal meaning is to be abandoned, that the communicator is shifting her intent and that hyperbole is being used to some purpose. The developmental literature on comprehension of this type of figurative language use is

74

more recent and briefer than the available literature on metaphor comprehension (see, for example Ackerman 1981; Demorest et al 1983).

However, the following generalisations can be made. Six year-old children often fail to recognise the discrepancy between what is said and what-is-the-case.

Eight-year-olds recognise this discrepancy but when asked why the speaker said what he did say they frequently give the wrong purpose. More importantly the wrong purpose was frequently that the speaker was mistaken (and not intentionally non-literal) and misleading (and intending to deceive the listener). It was not until 11 years of age that a complete understanding of figurative usage emerges.

In summary what I have done in this section is to place the issue of the child's comprehension of persuasive intent in the general context of the development of pragmatic aspects of communication and language, and in the particular context of the development of an understanding of the illocutionary forces inherent in speech acts. In so doing, a different, recent and less familiar literature than that normally associated with the psychology of the child's understanding of television commercials has been brought forward. It is my contention that this literature is extremely relevant to the problem posed at the beginning of this section, and that this literature is conceptually similar to analyses of advertising that have been provided by some critical theorists and linguists. However what originally was posed as the developmental problem of explaining the emergence of a single ability at a particular point in development, now appears to be a developmental sequence with several strands to it and a long period of associated development. In other words we are looking at the evolving nature of advertising literacy and it is this issue that will constitute the final section of this paper.

ADVERTISING LITERACY

If there is a broad developmental span during which an understanding of television gradually develops then when does it begin? Jaglom and Gardner (1981) conducted a small-scale naturalistic study of three pre-school children over three years, investigating their growing understanding of the world of television.

Using tasks of sorting and classification they concluded that advertisements were the first category acquired as early as 2½ years in one child. In other words in the developing differentiation of the experience of television, the earliest line is drawn between television advertising and the test. This of course, does not mean that the child comprehends advertising but what it does mean is that a cognitive frame or set of expectations for 'advertisements' as opposed to an expectation of 'other television' may be available very early in development. The content of this frame is still to be comprehended in full and it is the development of this comprehension that I shall call the development of advertising literacy. The term is deliberately chosen for various reasons. It is derived from the associated area of television literacy (see for example, Dorr et al 1980). Television

75

literacy is concerned with such issues as the understanding of forms and conventions used in programmes (such as cuts and flashbacks), comprehension of television narrative, distinguishing between fantasy, role-playing and reality as well as an appreciation of the processes underlying television production. Although many advertisements would have an episodic rather than a narrative structure it is inappropriate to exclude narrative from this list of issues as some children's advertising has a definite narrative in the sense of "the continuing adventures of ...", say the Weetabix cartoon characters in British commercial television advertising. To this list could be added the development of various figurative usages of language and communication that appear to be an intriguing mix of various abilities emerging at different ages. There is also no reason to exclude the development of social attributions from this list as television advertising constitutes a particularly rich sample of social situations involving children and families and (in British television advertising) speaking with a wide range of regional and socially categorisable dialects and accents. These social situations are unique in that they are often presented to practically all children in the medium of television and presented many times in exactly the same way.

Advertisements (in Britain) often employ humour and the development of the child's understanding of humour is an area that has an extensive literature associated with it (McGhee and Chapman 1980; pps 307-317). I have laid out this list as a set of headings for future research rather than offer a comprehensive theory of the development of advertising literacy at this stage in the hope that others will want to work in this area. To the list I should certainly add theoretical work extending recent advances in the pragmatics of language into media pragmatics, in particular pragmatics of moving visual images and how they are 'read' for intent.

There are advantages in conceiving of the relationship between television advertising and children as advertising literacy rather than the more traditional model of advertising having an 'effect' on children. The old relationship was born out of a stimulus-response psychology by the commercial interests of advertisers or protective desires of consumers. Advertising (the stimulus) was conceived of as impinging upon children who in turn behaved by buying (the response) and if this model was too simple then mediating constructs could be added such as the child's attention to the stimulus or the dynamics of family purchasing decisions. I am sure that this model will work under certain conditions and that it has an immediate appeal to advertisers who are concerned with the results or consequences of their intervention and consumer groups who are concerned for different reasons. The approach of advertising literacy is a different metaphor altogether with the child firmly at the centre rather than some link in a chain of cause and effect. Consequently it cuts across the old rivalries between advertisers and consumer protection groups and provides the researcher with a theoretical stance that, while not completely value-free, is relatively independent of both these groups' interests. Simply, whether you are for or against advertising you should be equally interested in how literate the child is in the media being used. Another advantage of the advertising literacy approach is that it focuses attention on issues of curriculum development if placed in an educational context whereas an 'effects' model suggests to the concerned parent or educationalist the need to put a protective shield around the child against the onslaught of commercial advertising, an approach that has regulatory consequences as opposed to the more positive consequences of the former.

In summary, this paper has attempted to demonstrate that the literature on television advertising and children is characterised by a particular model of child development and a particular image of childhood in relation to advertising. An analysis of the core issue of the child's comprehension or lack of comprehension of advertising's intent reveals some confused thinking in parts of the literature. Comprehension of advertising has two dimensions; a long developmental process that I have called the growth of advertising literacy and a radical developmental shift in middle childhood that appears more related to the development of metalinguistic abilities, than to a Piagetian transition for preoperational to operational thought, although these two may be linked by a more fundamental development of the ability to indulge in controlled cognitive processing. Finally what would constitute a research programme into advertising literacy is outlined and the advantages of approaching the relationship between advertising and children via advertising literacy is discussed.

MEDIA AWARENESS AND CRITICAL AWARENESS OF TELEVISION ADVERTISING:
An Abstract by Kaj Wickbom

I will start with a definition of Media Education. The concept means an essential understanding of how mass media works and how the process of mass media occurs in society. Children must understand who says what to whom and with what effect. Harold Lasswell's classical formula proves to be useful for many practical purposes, particularly, when students analyse the content of TV-advertising.

There is no doubt that mass media plays an important part in the lives of children and young people. Therefore it is desireable that mass media studies has a proper place in our educational school system. Similar discussions are being conducted in many other countries. Internationally, there is a movement towards an increase in the amount of time devoted to media education in school and in Scandinavia, media education has been integrated with the study of native language and General Studies. Since 1974-75 communications studies has, for example, been available in Norway as an optional subject at school.

Media Education also exists in other European countries such as West Germany, Great Britain, Spain and Scotland. Teaching is concentrated around individual creative activity. In the age group 7-17 in France there is an interesting experimental programme, called CYT project (Critical Young Televiewer). Organised by the government, young people and adults are being taught to analyse TV critically.

A pilot scheme in media education has been going on at Vaxjo Katedralskola, Sweden, since Autumn 1980. To a large extent the teaching has followed a basic course and an advanced course. The Vaxjo Katedralskola experimental project was the first in Sweden, (now there are four others). The "Sweden" project was initiated by the National Board of Education and will last until 1989. The students have three hours a week in the first year, and five hours a week in the second year - but Media Education is voluntary. The students can drop any other subject except physical training. During the first experimental year 1980-81 there were 29 pupils in the first year of the two-year General Studies course. In the second year there were 20 pupils.

The aim of Media Education is to teach the students to be consciously critical and therefore selective - thus protecting themselves against the fragmentation of information which reaches them via the mass media. But media education has a wider application than just school children. Basically this is a problem which concerns the older generation as well. Many people today watch television without questioning the reliability of the news and information programmes.

Critical awareness is by definition developed if a viewer understands how and why a programme is made. This relates to editing techniques which are used to dramatise the content of information. To develop critical awareness means to create a distance from television. Younger children find difficulty in understanding the reality behind what they observe on the screen. By understanding the process of mass media the viewer is supposed to become familiar with the medium, and, to achieve distance, children must ask questions.

The word critical is mostly negative – and to become critically aware has been seen as a way to escape the evil of television. But the word critical has, of course, other meanings. There is a positive dimension, which means, that the students are aware of the positive aspects of the press, radio and TV. The mass media can disseminate, in an uncomplicated fashion, knowledge of the world. It can improve people's ability to comprehend and strengthen their reading and writing skills in many parts of the world. Film and television are, for example, used as a means of reducing illiteracy. To be aware is also to become constructive and creative. By analysing the content of television the students will be aware of how to make better programmes and how to strengthen the quality of the products presented.

Awareness of how television works can start I suppose quite early, when the child is aged 7. Teaching must proceed from the elementary to the more complex (more structured) information. The child can write short scripts, produce fairy tales, combine colours, take pictures and even produce simple commercials. I think this is a way to build awareness of the aims of the communicator. Children must be able to understand the purpose of the sender in this productive way. They must be able to read the content of a message that the sender is trying to communicate. And the child must decide, whether or not they will be influenced by the sender.

In critical awareness of TV-advertising three components are important which indicate whether the students are able to evaluate certain commercials and information programmes. <u>First</u> , the wording of the aim should state a specific course of action, which means the child must be able to name and have knowledge of the advertisement's means of expression, historical date, influence of advertising. <u>Second</u>, the wording of the aim should state under which conditions this course of action should be demonstrated. This means that the students must be able to evaluate independently and critically the content of all advertisements. <u>Third,</u> the wording of the aim should state the quality standard demanded of the course of action. The students must have the ability to carry out certain advertising tasks themselves. They should be able, for example, to produce film or TV-advertising, radio programmes with commercials and also write advertisement copy for newspapers.

We have done an empirical test in a secondary school in Sweden. The aim of the investigation was to analyse how young people in the age group 15-19 years feel about Swedish TV-advertising, taking as a starting point our society's politically conceived cultural and social aims, that decides what kind of material is permitted to a Swedish audience. The investigation was carried out with 86 students from upper school in autumn 1982. The students were given the opportunity to study Swedish TV for one week. They had to evaluate a) information from state and civil institutions b) commercial advertising. Students worked in two groups, a beginners course and an advanced course. Every student watched television between 6 p.m. and 10 p.m.

The students noticed that official information was presented twice a day (14 times a week) before the news. The main message was to tell the

Swedish audience to obey law and order. However commercial programmes were more difficult to define, though almost every programme had some form of advertising. In all these programmes there were advertisements for certain commercial products, mostly presented either explicitly by the introduction of specific items (e.g. Abba - music) or implicitly as background to a football match.

The results of the test were as follows:

Most questions were aimed at analysing whether government information is really a reflection of Swedish culture and structure of our society and if age is a determining factor for when a student understands this.

It is obvious that the students exposed to previous knowledge of political systems and how they work, will easily be able to attempt to classify the content of the information. Also age is quite an important factor, when they analyse the content of Swedish TV-programmes. Young people have to understand concepts as commercial and as advertising. There is a difference between the two groups: the younger students were less motivated to classify the TV-content. The older ones were more aware of the inner structure of the explicit and implicit advertising. The investigation did however show that Swedish TV does make commercial impact on the individual.

My conclusions therefore are: Media Education is one, useful means of teaching children how to become aware of the influence of TV, especially how television advertising can manipulate a child's basic needs and buying habits. Education training in interpreting TV-advertising ought to begin in the primary school. Children have to consider exposure, perception, retention and decision as gateways to their cognitive awareness of the positive and negative effects of TV-advertising. Through media education training they will become more resistant and more constructive about the negative impact of television.

REFERENCES   THEO POEISZ

Atkin, C., & G. Heald. The content of children's toy and food commercials. Journal of Communication, 1977, 27, 107-144.

Berlyne, D.E., 'Novelty, complexity, and hedonic value', Perception and Psychophysics, 1970, 8, 279-286.

Berlyne, D.E., Conflict, aurousal, and curiosity. New York: McGraw-Hill, 1980.

Budner, S., 'Intolerance of ambiguity as a personality variable', Journal of Personality, 1962, 30, 29-50.

Cairns, R.B., & J. Valsiner. 'Child psychology', Annual Review of Psychology, 1984, 35, 553-577.

Chestnut, R.W., 'Television advertising and young children': Piaget reconsidered. In: J.W. Leigh and C.R. Martin Jr. (eds.), Current Issues and Research in Advertising. 1979, Ann Arbor, University of Michigan.

Flavell, J.H., & H.M. Wellman. Metamemory. In: R.V. Kail & J.W. Hagen (eds.). Perspectives on the development of memory and cognition. Hillsdale, N.J.; Lawrence Erlbaum Associates, 1977.

Grush, J.E., 'Attitude formation and mere exposure phenomena: a non-artifactual explanation of empirical findings', Journal of Personality and Social Psychology, 1976, 33, 281-290.

Harrison, A.A. Mere exposure. In: Z. Berkowitz (ed.). Advances in Experimental Social Psychology, 1977, Vol. 10. New York: Academic press.

Harrison, A.A., 'Response competition, frequency, exploratory behaviour, and liking', Journal of Personality and Social Psychology, 1968, Vol. 9, 4, 363-368.

Hale, G.A., Development of children's attention to stimulus components. In: G.A. Hale & M. Lewis (Eds.). Attention and cognitive development: New York: Plenum Press, 1979.

Jacoby, J., & L.B. Kaplan. 'The components of perceived risk', In: M. Venkatesan (ed.). Proceedings of the IIIrd Annual Conference of the Association for Consumer Research, 1972.

Jolibert, A.J.P. & G., Baumgartner. an empirical comparison of the properties of three scaling techniques. Institut des Etudes Commercials, Universite de Grenoble, 1979, p. 39-57.

Matlin, M.W., 'Response competition as a mediating factor in the frequency-affect relationship'. Journal of Personality and Social Psychology, 1970. Vol. 14, 3, 536-552.

Mook, D.G., 'In defence of external invalidity', American Psychologist, 1983, 38, 4, 379-388.

Poiesz, Th.B.C. 'The Relationship between exposure frequency and consumer affect: toward a functional interpretation', Dissertation Tilburg University, 1983.

Ross, A.O., Psychological aspects of learning disabilities and reading disorders. New York: McGraw-Hill, 1976.

Rossiter, J.R., The effects of volume and repetition of television commercials. In: Adler et al. (Eds.). The effects of television advertising on children. Lexington, Massachusetts, Lexington Books, 1980.

Stang, D.J. 'Intuition as artefact in mere exposure studies', Journal of Personality and Social Psychology, 1974, vol. 30, 5. 647-653.

81

Stang, D.J., 'Six theories of repeated exposure and affect', Catalog of selected documents in psychology, 1973, 3, 126.

Stevenson, H.W., Children's learning, New York: Appleton-Century-Crofts, 1972.

Van Beselare, N. Mere exposure: a phenomenon in search for an explanation. In: Doise, W., & S. Moscovici (Eds.). Current issues in European social psychology. Vol. 1. Cambridge, Cambridge University Press, 1983.

Winer, B.J., Statistical principles in experimental design, 2nd (Ed.), New York: McGraw-Hill, 1971.

Zajonc, R.B., 'Attitudinal effects of mere exposure', Journal of Personality and Social Psychology. Monograph Supplement, 1968, Vol. 2, 1-27.

REFERENCES : BRIAN YOUNG

Ackerman B.P., (1981) 'Young children's understanding of a speaker's intentional use of a false utterance', Developmental Psychology 17, 4 472-480

Adler R.P., (1980) 'Children's television advertising: history of the issue' , in Palmer EL & Dorr Aimee Children and the Faces of Television : Teaching, Violence, Selling. New York: Academic Press pps 237-249

Adler R.P., Lesser G.S., Meringoff Laurene K, Robertson T.S., Rossiter J.R. & Ward S. (1980) The Effects of Television Advertising on Children: Review and Recommendations Lexington Mass: DC Heath & Co.

Austin J.L., (1962) How to do Things With Words Oxford: Clarendon Press

Barry T.E., (1977) Children's Television Advertising, American Marketing Association Monograph Series 8 American Marketing Association: Chicago

Demorest Amy, Silberstein Lisa, Gardner H. & Winner Ellen (1983) 'Telling it as it isn't: children's understanding of figurative language British Journal of Development Psychology 1, 121-134

Donaldson margaret (1978) Childrens Minds London: Fontana

Donohue T.R., Henke L.L., Donohue W.A. (1980) 'Do kids know what TV commercials intend'? Journal of Advertising Research 20 (50 51-57)

Dorr Aimee, Graves S.D., and Phelps E (1980) 'Television literacy for young children', Journal of Communication 30, 3 71-83

Esserman June (ed), 1981) Television Advertising and Children: Issues, Research and Findings New York: Child Research Service

Federal Trade Commission (1978) Federal Trade Commission Staff Report on Television Advertising to Children. Washington DC: Federal Trade Commission

Federal Trade Commission (1981) FTC Final Staff Report and Recommendation in the matter of Children's Advertising 43 Fed. Reg. 17967 Washington DC: FTC

Gardner H, Winner Ellen, Bechhofer Robin & Wolf Dennie (1978) 'The development of figurative language' in K.E. Nelson (ed), Children's Language Vol. 1 New York: Gardner

Geis M (1982) The Language of Television Advertising London: Academic Press

Hakes D.T., (1980) The Development of Metalinguistic Abilities in Children Berlin: Springer-Verlag

Jaglom Leona M & Gardner H. (Eds) (1981) 'The preschool television viewers as anthropologist' in Kelly Hope & Gardner H (eds)., Viewing Children Through Television San Francisco: Jossey-Bass Inc Chapter 1.

Levinson S.C., (1983) Pragmatics Cambridge: Cambridge University Press

McGhee P.E. & Chapman A.J. (1980) Children's Humour Chichester: John Wiley

Packard V., (1957) The Hidden Persuaders London: Longmans

Pateman T., (1980) 'How to do things with images: an essay on the pragmatics of advertising'Theory and Society 9, 603-622

Robertson T. & Rossiter J. (1974) 'Children and commercial persuasion': an attributional theory analysis Journal of Consumer Research 1, 13-20

Roedder Deborah L.(1981) 'Age differences in children's responses to television advertising' : an information processing approach Journal of Consumer Research 8, 144-153

Rossiter J.R., (1980) Children and television advertising: policy issues, perspectives and the status of research in Palmer EL & Dorr Aimee (op cit) pps 251-272

Searle J.R. (1969) Speech Acts Cambridge: Cambridge University Press

Shaw J.H. (1983) Political and commercial influences on dental health: the Federal Trade Commission looks at television advertising to children Journal of Dentistry 11, 2, 168-174

Soldow G.F., (1983) The processing of information in the young consumer: the impact of cognitive developmental stage on television, radio and print advertising. Journal of Advertising 12 (3) 4-14

PART IV
MICRO-PROCESSES OF
CHILDREN'S RESPONSE

Session summary

This session was concerned with the question of how children process information in advertising. In particular, what mental (cognitive) operations occur as children watch television, as they interpret and evaluate what they see, as they forget or remember information in advertising, and as they ultimately may use the information in some way?

Lisa Uusitalo reviews a number of models which have been used, or could be used, to study children's responses to television advertising. She notes that much past American research focuses very narrowly on children's reactions, and does not take into account the broader "holistic" context of children's television viewing. Rather than looking for specific effects of commercials on children, Uusitalo suggests that we examine how children use television, and what gratifications they obtain from the medium. Explorations in this "uses and gratifications" research approach would do much to increase our understanding about children's emotional gratifications from television, and about how children acquire "cultural competences", that is, learn the social and stylistic codes of a culture.

Fred van Raaij presents a model of children's responses to television advertising. The model portrays the interacting effects of four sets of variables: commercial variables (such as information content, repetition, etc.) environmental variables (such as how involved a child is with watching television), processing variables, (such as children's reactions to what they see, whether they like or dislike a commercial, whether they counter-argue while they watch, etc.) and consequences or outcomes of viewing, such as the formation and change in children's attitudes, and so forth. Van Raaij explains how these variables interact to shape children's responses to advertising, and offers various hypotheses about how children may elaborate on what they see (for example, pose internal arguments for or against what they are watching), how they may learn social codes and skills as a function of portrayals in commercials, and how they may have affective reactions (liking and disliking) to commercials as a function of the child's age and interest in the advertised product.

Professors Vitouch, Sturm and Grewe-Partsch review empirical studies they have done of children's reactions to television. Vitouch presents provocative research results which show that children exhibit different physiological and cognitive responses, depending on the nature of what they see on television. Children are in general more responsive to emotional portrayals, rather than to "matter-of-fact" portrayals. Interestingly, Vitouch finds that children are selective in their viewing, in that they are more likely to remember pleasant scenes, rather than unpleasant scenes.

Professors Sturm and Grewe-Partsch also note differences in children's recall of television. For example, they quickly forget factual information, but remember emotional states for as long as three weeks. They present evidence to support the notion that children categorize and internally "label" what they see on television, when the programming is paced in order to allow the half-second for these responses to occur.

Taken together, these papers rather dramatically support the idea that children are active viewers of television. They are not passive recipients of television content. Rather, they selectively attend to, evaluate, and store information they see, and actively categorize television stimuli in various ways.

The symbolic dynamics of TV viewing

PROFESSOR LIISA UUSITALO

Several types of discourse can be distinguished regarding children and TV-advertising. These discourses usually take place independently of each other and can hardly be brought together under a uniform theory. The "consumer policy discourse" is aimed at restriction or control of advertising because of the negative side effects of advertising on children. Borrowing from applied economic theory, it often emphasises a normative model of rational decision making, and sees information seeking and receiving from this angle only, as an instrumental stage of the decision process (31). Impacts of TV advertising that do not contribute to rational consumer behaviour are considered harmful. However, the understanding of these impacts is still poor in this approach, due to the underlying assumption of rational, concious behaviour.

The "creative advertising discourse", on the other hand, can be seen as a counterargument to the consumer policy - discourse. It usually represents the views of the advertising and marketing research branches which, at the same time, try to increase the marketing capacity of advertising and legitimate advertising practice (29). In this discourse, models of advertising are applied which emphasise recognition, recall and buying behaviour effects of advertising rather than try to understand how and why these affects come about. However, be it intuitively or with the help of tests and experience, the experts of suggestive advertising seem to come closer to the realist view of communication behaviour than does the consumer policy discourse. This is manifested in the emphasis on different suggestive methods in advertising practice, and in the trend where advertised products are connected to different emotionally appealing life styles or holistic images of life. At the same time communication via the television media is undergoing an explosive growth due to the new video and sattelite techniques.

The "scientific discourse" and research has been somewhat lagging after these world-wide developments in the communication practice. What we would like to call "communication rationalism" in research, limits itself very much to the analyses of the "information" sent, either on micro or macro level (e.g. programs, commercials). At the previous stages of television research, e.g. in the 1950's, TV was criticised for being a form and vehicle of popular culture in contrast to what was appreciated as "high culture". In the 1960's and 1970's TV research came to include both sociological description of the audience and physiological research of the impacts of TV violence on aggressive behaviour. However, the holistic approach to the TV-viewing situation was still missing. It is only lately that the particular relation between the viewer and the television, the so-called TV-relationship has received more attention. Semiotic and psychoanalytic concepts have been proposed for the analysis of this relationship (28).

A purely positivistic approach, i.e., the measurable-effects-approach, has received criticism as well as the purely theorising Marxist approach. Both can be blamed for the already mentioned rational behaviour assumption bias.

I share the above mentioned critical view of television research and admit the importance of analayzing the TV-relationship as a whole. However, I do not wish to advocate a research on purely psychosemiotic basis either. In analysing the psychological dynamics and mechanism of the TV-relationship, the cultural dependence of this relation should also be taken into account. This is important especially in the late stages of market culture, when cultural institutions (press, publishing, television, advertising etc.) are no longer marginal but are by themselves, as well as in their interlocking and integration with other productive organisations, integral parts of the general social organisation (39). Moreover, when we quite rightly emphasize the non-rational, unconscious aspects of the TV-relationship, this should not lead to total ignorance of the conscious, analytic elements of the communication behaviour.

CULTURAL DEPENDENCE OF TV-VIEWING

In the way-of-life research consumption patterns are seen as culturally dependent and changing over time (32). The same basic ideal of the cultural relativity of the different explicit forms of need satisfaction can be applied to the analysis of communicative behaviour. For example, the way people receive mass communication is influenced by the type and amount of it in their past everyday life. Existing communication structures, during childhood learned ways of viewing and "seeing", as well as learned expectations concerning the communication contents very much determine both communication preferences and actual communication behaviour in adult life (30). Not only does mass communication effect our way of life (9, 10); our way of life more and more is (i.e., consists of) communicative behavior in one form or other (7, 8, 13).

90

Therefore, when studying the impacts of TV advertising on children, we would need more comparative research on children's behavior in countries with different level and history of TV advertising. The impact of TV commercials should not be studied isolated from other TV viewing behaviour. The whole flow of television events forms one universal experience (38). Children do not easily differentiate between TV programs and TV commercials. Neither do they differentiate between the central issue and peripheral, symbolic elements of the messages (22, 26). It is the whole relationship between the child and TV which is interesting.

In the study of children's TV relationship and reception processes, one can apply either the psychoanalytic approach or the "uses and gratifications" approach. Basically both approaches share the idea of analysing the type of need satisfaction which is involved in the TV - viewer relationship. Both approaches can be characterised as belonging to the research tradition of reception aesthetics which is gaining importance within cultural research.

PSYCHOANALYTIC APPROACH AND THE "PASSIVE TRANSFERENCE"

The psychoanalytic approach strongly emphasises TV viewing as a transference process by which unconcious sexual instincts and desires are satisfied, infantile fixations and traumatic experiences reflected or acted out in the flow of television events.

The TV-viewer relationship is described as a passive transference relation including both symbolic and imaginary elements. However, the imaginary elements are far more dominant. The viewer transfers into the flow of TV events imaginary elements that originally characterised his first instinct objects or part of them. Either a person, a program or the whole flow of TV events can act as an object. It has been claimed that the passive transference upholds, in a defensive way, existing conflicts; the viewer sees in the events what he wants to see. However, the viewer is not conditioned by the flow of events because he determines how to interpret the contents according to his own imaginary order. Therefore, only the position of the viewer is passive and subordinate in a TV relationship, but his fantasy world is far from being a passive one.

Because the passive transference of the TV relationship encourages satisfaction of desires on the imaginary level, it seldom leads to a deeper knowledge of oneself. It rather leads to continuous search for new imaginary satisfaction in the flow of TV events. The contents of any specific program (or commercial) are not very relevant because the key importance lies in the TV-relationship as a whole. A typical feature of the TV relationship is the compulsion of repetition. The viewer repeats regularly the passive viewing situation because the instincts on which it is based are very conservative by nature; they help one to regress to a more primitive stage of development. The television relationship mainly appeals to the "pleasure ego", not to the "reality ego" of the

---

1) This chapter borrows its main ideas from the recently published dissertation of Steinbock (28).

viewer. Therefore, it is closely connected with early narcissistic experiences.

It has been proposed that passive TV-viewing and fantasies associated with it are substitutes for children's own active playing. Moreover, the preference for non-verbal forms of expression and subjectivism are claimed to be associated especially with the new TV generation (37). These hypothesis remain to be tested, but they are probably valid only for some heavy-viewer groups among children.

In the constitution of the (passive) "viewer", a central role has been given to the traditional narrative form (classic, formalistic realism, novel style and identification, (i.e., illusionism) which is followed in most TV-films. One can add that the narrative style, the use of drama and identification have also been transferred into TV-advertising, which all makes it much more effective. The fiction and drama going on in the TV advertising becomes assimilated by the programs and vice versa.

According to Steinbock, the passive transference can, however, be broken and the view "deconstituted" - as several anti-illusionist movie directors have shown us (e.g., Brecht, Strauch and Huillet, Godard, Fassbinder)- by breaking the narrative form, identification or novel style, or any combination of these. Anti-illusionism is writer-centered rather than receiver-centered, and it leads more often to structural-materialistic film than to fictive narrative film.

It remains still questionable how well "anti-illusionists" will succeed in breaking the passive TV-relationship. Usually they have to work through compromises between illusionism and anti-illusionism. Moreover, their works frequently seem to appeal to intellectuals only. The impact of anti-illusionism on program policies, i.e. through problematizing the whole TV-relationship, has so far been minimal.

By way of summing up one can say that the psychoanalytic approach has deepened our understanding of how and why a passive transference relationship develops in TV-viewing. However, it possibly somewhat over-estimates the role of the unconscious and neglects some other functions of television to the viewer.

THE USES AND GRATIFICATION APPROACH AND THE AFFECTIVE-AESTHETIC FUNCTION

In the "uses and gratification approach" or "functional approach" researchers have tried to define some common functions of communication in all societies. Based on the more detailed classification in Figure 1 a distinction can be made between three different major functions (30, 7): 1. the cognitive-informative function, 2) the integrative-social function, and 3) the affective-aesthetic (emotional) function of communication. These functions can be studied both at individual level and in society as a whole.

It has been found out that the major perceptual dimensions on which people tend to evaluate commercials reflect all the above mentioned theoretical functions. (30)

92

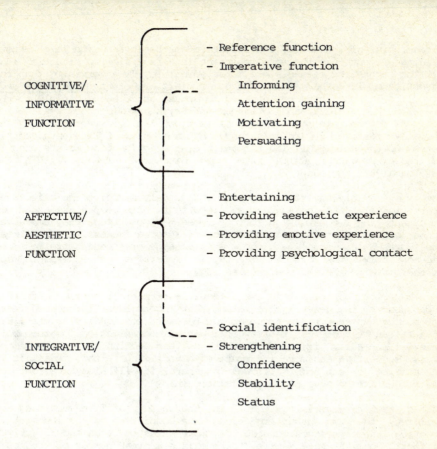

COGNITIVE/
INFORMATIVE
FUNCTION

- Reference function
- Imperative function
    Informing
    Attention gaining
    Motivating
    Persuading

AFFECTIVE/
AESTHETIC
FUNCTION

- Entertaining
- Providing aesthetic experience
- Providing emotive experience
- Providing psychological contact

INTEGRATIVE/
SOCIAL
FUNCTION

- Social identification
- Strengthening
    Confidence
    Stability
    Status

Figure 1

Functions of communication

Not surprisingly, however, the <u>affective-aesthetic function</u> (e.g. entertaining elements) is the most important in a real viewing situation (30,
7). The suggestive elements are more typical for TV-advertising than for
advertising in other media. <u>TV commercials are often using codes and
symbolic</u> images that are intended to appeal as much as possible to the
viewer's unconscious and to launch off psychodynamic processes in him/
her. As stated in the previous section, this is reinforced by the
normally passive TV relationship; the whole flow of TV events contributes to the same goal. The affective-aesthetic function refers exactly
to those processes which have been discussed already within the
psychoanalytic approach.

The viewers of advertising do not consciously perceive the affective/
aesthetic elements as the most important. When people are asked how
important they consider different message properties, they emphasise
either cognitive or integrative elements (informativeness, truthfullness
and worthwhile issue). However, when message preferences are measured
independently, the affective/aesthetic properties seem to explain most
of the variation in the preferences (30).

The superior position of the affective-aesthetic function is further
supported by the general observation that modern advertising uses facts
not so much to support an argument but to exert emotional pressure (18).
Because suggestion is the typical way of communication for the whole
television media, it seems rather useless and frustrating to demand
"less suggestive and more informative" advertising in this media. If TV
advertising exists and is allowed in general it will always be (decoded
as) suggestive because of the TV relationship.

It is rather surprising that, in the study of TV advertising and
children, the two other functions, the cognitive and the integrative
function, have received considerably more attention than the affective-
aesthetic one. [1] For example, there exists a great number of studies
on the cognitive abilities of children in regard to advertising (1, 22,
23, 24, 25, 27, 34). Moreover, the effects of TV commercials on
children's consumer choise and attitudes have been studied mainly in
terms of the cognitive-informative function (2, 11, 12, 26). The
theoretical basis of these studies is usually provided by theories of
developmental and cognitive psychology (especially Plaget's theory) or
by learning and information processing theories.

The recognition of the importance of the affective/aesthetic function
could give new insights also when studying children's cognitive
abilities. Education scientists have proposed that deep learning
orientation requires that the subject - after overcoming the stage of
more reproductive learning (repetitive learning) - should not only learn
how to do <u>conceptual analysis</u> but also have to do <u>analysis of relevances</u>
(16). This requires the ability to place the object in a larger context
and to do active exploratory thinking. This can take, for example, the

---

1) In contrast, <u>art reception</u> studies often <u>over</u> emphasise the
affective/aesthetic function and neglect the cognitive and social
functions of art: its ability to establish relationships between
person, ideas and patterns of behaviour.

form of affective criticism but it can also mean new ideas and new ways of feeling. Thus learning of relevances is probably associated more with the affective/aesthetic dimension than with the cognitive dimension of communication.

The integrative-social function has been studied by examining the socialisation effects of TV advertising (3, 20, 21, 22, 24, 33, 35, 36). These studies often implicitly or explicitly apply a S-R model borrowed from learning theory. The research has paid some attention to the mediating factors (e.g. the behvaiour of parents) in addition to different variables describing the children in question. Of the socialisation effects, TV's influence on children's aggressive behaviour has probably received most attention also in recent years (14, 15, 17). Moreover, there are findings concerning TV's long-term effects on other values, e.g. materialism and sex role perceptions (20). Socialisation studies, especially aggression studies, also come close to the category of research on the affective function.

In the analysis of messages attention has been paid to the effectiveness of certain separate message properties. In some countries efforts have been also made to define normatively features which are not suitable in commercials directed to children (19, 4). However, what is missing is a more systematic analysis of TV advertising from the viewpoint of theory of film and other media. This sort of study would include the analysis of the product-specific characteristics of commercials (e.g. codes), their type-characteristics (drama, dialogue, life style advertisements, etc.), and their narrative characteristics (visualisation, sound). Equally important is the study of how all these elements are combined (staging, editing, synchronisation, contrast, etc.). The film analysis can be combined with the psychodynamic analysis of the reception processes, that is, the detailed analysis of the affective-aesthetic function.[1]

STUDY OF CULTURAL COMPETENCES: DECODING AND ATTACHING MEANING

The uses and gratifications approach or functional approach would very much suggest sociological and semiotic analyses of the viewers' cultural

---

1) An interesting example of empirical analysis along these lines has been presented concerning the development of Coca-Cola commercials (29). The changes from the beginning of 1970's until 1980's have been considerable. The average length of shots was shortened from 6, 7 to 2, 0 seconds, and their number in a commercial was accordingly increased. The tempo of suggestive advertising thus follows the general acceleration of the life rhythm. The emphasis on the last shots remained unchanged. The more rapid tempo can be observed also in the music. The shifts from one shot to another became much sharper, and the tempo of picture and music were synchronised to emphasise the key points. Other major changes include increased emphasis of female voice, eroticised atmosphere and younger identification objects. Moreover, the commercials adapted the narrative form; the commercial presents a story with its own dramaturgy.

competence, i.e. their command or lack of different social and stylistic codes which are necessary to decode and understand the underlying meaning and nuances of the object (5).

The combining of the two types of analysis, film/media analysis and the analysis of psychic processes, makes it easier to understand, for example, why certain type-characteristics or narrative styles of TV commercials are preferred to others (for instance, because of their ego-supportive function). It also helps to understand the importance of the cultural gaps between the encoded messages and the viewers' competence to interpret them.

The marketers are aware of the different sensitivity of various age groups to different spots and use this knowledge in the segmentation. Underlying this practice is the importance of different previously acquired cultural competence (e.g. familiarity with the connotation of symbols). The viewer must behold them in order to give meaning to what is perceived. There is no perception which does not involve an unconscious code. Bourdieu, for example, has strongly criticised the illusion of "fresh eye" or "naked eye" in the reception of art works. Whenever competences are missing, the illusion of immediate comprehension leads to illusory comprehension based on a mistaken code (6). If information exceeds the cultural competences of the viewer, he perceives it as being without significance, structure and organisation, because he cannot decode it. Obviously, this fact forms an important obstacle to the distribution of cultural experience in a democratic way.

Correspondingly, the study of cultural competences and differences in decoding abilities can be of central value in the efforts to deconstitute the passive TV relationship.

It has been proposed that the TV viewing situation is a reverse form of psychoanalysis (28). The passive transference, "TV-relationship", encourages the viewer to reproduce, not uncover his/her conflicts in the flow of TV events. The viewer does not actively seek experiences but rather rediscovers them. Especially the affective-aesthetic elements (e.g. entertainment), in turn, more or less resemble supportive therapy in many respects (use of suggestion, catharsis and manipulation).

If it is a fact that television and TV commercials are capable of appealing to the unconscious of adult viewers and easily advance their regress to earlier developmental stages, the impact obviously is even stronger for children whose ego-development is only under way. The problem is not in the first place how to develop children's cognitive information processing abilities or rational decision making. Neither is it of much use to bring under control some separate elements in commercials (such as children's appearing in them). Instead, more attention should be paid to the holistic impact of constant exposure to the flow of TV programs and TV commercials which children only with difficulty, if at all, can differentiate from each other. Programs and commercials are both heavily dominated by the affective-aesthethic codes and styles which appeal to the unconscious fantasy world of the viewer. From the children's point of view, it is important to find out how to break the normally passive TV viewing situation and thus "deconstitute" the passive spectator. Increased awareness of the symbolic codes presented in the TV flow of events and of the symbolic position of the TV relationship itself in the viewer's life could help to break the passive transference on the personal level. This requires education in the cultural codes which are specific to the television media and to the life in a society dominated by this media.

Cognitive and affective effects of TV advertising on children

PROFESSOR F. VAN RAAIJ

Modern theories of the effects of mass communication assume a more active role on the side of the receiver and more intervening cognitive and affective processes. The message as such triggers a process, in which situational variables, medium factors, social interaction, knowledge and memory of the receiver play an important part. New information in the advertising message will be linked with existing information about the product, argumentation will take place to support or to refute the advertising claims, the information source will be evaluated, and fourthly, social conversation about the product may be enhanced. Note that these intervening cognitive and affective processes are a possible or a negative reinforcement of the advertising claim.

While these intervening processes have been studied with adults (Mitchell, 1983; Wright, 1974), limited research has been done with children. The degree of product involvement of children is probably restricted to toys, candy, soft drinks, clothing, audio-video equipment, and sports equipment, but may be high for the mentioned product classes. Age and developmental differences are expected for product classes, with more extensive cognitive and social elaboration of advertising for the higher age groups.

In this paper, we describe cognitive elaboration (argumentation of advertising claims, source derogation); affective reactions; differences of intervening processes depending on levels of involvement; social elaboration (conversations with peers); effects of media factors (print-electronics; speed control of transmission); and the type of dependent variables measuring advertising effects. Not only the assessment of advertising effects, but also copy editing and testing may benefit from knowledge on how consumers process advertising information.

COGNITIVE ELABORATION

Cognitive elaboration is the active formulation of pro or contra arguments, being exposed to advertising information, especially claims. Only if enough time is available, and the involvement of the receiver is high enough, one may expect cognitive elaboration to take place. In the cognitive elaboration process, the receiver tries to connect the new information with existing beliefs in memory and own experiences with the advertised product or service. Four types of cognitive elaboration may be distinguished:

1) Pro-argumentation or support argumentation. The receiver links the advertising information with existing beliefs that are consonant with the advertising claims. Thus, the advertising claim is enhanced and a positive effect of advertising on product beliefs is the result. Not only existing beliefs, also information from other sources (other advertisements, consumer tests, experiences of others) may increase pro-argumentation. An attribution process (consensus, consistency over modality and time) results in the conclusion that the advertising claim must be true.

2) Contra-argumentation. The receiver confronts the advertising information with existing beliefs and experiences and forms a dissonant relationship. The advertising information will probably be discounted as "not true". In this way, the advertising effect is reduced, or might be even negative, in the sense that the advertising message evokes the negative experiences and makes them more manifest. Advertising as a source of information will be readily discounted, because consumers are aware of the persuasive purposes of the advertiser. Advertising against a dominant trend in public opinion will have adverse effects.

3) Source Derogation. Dissonant advertising information may lead to source derogation, i.e. discounting the information based on its unreliable, untrustworthy source, motivated by self-interest. Negative attributions to the source are common with advertising and are a way to reduce cognitive dissonance. An important aspect of source derogation is the perception of intent of the advertiser. Perceiving a persuasive intent will generally decrease the effectiveness of the commercial. Perceiving an assistive intent ("commercials tell you about products") will increase the effectiveness (Robertson and Rossiter, 1974). The development of persuasive intent attributions reinforces the cognitive defense to persuasion. Older children will be less persuadable than younger children.

4) Curious disbelief is a weak form of contra-argumentation. Humor, double meaning, or an ambiguous opening statement in advertising create curious disbelief. This disbelief may be "solved" in the

advertising content and changed into pro-argumentation.

Advertising will have a positive effect on consumer beliefs, if enough pro-argumentation has been evoked and sustained, while contra-argumentation and source derogation are relatively low. Curious disbelief might be developed into pro- or contra-argumentation. The result of cognitive elaboration is a change in the beliefs about the product or service, and thus a change in preferences, intentions, and ultimately purchasing behavior.

The level of cognitive elaboration depends on product involvement, situational facilitation, especially processing time and absence of distractions and concurrent activities, and mode of presentation. With regard to children, we expect an increasing level of cognitive elaboration with increasing age, due to cognitive development, differentiation, and personal experience with the product. For very young children (below 6 years of age), cognitive functioning may be restricted to enactive (motor) and imagery codes of information. An enactive (motor) code is imitation of behaviours that seem to work to reach a goal, e.g. obedience or disobedience to parents, repetition of slogans and jingles, in the sense that they represent the product, and may become active in the store, where the child recognises a product, known from television (Calder, Robertson, and Rossiter, 1975).

Older children (6 - 12 years) will exhibit a higher level of cognitive elaboration, although probably not including source derogation. Children over 12 years of age will probably develop more contra-argumentation as compared with pro-argumentation.

However, we should be aware that the cognitive functioning of children may be qualitatively different from adults, and not just a more constrained adult model (Calder, Robertson, and Rossiter, 1975).

AFFECTIVE FACTORS

While the cognitive elaboration process may lead to a revision of beliefs, this process is not independent of affective factors. Affective factors pertain to evaluations, attitudes, preferences, and other types of evaluative judgement. Traditional models of advertising effects assume that the affective reaction comes after the cognitive elaboration and belief formation or change, cf. AIDA (Palda, 1966). Fishbein and Ajzen's (1975) attitude model of reasoned action starts with beliefs about the attitude object, followed by an evaluation of beliefs. However, evidence exists that an affective reaction preceeds the cognitive reaction and elaboration. After that, a more developed secondary affective reaction may follow. For most cognitive and social psychologists, cognitions are first and affect (attitude, evaluations) is secondary. Wundt (1905), however, already argued that "Gefuhls-elemente" (feelings) are primary in human and animal behaviour, "ehe noch von den Vorstellungselemente etwas wahrgenommen wird" (before anything cognitive is perceived). People develop an evaluation about a person, a product, an advertisement, and develop cognitions afterwards.

In the primary affective reaction, the advertisement and/or the product are evaluated, and a subsconscious decision is made, whether it is necessary, useful or interesting to collect and to process more information about the object. The cognitive elaboration process that follows, is not neutral but serves to support and to justify the primary affective reaction (Van Raaij, 1983). The secondary affective reaction need not be different from the primary affective reaction, but is often more detailed and supported by cognitive elements.

The sequence of effects of advertising is modeled in Figure 1. Stimuli from the environment will be received and coded by the sensory system (A). Coded stimuli will be evaluated (B). The primary affective reaction is both a selection filter and a first reaction to the stimulus. Cognitive elaboration (C) contains recognition, recall of memory traces, discrimination or differentiation of stimulus attributes. The cognitive elaboration process leading to belief change or support has been described in the section above. After the cognitive elaboration, the secondary affective (D) may follow, and after that buying intention and purchasing behaviour (E).

Advertising effects are usually measured as recognition (C1), discrimination (C2), recall, attitude (D), buying intention or behaviour (E). The primary affective reaction is usually not considered, just as the receivers themselves do not consciously consider or rationalise the primary affective reaction.

Broadbent (1977) uses the expression "the hidden pre-attentive processes". He argues that the primary affective reaction not only determines the process, but also functions as a global, fast, passive analysis of information ("scanning") preceding a more elaborate, slow, and active type of information processing ("focussing"). The primary affective reaction may be biased and misperceived, due to motivational factors (physiological, expectational, or functional) one is not always aware of.

The scanning-type of information processing is said to occur in the right brain hemisphere, whereas the focussing takes place in the left brain hemisphere.

Affective reactions cannot be avoided and are difficult or impossible to control. It may be somatic (blushing, trembling); body reactions interpreted afterwards may be attributed to elements of the advertisement. The affective reaction is never "wrong". Beliefs and cognitions may be wrong; preferences may change; but tastes are never wrong (de gustibus non est disputandum). While beliefs are based on reasoning, the verbalisation of affect and emotions is difficult. The usual way of "measuring" affect is a post-hoc rationalisation process, why we like or dislike something. The common question of lovers is "why do you love me?". It is difficult to accept an affective reaction without any explanation.

The first impressions of an advertisement, product, package, magazine, salesperson may be crucial for the rest of the process. In the later cognitive elaboration, this first impression may be refined or altered, although probably not too much. The cognitive elaboration process may

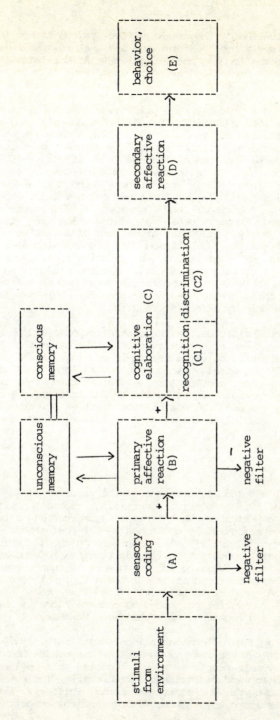

Figure 1. Model of the receiver of information

serve as a justification of the primary affective reactions. It is not true that we collect "cool" information and evaluate the information afterwards. Most information is "hot", emotional, affect-laden. We don't see a "house", we see a "home" and refer to ourselves: "Should I like to live there?"

Affective reactions are probably more primitive and come earlier in the development process of children. The distinction of good and bad, friendly and unfriendly is the first reaction a baby learns (Izard, 1978). Emotional reactions exist before the development of thinking and language. The nonverbal communication of the affective system is effective, although the repertoire may be limited. One may expect that even young children have their preferences which they are unable to verbalize. In choice and play situations, one may learn about these preferences. Calder, Robertson, and Rossiter (1975) stress that the enactive (motor) and imagery codes of information are important. Enactive codes in early development are a form of imitative modeling, including verbal imitation. Repetition of slogans without attaching meaning to them is an example of an enactive code. Imagery codes constitute a more truthful representation of the product. An imagery code acquired from television commercials may become active in the store, where the child recognises the product. This may lead to a positive or negative primary affective reaction.

Somatic measures (pupil dilation, galvanic skin response, and observation of behaviour) may tap these affective reactions. The older the children, the better they are able to verbalise their feelings. Market research questionnaires will generally measure the rationalised affective reactions only. The more emotional and global reaction that triggered the process is lost by that time. It would be informative to know which advertising factors caused the positive or negative primary affective reaction; this is crucial to the success or failure of an advertising campaign.

SOCIAL ELABORATION

Until now the reactions and elaborations of the receiver of advertising have been individually, confronting advertising information with their own knowledge and experiences. The elaboration process might be social as well. Social elaboration is the confrontation of preferences, beliefs in a social context. Advertising has been said to provide information and topics for social conversation (agenda setting; McCombs and Shaw, 1972). An objective for advertising is not so much to change beliefs and evaluations, as to make the product or service a topic of conversation. Attitude change and product adoption will then take place in a social context. In social conversation, pro- and contra-arguments may become dominant, supporting and negating the advertising message.

Two-step or multi-step flow of communication models (Katz, 1957) also assume an interaction between mass communication and social conversation. Advertising may make people aware of products; opinion leaders receive this information and disseminate it to others ("followers"), together with their own pro- and contra-arguments. Followers, then, may become aware of advertising as a source of information, supporting social conversations. After product adoption advertising is a source of information to legitimize the purchase and to counterargue the critical remarks of others.

Churchill and Moschis (1979) test a model of consumer socialisation and conclude that family and peer communication about consumption mediate the effect of amount of television viewing on the social and economic motivations for consumption, and on a materialistic attitude. Only the frequency of interactions, not the content of the family and peer communication is, however, considered in their study. Social elaboration is more vivid and personal than the more abstract and impersonal information in advertising. Parents and peers are probably judged to be more trustworthy and reliable.

A specific case is the parent child relationship, in which the parents try to shape the beliefs, evaluations, and behaviour of the child, and the child tries to convince the parents. Older children might even teach their parents about fashions and the symbolic meaning of goods (retro-active socialisation). This information then, is acquired from peers and passed on to the parents.

Social elaboration is part of the consumer socialisation and learning processes, described by Ward (1974), Ward, Wackman, and Wartella (1977).

MEDIA CHARACTERISTICS

Elements of mass communication are image and text. Images are pictures of persons or objects, brand images and other forms of visual information. Text and numbers refer to concepts and amounts in a more abstract way. Paivio (1975, 1978) developed the "dual coding" hypothesis for images and text. Images are processed in an analog manner as "perceptual isomorphs" with a synchronous, spatially parallel representation. Text, however, is processed in a discrete, sequential manner.

Images may directly create an affective impression with the person (nice, attractive, or not), whereas for text, one needs an internal transformation to create an image. The internal representation of a text may be in the form of images, just as one remembers images after reading a book without illustrations. The information processing of texts will be longer than for images.

Another distinction of media is internal vs external pacing (Van Raaij, 1979). With internally-paced media, the receiver controls the speed of information transmission, e.g. the printed media. The receiver may read slowly or fast and processes the information at the desired speed. With a slow speed, more cognitive elaboration is possible. The affective reaction will be faster than the cognitive elaboration. This may mean that with a high speed of information transmission ("walking through a magazine"), an affective reaction but no cognitive elaboration may take place. A controversial message may only be evaluated in an affective way (approval or disapproval) and not or only very minimally elaborated in a cognitive way.

With externally-paced media the sender controls the speed of information transmission, e.g. radio and television. The receiver forms an affective reaction and, if the speed is not too high, a cognitive elaboration. Large individual differences exist with external pacing in the degree of cognitive elaboration of the messages. Time compression of the message (Riter, Balducci en McCollum, 1983) reinforce the effects of external pacing.

According to the above distinction, media may be classified in four groups (Figure 2): Media of type I contain images to be processed by the receivers in their own speed (posters, picture book).

Type II media are mainly texts to be processed at one's own speed (book, newspaper, magazine). Type III media contain images, speed-controlled by the sender (radio). Affective reactions are likely to occur in all four types. Cognitive elaboration will be strongly influenced by the sender in type III media. The cognitive elaboration of type II media is probably receiver-controlled, provided that the receiver is involved to engage in cognitive elaboration.

Type III media are probably most persuasive. The sender has the power to influence the primary affective reaction. Type II media may be persuasive, provided that the receiver is motivated and the primary affective reaction is favourable for the message.

Young children will mainly use the media of Type I and III (comic books, television). Images are easier to process and to retain than texts, but it is more difficult to assess the affective impact of images in advertising and the way an image creates a positive or negative primary affective reaction. Type I media allow for more cognitive elaboration than Type III media. We expect as a consequence, more extreme product evaluations for Type I media as compared with Type III media, allowing enough time to process the print (Type I) advertisement.

For older children, type II and IV media will be become more important, and thus the need for an internal transformation of words into images. One may expect a longer processing time for words as compared with images.

	Pacing:	
	Internal	External
Images	I poster comical strip cartoons	III television movie slides
Content:		
Text	II book magazine newspaper	IV radio

<u>Figure 2</u>. Four types of media according to internal/external
pacing and content of media.

For more complex and meaningful products (toys, electronics), Type I
media will be able to convey more information. If this information is
relevant and understandable for children, and if pro-argumentation may
be expected, a print medium (type I) should be selected. If otherwise,
the information is simple (candy, soft drinks), a slice-of-life, more
entertaining approach to the product usage situation is more
appropriate.

INVOLVEMENT

Product involvement is an important factor for the degree of
information processing of advertising. <u>Product or service involvement</u>
will be defined as the degree of interest in a product depending on the
technical and social functionality of a product for the consumer.
Consumers will be more involved with products that require a large
financial outlay that are perceived as having social or physical risk.
<u>Advertising involvement</u> is the degree of interest in advertising due to
the plot, actors, humor, newness of the advertisments. The number of
products and services children are interested in, may be limited but
involvement in these products may be high.

We distinguish three types of processes:

(1) Most cognitions and beliefs will be developed with a <u>high</u> level of
     product involvement and prior knowledge, with ample processing time
     (relatively low speed of information transmission or internal
     pacing), and absence of disaction and simultaneous activities. The
     new information from advertising will be combined/integrated with
     prior knowledge in memory. Argumentation and elaboration procedures
     include pro-argumentation, counter-argumentation, and source dero-
     gation. Advertising will have a positive attitudinal and inten-
     tional effect, if enough pro-argumentation is developed, and
     counter-argumentation or source derogation is relatively low.

(2) With an <u>intermediate</u> level of product involvement, more situational
     distraction, and less processing time, the advertisement or commer-
     cial should attract attention by creating unexpected combinations
     (collative properties, such as humor, newness, tension). The
     attracted attention should be directed toward the product and
     should overcome cognitive argumentation of the type of curious
     disbelief and elaboration toward relevant and characteristics and
     message.

(3) With a <u>low</u> level of product involvement, not many cognitions will
     be developed. Mere exposure of brand name and product in a repet-
     itive schedule may enhance a positive affective reaction or rein-
     forcement of an existing positive affective reaction (attitude).
     Poiesz (1983) concludes that the functionality of the product
     enhances an exposure-affect relation.

It is generally not true that advertising is more effective in high-involvement situations. As we have seen, in a high-involvement situation contra-argumentation might be developed decreasing the effects of the advertising message. In a low-involvement situation not many cognitions will be developed, <u>and, thus, the advertising message might have more effect,</u> depending on the number of repetitions and the difficulty of the message.

Research should be directed to assess the type of information processing enhanced with children confronted with advertising. The following groups of factors should be studied.

COMMERCIAL:
1. information content of commercial
2. attention value of commercial
3. repetition schedule

ANTECENDENTS:
4. product involvement
5. processing time
6. situational distraction

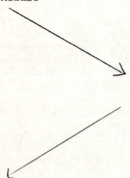

PROCESS:
7. cognitive elaboration number and type of cognitions
8. argumentation (pro/contra/source)
9. Response latency

CONSEQUENCES:
formation and change in:
10. cognitions
11. attitudes
12. preferences
13. intentions
14. buying behaviors

NEEDED RESEARCH

Research is needed with children as compared with adults to assess the spontaneous thoughts evoked by advertising. These thoughts could be classified as: pro- and contra-argumentation, source derogation, curious disbelief, and attributional processes. We expect for this type of research on <u>cognitive elaboration</u> that:

H (1):   More cognitive elaboration with high as compared with low product involvement.
H (2,3,4):   More cognitive elaboration with ample as compared with restricted processing time, due to distraction, concurrent activities, or internal pacing.
H (5):   More cognitive elaboration with increasing age of children.

H (6):   No contra-argumentation and source derogation for very
            young children (<6 years).

The measurement of <u>affective reactions</u> will make it possible to test:

H (7):   Affective responses dominate cognitive responses with
            young children.
H (8):   Less affective responses with increasing age.
H (9):   More affective responses under low-involvement conditions.

With regard to <u>social elaboration</u> we expect:

H (10):   Social elaboration increases with age.
H (11):   More social elaboration with peers with increasing age.
H (12):   More active search of advertising information with
            older as compared with younger children, as a
            consequence of social elaboration.

THE INFLUENCE OF "WORD PICTURE" RELATIONSHIPS OF TV FILMS ON THE EMOTIONAL REACTIONS AND RETENTION PERFORMANCE OF CHILDREN
AN ABSTRACT: PETER VITOUCH

The investigative material was a film of 28 minutes' duration produced by the Bavarian Broadcasting Corp. and shown on an afternoon program of the German General Broadcasting Corporation (ARD).

The nonverbal film relates the story of "Bibi Bitter" and his snowman in quite emphatical and emotional style. Without the aid of any spoken or written text, the story is told solely by means of photography, supplemented by sounds and background music. This peculiarity allowed us to produce two further film versions, each varying from the original according to one of the variables. Both additional versions were characterised by sparing off-texts; the one was held purely informational, matter-of-fact verbal content; the distinguishing feature of the second was the emotional style of its language. Fifteen sentences were integrated into each film at the same exact scene for each type of text. (Picture, music, and sounds matched in time).

Three versions of the film were at our disposal (first independent variable):

- the nonverbal original version
- the version with matter-of-fact text-style
- the version with matter-of-fact text-style combined with a short emotional supplement

The Second Independent Variable

To gain differentiated information about the effect of the sequence of scenes, the three versions were divided into 10 sections at the same points (scenes). We therefore were able to measure the emotional reactions to each separate section as well as to the film as a whole. These sections correspond to the "dramatic flow" of the story, and thus serve as a second independent variable.

Aside from the above-mentioned independent variables, it was assumed that the previous experience of the children with the medium "television" as also their personality, could influence their emotional reactions; these data were used as the covariates in the statistical evaluation via analysis of variance.

Experimental Design

The films were presented to each child separately, who saw one of the films. In all, sixty-two children, 9 years of age +/- 6 months, participated in the investigation. The subjects were divided into three separate experimental groups after a trial run. This trial served the purpose of gathering information for parallelising the groups according to the children's physiological base values as also to acclimatize the children to the experimental setting.

The dependent variables were the children's emotional reactions and their retention performance (regarding the content of the film). The

110

emotional reaction was simultaneously measured on two levels:-

1. On the physiological level by:
    a) registering the heart rate via finger pletysmography
    b) registering the breathing frequency via respiration belt
    c) registering the galvanic skin responses

2. On the cognitive level by:
    a) verbal interviews along the dimension "cheerful - sad"
    b) scaling the dimension "pleasant - unpleasant" via placement of a pointer on a continuous scale.

Significant results were the answer to the following questions:-

1. How do differentiated verbal formulations of a text (word-picture-relationship) influence the emotional reactions of children when the pictorial content remains identical?

2. How great is the difference in the intensity and/or quality of emotions as a dependent of the specific word-picture-relationship?

3. Does the measure of the emotional reaction have an influence on retention performance?

4. How greatly is the capability to react determined by:
    a) prior TV-viewing experience
    b) personality factors?

5. Which physiological measures best reflect quality changes in emotions?

RESULTS

For the Communciations Researcher

   The matter-of-fact version of the film elicited heart rate and SCR reactions significantly different from those observed to the other two styles of presentation. Together with the cognitive ratings, the differential emotional responses of the children could be objectified.

By including <u>physiological measures</u>, the comparison of the styles of presentation availed us of further objective information.

For the Psychologist of Emotions:

   The dramatic sequence, as defined by the progression from scene 1 to scene 10, reveals a significant covariation of respiratory amplitude with the ratings "cheerful - sad". The sadder the scene was rated, the higher the respiratory amplitude.

For the Media-Practitioner:

   Even relatively minute modifications of texts matched with the same pictorial contents can lead to a significantly different experience and also to poorer memory (retention performance). Particular attention must be paid to the interference of matter-of-fact texts on emotional pictorial material. These relationships deserve to be studied in greater detail. (A study on the effects of emotional information presented visually and underscored by different text versions on affective reactions and memory performance is already underway at the Institute for Psychology, University of Vienna). Personality factors and previous TV-viewing behaviour do have a certain effect on the way a particular presentation is experienced, but the emotional reactions of children are to a much greater extent a reflection of the scenario of the material actually being viewed. The film with a sober text generally elicits a higher level of activation and is therefore felt to be less pleasant.

The paper from which this abstract was taken was sponsored by the Bavarian Broadcasting Corporation and realised in collaboration with H. Bauer and the research group STURM-GREWE at the Institute for Psychology, University of Vienna, AUSTRIA.

CHILDREN'S PERCEPTION-PROCESSING OF T.V. PRESENTATION
THE MISSING HALF-SECOND
AN ABSTRACT: HERTHA STURM

Human perception is in part determined by past experiences and expectations. Such experiences can be quite varied dependent on whether they
relate to the perception of televised or non-televised material. In
real life-situations, a person usually has a certain short period of
time between the expectation of an event and its recurrence. Television
presentations are a different matter. As we perceive them, we are unable
to predict what is going to happen next. Cues are necessary for the
comprehension and retention of a presentation, particularly when there
is little time for a sequential decoding of picture and sound.

A comparison of real life versus television mediated perception reveals
a phenomenon which simply can be called "The missing half-second of
televised presentations". This missing half-second effects the behaviour of a recipient who is confronted with television-mediated stimuli.

Even our own introspection will reveal that we apply internal labels to
televised events. Such internalised labelling involves an attempt to
generate one's own expectations or experiences while watching a program.
This means that without such verbalisations (and its associated categorisation), comprehension and retention of the perceived material will be
greatly impaired. This assumption was confirmed by our study "Emotion
and arousal - children as TV viewers".

We were able to show that gaps of disruptions in televised textural
materials result in significant reduction in retention. These results
also showed that the recipient relies on internalised verbalisation in
order to comprehend a sequence of events, this requires a congruence
with the pictorial material. A mismatch between picture and sound confronts the viewer with two incongruous messages which make decoding
particularly difficult. In view of these findings, it should be clear
that a rapidly changing presentation impairs verbalisation.

In such cases, the individual acts and reacts with an increasing physiological arousal resulting in a reduction of comprehension, impeded
retention, and emotional dissatisfaction. This is obvious as we can
prove now that viewers are able to use mediated information significantly better if a transitional pause of two seconds has been inserted
between two sequences.

EMOTIONAL AND COGNITIVE ASPECTS OF TELEVISION
AN ABSTRACT: MARIANNE GREWE-PARTSCH

Summarizing the results of ten years media-research of the project group Sturm/Grewe with regard to television, advertising and children I would like to focus on the following topics:

1)   Television as an emotional medium
2)   Understanding televised information and understanding televised emotions

Television As An Emotional Medium

Television's role in affective development and functioning is one of the areas which have not received much attention in the past decade. Three studies of the product group Sturm/Grewe have been dedicated to this subject. Two empirical studies related to radio and TV were conducted on the topic "Media specific learning effects". The second study confirmed the results of the first (see Sturm et al., 1972).

This study showed that information conveyed by the media is retained or forgotten in accordance with long established forgetting curve of Ebbinghaus, that means reflecting a high rate of forgetting immediately after learning which decreases as a function of time. In contrast, emotional states, which were induced by radio and television programs remain stable and unchanged over the three-week-period of the study. That's why TV can be called an emotional medium: There is no forgetting, no alteration, while knowledge conveyed by television chiefly is forgotten by this time. This holds true for the emotions associated with the mediated program as well as for the emotions associated with the acting characters of TV. It was shown that audiences endow television actors - even marginal characters with stable and lasting emotions.

But, emotions demand to be confirmed. If one has formed an emotional attachment to a person one wants to see him or her again, preferably unchanged. From this perspective, television actors are usually un-reliable reference persons, because the viewer can never be certain, whether and under what circumstances they will re-appear. This repre-sents a media-specific example of the psycho-analytic concepts of loss - and separation - anxiety (Sturm 1973 and 1979). For children, this seems to be of particular importance. For advertising-communication via tele-vision, the fact seems to be remarkable that the emotionally effected period mediated by television lasts longer than the period that the young viewer knows why he has been excited.

I am coming to my second item: Understanding content, understanding one's own emotions as well as the emotions of others.

Considering the differences in the responses of children of various age groups to television, the developmental approach of Piaget seems to be a very useful method of discrimination. If we accept Piaget's reasoning then it becomes clear why the same television programs are comprehended differently by various age groups, contents become structured according to the level of cognitive and emotional development. And another aspect:

114

Understanding context depends chiefly on the format of presentation. These two aspects indicate two crucial points: Age related responses of children to mediated material and the presentation modes of television. Collins (1982) find age related aspects with children:

- in their cause of retention of television content
- in the processes of segmentation by viewing
- in influences about implicit events and their relations to retention
- in the ability to imply motive formation

Researchers nowadays agree that children's perception, attention and comprehension of media-presentations are age-related. To prove this, we tested the cognitive state of "intuitive thought" attributed by Piaget to the four-to-seven-years old age group (Sturm; Jorg: Information processing by young children, Piaget's theory of intellectual development applied to radio and television, Munich 1981).

We found that five-years-olds differ from six-and seven-years-olds in thier ability to process pictorial material. The young children appear to rely more on verbal cues which direct their attention. An explanation of this might be that pre-school children encounter difficulties in distinguishing between important and unimportant aspects of visually presented information. This suggests that the spoken word can play an important role in directing the child's attention to particular aspects of the mediated situation.

Understanding Ones Own Emotions

Hertha Sturm did refer to a special activity of the viewer who follows TV presentations with internal labelling. The emotional side of this internal labelling has particular salience. It helps to get to know owns own emotions. According to contemporary psycho-analytic and cognitive psychology the human infant's feelings are largely undifferentiated, consisting only of pleasure and displeasure. It is only through recognition and simultanuous labelling, that means through categorization, that these basic feelings become differentiated, for instance, pleasure becomes differentiated as joy, happiness, luck; and displeasure as fear, sadness and rage. These conclusions indicate a need for extended television specific pauses. This is, where the half-second for internal labelling gains its importance - to identify ones own emotions. Children particularly need these possibilities for affective development.

Modes of Presentation

A television program, which presents a story or a factual case on a one-track, undirectional manner, moving step by step, sequentially, without gaps, will be understood according to our study of a five-year-old. But the same story can also be presented with different levels of salient formal features - action, pace, visual special effects, loud music. Such presentations would be addressed to different periods of intelligence development in Piaget's terms. Hertha Sturm - as you have heard - introduced the concept of media-specific forms of presentation to media in Germany. It was good news to find, that the Centre for Research on the Influence of TV on Children in Kansas did corresponding empirical research in this field. That way, there are studies about levels of representation, analyses of television forms, linguistic codes, the impact of attention, comprehension and on social behaviour by Aletha Huston and John Wright.

It has been found that salient formal features can instigate aggressive behaviour in children, even in the absence of violent content - according to a study which dealt with advertisements with different levels of salient formal features. These findings provide support for the notion, that arousing form can lead to increased aggression even without the modelling of violent content. If form and content have somewhat different effects - as the conclusion of Aletha Huston - then commercial producers might reduce the violence in children's programs and substitute non-violent content presented with salient features.

Salient formal features lead - as we know - now to a state of generalized arousal. And here we have the discrepancy which Dr.Vitouch, the co-worker of our study - did refer to, a mismatch between information and formal presentation with the result that the young viewer is dissatisfied, so the advice to substitute non-violent content presented with salient features is not a good one.

REFERENCES: LIISA UUSITALO

Adler, R. & Ward, S. & Lesser, G. & Merringgoff, L.& Rossiter, J.
  (1980), "The effects of television advertising on children: review and
  recommendations", Lexington, MA: Lexington Books.
Atkin, C. & Heald, G. (1977), "The content of children's toy and food
  commercials", Journal of Communication 27.
Banks, S. & Gupta, R. (1980), "Television as a dependent variable, for a
  change", Journal of Consumer Research 7,327-330.
Billgren, J. (1980), Reklam till barn och ungdom (Advertising for
  children and adolescents). Lund, Sweden.
Bourdieu, P. (1974), Zur Soziologie der symbolischen Formen. Frankfurt
  a.M.: Suhrkamp.
Bourdieu, P. (1968), "Outline of a sociological theory of art
  perception," International Social Science Journal vol. 20, no.4, 589-
  612.
Eco, U. (1971), Den franvarande strukturen (La strutture assente). Lund:
  Berlinska Boktryckeriet.
Eco, U. (1972), "Towards a semiotic inquiry into the television message"
  Cultural Studies 3 (August 1972), Birmingham University.
Gerbner, G. (1969), "Toward 'cultural indicators': the analysis of mass
  mediated public message systems", In: Gerbner, G., The analysis of
  communication content. New York: John Wiley & Sons, 123-131.
Gerbner, G. (1972), "Communication and social environment", Scientific
  American 227:3 (Sept. 1972).
Goldberger, M. & Gorn, G.J. (1974), "Children's reactions to television
  advertising: an experimental approach", Journal of Consumer Research
  1, 69-75.
Gorn, G.J. & Goldberg, M.E. (1982), "Behavioural evidence of the effects
  of televised food message on children", Journal of Consumer Research 9
  (Sept. 1982), 200-205.
Habermas, J. (1981), Theories des kommunikativen Handelns, vols I-II.
  Frankfurt a.M.: Suhrkamp.
Huesmann, L.R. (1982), Television violence and aggressive behaviour. In:
  Peral, D. & Bouthelet, L.& Lazar, J. (eds.),Television and behaviour.
  Ten years of scientific progress and implications for the eighties,
  Vol.2. Washington D.C.: U.S. Government Printing Office.
Huesmann, L.R. & Lagerspetz, K.M.J. & Eron, L.D. (1983), Intervening
  variables in the television violence-aggression relation.
  Developmental Psychology 19.
Hayrynen, Y.P. (1980), Aesthetic activity and cognitive learning.
  Adult Education in Finland, Vol. 17, No.3, 5-13.
Lagerspetz, K.M.J. & Viemero, V. (1982). An international investigation
  of televised violence and aggression in children. The NORDICOM
  Review, 2, 11-13.
Lasch, Ch. (1979), "The culture of narcissism", New York: Warner Books.
Miller, J.H. & Bush, P. (1979), "Host selling vs. premium TV
  commercials: An experimental evaluation of their influence on
  children", Journal of Marketing Research 16 (August 1979), 323-332.
Moschis, G.P. & Moore, R.L. (1982), "A longitudinal study of television
  advertising effects:" Journal of Consumer Research 9, 279-286.
Robertson, T. (1979), "Parental mediation of television advertising
  effects", Journal of Communication 29, 12-25.

Robertson, T. & Rossiter, J.R. (1974), "Children and commercial persuasion. An attribution theory analysis", Journal of Consumer Research 1, 13-20.

Robertson, T. & Rossiter, J.R. (1976), "Short-run advertising effects on children: a field study", Journal of Marketing Research 13 (February 1976), 68-70.

Robertson, T.S. & Rossiter, J.R. (1977), "Children's responsiveness to commercials", Journal of Communication 27, 101-106.

Roedder, D. (1981), "Age differences in children's response to television advertising: an information processing approach", Journal of Consumer Research 8, 144-153.

Roedder, D.L. & Sternthal, B. & Calder, B. (1983), "Attitude-behaviour consistency in children's response to television advertising", Journal of Marketing Research 20, (Nov. 1983), 337-349.

Rubin, R. (1974), "The effects of cognitive development on children's response to TV advertising", Journal of Business Research 2, 409-419.

Steinbock, D. (1983a), Television ja psyyke: Televisio, illusionismi ja anti-illusionismi. (Television and psyche) Helsinki: Weiling & Goos.

Steinbock, D. (1983b), "Suggestive advertising, society and research", Mimographed working paper (in Finnish).

Uusitalo, L. (1977), Consumer perception and preferences of message structure. Helsinki School of Economics Series B:21.

Uusitalo, L. (1978), "Consumer information - prerequisite and determinant of need satisfaction (in Swedish)", In: Konsumenten i samhallet, Stockholm: Raben & Sjogren, 90-97.

Uusitalo, L. (1979) "Consumption style and way of life", Helsinki: Helsinki School of Economics Series A:27.

Wackman, D.B. & Wartella, E. & Ward, S. (1977), "Learning to be consumers: the role of the family", Journal of Communication 27, 138-151.

Ward S. (1972), "Children's reactions to commercials", Journal of Advertising Research 12 (April 1972), 37-45.

Ward, S. (1974), "Consumer socialisation of children:, Journal of Consumer Research 1, 1-13.

Ward, S. & Wackman, D.B. & Wartella, E. (1977), "How children learn to buy", Beverley Hills, Cal: Sage Publications.

Winn, M. (1977), "The Plug-In Drug", New York: Bantam.

Williams, R. (1974), "Television: Technology and Cultural Form", London: Fontana.

Williams, R. (1981), "Culture", Cambridge: Fontana.

REFERENCES: FRED VAN RAAIJ

Broadbent, D.E., "The hidden preattentive processes", American Psychologist, 32, 1977. 109-118.

Churchill, G.A. & Moschis, G.P., "Television and interpersonal influences on adolescent consumer learning", Journal of Consumer Research, 6, 1979. 23-35.

Fishbein, M., Ajzen, I., "Belief, attitude, intention, and behavior", Reading, Mass.: Addison-Wesley, 1975.

Izard, C.E., "On the development and emotion-cognition relationships in infancy", in: M. Lewis & L. Rosenblum (Eds.), The development of affect", New York: Plenum Press, 1978.

Katz, E., "The two-step flow of communication: An up-to-date report on an hypothesis", Public Opinion Quarterly, 21, 1957. 61-78.

McCombs, M.E. & Shaw, D.L., "The agenda-setting function of mass media", Public Opinion Quarterly, 36, 1972. 176-187.

Mitchell, A.A., "Cognitive processes initiated by exposure to advertising", in: R.J. Harris (Ed.), Information processing research in advertising, Hillsdale, N.J.: Erlbaum. 1983. 13-42.

Paivio, A., "Perceptual comparisons through the mind's eye", Memory and Cognition, 3, 1975. 635-647.

Paivio, A., "Dual coding: Theoretical issues and empirical evidence", in: J.M. Scandura & C.J. Brainerd (Eds.), Structural Process Models of Complex Human Behaviour, Alphen a.d. Rijn: Sijthoff & Noordhoff,

Palda, K.S., "The hypothesis of a hierarchy of effects: A partial evaluation", Journal of Marketing Research, 3, 1966. 13-24.

Poiesz, Th.B.C., "The relationship between exposure frequency and consumer affect; toward a functional explanation", Dissertation, Tilburg University, 1983.

Raaij, W.F. van, Consumenteninformatie: "Hoeveel en in welke vorm?", Tijdschrift voor Marketing, 13, 1979. 10-16.

Raaij, W.F. van, "Affective and cognitive reactions to advertising", Rotterdam: Erasmus University, Papers on Economic Psychology 28.

Riter, C.B., Balducci, P.J. & McCollum, D., "Time compression: New evidence", Journal of Advertising Research, 22, 1982. 39-43.

Robertson, T.S. & J.R. Rossiter, "Children and commercial persuasion: An attribution theory analysis", Journal of Consumer Research, 1, 1974. 13-20.

Ward, S., "Consumer socialisation", Journal of Consumer Research, 1, 1974. 1-14.

Ward, S., Wackman, D., & Wartella, E., "How children learn to buy", Beverly Hills, Cal.: Sage 1977.

Wright, P., "Analysing media effects on advertising response", Public Opinion Quarterly, 38, 1974. 192-205.

Wundt, W., "Grundriss der Psychologie", Leipzig: Wilhelm Engelmann, 1905.

REFERENCES: HERTHA STURM

(Sturm, H.; Vitouch, P.; Bauer, H.; Grewe-Partsch, M:
Emotion und Erregung - Kinder als Fernsehzuschauer. Eine psychophysiologische Untersuchung. (Emotion and arousal - Children as television viewers. A psychophysiological study). In: Fernsehen und Bildung, 16 (1982) 1-3, pp. 11-30).

PART V
PARENT-CHILD
RELATIONSHIPS

Session summary

This session focused on the general issue of how parent-child relationships mediate the impact of television on children, and conversely, how television might influence parent-child relationships. For example, children may ask their parents to buy things for them that they see advertised on television, and this asking behaviour may be functional or dysfunctional. It is functional if knowing their children's desires helps parents to make choices which will be satisfying and not result in waste. American research shows that parents actually encourage their chldren to watch television in order to make a list of products children might wish to receive at Christmastime. On the other hand, asking behaviour might be dysfunctional if it causes stress in the family relationship beyond the "normal" stresses within families.

More broadly, the nature of rules that parents set regarding their children's television behaviour, and the general "climate" regarding television within the household, forms a context in which children use television. Papers in this session address this question of the context for television in families, and how this context mediates the medium's impact on children.

Professor Thomas Robertson reviews American research in this area. He notes that a potentially powerful mediator of televisions's effects is the extent to which parents and children watch television together. However, such co-viewing does not occur frequently. Another powerful mediator is the extent to which parents and children discuss advertising and purchasing behaviour. Such discussions occur more frequently than co-viewing, and such directed discussions are particularly useful to younger children (under 7 years). Parents seem to expect older children to model their behaviour. Older children ask for fewer things than younger children, probably reflecting greater purchasing autonomy and reflecting the fact that older children's preferences are known to parents, so that they do not have to make product requests as often as younger children.

American research has shown that children ask their parents to buy things for them an average of 13 times per month. Their requests reflect their developing interests, so that older children are likely to ask for clothing, records, and the like. Research has shown that such intra-family requests rarely result in conflict. Parents often simply agree to buy things, although they report more discussions about the purchase with their children when the goods requested are relatively expensive.

Jean-Noel Kapferer challenges previous research which has shown that children who are heavy viewers of television develop more "materialistic" attitudes than do light viewers of television. He presents data which show that materialistic attitudes are more shaped by parental attitudes than by television.

Professor Philip Graham brings the perspective of a child psychiatrist to bear on the question of advertising and family relationships. While his experience is mostly with seriously disturbed children and families, he notes that many issues, such as product requests, can be a source of tension and stress within families. However, the question is whether children's requests for products are a more or less powerful source of stress than other family issues, such as children's choices of friends, drug abuse, and potentially more serious issues.

Taking the papers in this session as a set, the dominant message is that simplistic models of the family's influences on mediating advertising effects, and of children's influences within families, are not appropriate. There was consensus that the family unit exerts a powerful influence to mediate the effect of television advertising and programming, but the mechanisms by which this mediating influence occurs remain unclear. It would appear that directed discussions, parents acting as role models, and more subtle processes all play a role in mediating television's impact.

Conversely, the linkage is complex between a child's seeing a desirable product in an advertisement, and asking one or both of their parents to buy it for him or her. Such asking behaviour depends on the child's age, and the context of the request. For example, parents may discourage children from asking for products, but there are occasions when such asking behaviour is actually encouraged. In any case, it seems clear that advertising does provide a source of information about products for children; it also seems clear that children's interests in products they see advertised depends upon their age-related interests, and it seems clear that such asking behaviour is only rarely a source of serious tension or conflict within the family.

A comparison of TV advertising and mothers' influence on children's attitudes and values

PROFESSOR J. N. KAPFERER

This paper addresses the issue of comparing television and parental influence on the acquisition (or non acquisition) of children's consumer skills and values related to consumption. It stems from the recognition that the debate between critics of advertising to children and marketing researchers is basically a debate between two theoretical models of television influence. It reports a research specifically undertaken to allow an empirical testing of these two conflicting models [1].

THE TWO MODELS OF TELEVISION INFLUENCE

Be it in the context of advertising, of violence, of sexual stereotyping, of basic values, the critics of television share the same implicit model : television has strong carving effects on children, and is considered as the major socializing agent of children. In this model, the role of the parents is difficult. They are presented as disapproving witnesses of the alleged effects of television, having given up the frontal fight against the video-intruder. In this model, nothing stands between television and the child : its influence is direct and un-mediated.

When one looks at sociological research concerning the effects of television on children (Southon 1978 ; Chombart de Lauwe and Bellan 1981), a different model is emerging. All sociologists consider that no influence of television can be predicted unless the conditions of its reception are known. In other words, the most important variable is the family context around exposure to television : are the parents present, do they speak with their children about the programs, what are the values held by the parents....?

Because it tried to empirically assess the validity of the criticisms emitted against advertising aimed at children, early marketing research de facto adhered to the first model, the one of the critics. Most research on heavy viewing or on repetition effects had an S - R look. Typically, experiments varied the repetition rate of specific commercials and assessed its effect on cognitive, affective or behavioural outcomes. Survey research examined the correlations between indicators of television exposure and variables related to the acquisition of consumer skills and values. In both methodologies, the context of exposure, the conditions of reception, the parental habits and culture are generally left aside. The focus is on television advertising and the child, thus reinforcing the implicit idea that there is nothing else to study between these two protagonists.

LITERATURE REVIEW

Through comparisons of heavy and light viewers, holding age constant, or through correlational analyses, what are the conclusions of research addressing the issue of television influence on children's consumer skills and values?

At the cognitive level, in a recent Belgian experiment, heavy viewers perceived less than light viewers the selling purpose of three specific advertisements (Mars chocolate bar, Lego toys, Pepsi-Cola soft drink). This finding held true both for French and Dutch speaking children (Crioc, 1983). The authors concluded that heavy viewing far from making people more resistant to advertising (through increased recognition of the selling purpose), actually did exactly the contrary. heavy viewers' vigilance is reduced : they tend to forget the "real" aim of advertising.

Using multiple indicators of cognitive understanding of advertising (its purpose, the nature of the differences with regular programs....), Rossiter and Robertson (1974) report a non significant correlation with television viewing ($r = -.06$). If one considers that disappointment after the purchase of advertised products is an indicator of trust in advertising content, or of the ability of making realistic expectations, Rossiter and Robertson (1976) found that, within age-groups, dissatisfaction was higher among those children who were above average television viewers.

At the affective level, it has been repeatedly found that, within age groups, heavy viewers hold more positive attitudes than their peers (Adler et al., 1981).

Evidence concerning the acquisition of various consumer skills (Ward, Wackman and Wartella, 1977) is equivocal. No systematic pattern was found:for some skills, TV viewing actually decreased the speed of acquisitions. Finally, at the value level, Atkin, (1975) showed that materialism among children was positively related to television exposure (r=. 10, p< .05), thus providing support for the critics' contention about the negative effect of advertising on childrens's values.

Whatever the direction of the results, the above studies are inconclusive for they do not control for a major variable that could possibly explain alone the observed differences between heavy and light viewers' opinions and attitudes vis a vis advertising and consumption : the parents' own opinions and attitudes. One could pretend, for instance, that materialistic values observed among children would only mirror their parents' differences, and not the effects of television viewing. Any relationship between a child's exposure and attitudes is likely to be spurious as long as his (or her) parents' attitudes are not controlled, as shown in the accompanying figure. In any study concerning the alleged effects of television on children's attitudes and values, the parents must be included.

PARENTS' ATTITUDES/CHILD'S EXPOSURE LEVEL/CHILD'S ATTITUDES

Objectives of the research

The present research purported to answer the three following questions:

1. To what extent are children's attitudes, behavior and values as consumers related to their mother's attitudes, behavior and values?

2. Do heavy viewers differ from light viewers in terms of attitudes, behavior and values?

3. In case such differences appear, would they hold true, if one controls for the mother's own attitudes, behavior and values?

To answer these questions, two parallel forms of the same questions were used to tap mother's and child's attitudes, behavior and values. In addition, children's exposure data were collected. This methodology is now detailed.

METHODOLOGY

Dependent Variables

On what specific child's attitudes, behavior and values did the research focus? Table 1 presents the conceptual variables and the items selected to operationalize them. On the whole, 17 items tap five major conceptual areas.

1. Understanding of advertising

Do children perceive the selling objective of advertising, its informative function? Do they perceive themselves as targets? Do they realise that there are more than formal differences (i.e. : shortness) between TV advertising and the other programs? Do they develop realistic expectations concerning advertised products or unrealistic ones leading to frequent disappointment once the

TABLE 1

OPERATIONALIZING THE ATTITUDES AND OPINIONS VIS A VIS ADVERTISING, CONSUMPTION AND TELEVISION.

VARIABLES	ITEMS
Understanding of Advertising	
- Information Purpose of Advertising	Advertising allows knowledge of objects and products which exist.
- Selling Purpose of Advertising	On TV, the difference between advertising and the other programs is that it tries to sell things.
- Formal Differentiation of Advertising	Shortness apart, advertising is like the other programs on TV.
- Realistic Expectations	One is often disappointed after purchasing products seen in advertising.
- Self Perception as Target	There are advertisements especially made for children
- T.V. and Manufacturers relationship.	It is TV itself which asks manufacturers to show their products on TV.
Attitudes Vis a Vis Advertising	
- Like/Dislike	On the whole, I like advertising
Perception of Advertising as a Fairytale	
- Pleasant Experience	In advertisements, people are always sympathetic (nice).
- Magic Experience	In advertising, what is shown is almost like magic.
- Happy Ending	In advertising, the naughty people are always punished.
Personal Values	
- Materialism	People are much happier if they can buy a lot of things.
- Self Restriction Morality	One may not get all things one desires.

– Liking of School	Going to school is fun.
– Sensitivity to Violence	TV news often scares me.
– Self Tolerance for Negative Behavior	One may be a bit naughty.

Decision Process

– Information Seeking	To purchase something I look for information from all possible sources.
– Price Sensitivity	To purchase something, I pay attention especially to price.

advertised product is purchased? Finally what is their understanding of the advertising buying process : do they believe that it
is television itself which asks manufacturers to show their products
or the opposite?

Thus understanding of advertising was measured by six indicators.
The children had to answer on Likert-type 5 point items (from
totally disagree (1) to totally agree (5). These six items were not
intended to build up a single scale. Actually, pilot testing of a
larger number of items on a convenience sample had shown that the
six selected items were rather independent.

2. Perception of advertising

It has often be said that television advertising, by its format,
its repetition and its plot, functions a bit like a fairy tale. In
fact, many critics consider that this fairy tale appearance is the
base of advertising seduction among children. But do children
perceive advertisement as such tales? Three items purported to tap
this perception. From the author's previous qualitative work on
structural comparisons between TV advertisement and fairy tales,
three items were selected. Do they perceive that advertisements
always have a "happy ending"? Do children perceive that, unlike
regular programs, people in advertising are very sympathetic and
nice? Finally, do they experience some advertisements as magic?
Actually some "before-after" comparisons of the product effect could
be decoded as such by a child, unaware of the techniques and
language of advertising.

3. Attitude vis-a-vis Advertising

A single item measured this affective dimension. Do children like
advertising?

4. Pre-purchase Decision Making

Critics of advertising to children often contend that advertising
leads to purchases on the basis of advertising "information" alone
(the critics would certainly question the legitimacy of using the
word "information" to describe advertising content). In other words
the child would not be getting information from all possible sources
before making a purchase. In addition, critics believe that
advertising emphasis on "image" dimensions of differentiation lead
children to make less use of functional dimensions of choice, and
especially on the economic front - price. Two items purported to
measure these two facets of consumer pre-purchase decision-making.

5. Values

Because of its emphasis on products and the satisfactions brought
about by getting them, does advertising breed materialistic values
among children? In addition does advertising go against the integration of a "reality principle" by children? In Freudian theory,
psychological development as an adult involves a balance between the
pleasure principle (the id) and the reality principle (the superego):

children slowly internalize self restriction norms and morality and accept delayed gratifications. Since advertising brings to the home a constant flow of inducements to buy, it can be considered as going against the development of the ethics of self-restriction.

Three other values included in the study relate to television in general and not only to advertising. Because television is easy leisure, is permanent pleasure and fun, does it make, by contrast, going to school no fun at all, - even a painful experience? Many educationalists have been prompt to point to the competition between television experience and school experience (Chalvon et al. 1981). Finally do children perceive television as violent (especially the news) or does heavy viewing lead to habitualisation (Winick and Wineck, 1979)? Does seeing violence on TV create some self-indulgence or tolerance for naughty, mischievous or malevolent behaviour (Liebert et al., 1973)? On the whole, five items measured the children's general attitudes.

B. **Independent variables**

Children's answers to the seventeen attitude, behavior and value items may reflect either TV or parental influence.

The first independent variable was mother's own answers to these seventeen items. Since mothers have much more contact with their children than fathers, it was decided to tap parental microculture through their answers only.

The second independent variable is the child's exposure level to television. It was measured by nine questions of reported exposure behavior (on week days, Saturday, Sunday and Wednesday afternoon - the French kid-vid prime time). Actually, the exposure data had been collected prior to the research, in the context of a national survey of children's media habits, by the C.E.S.P. the French equivalent of the American Simmons Marketing Research Bureau (SMRB) or Mediamark Research Incorporated (MRI).

C. **Data collection**

In the first quarter of 1982, the C.E.S.P. interviewed a national sample of 2,500 children between eight and fifteen years old. All media exposure data were obtained by face to face interviewing procedure. In each family, in case of multiple children falling within the age bracket, one child was selected by a random procedure.

In April 1982, our dual questionnaire was sent by mail to these 2,500 families, thanks to the cooperation of the C.E.S.P. authorities. 362 families returned the questionnaire - one page for the mother, one page for the child. Since socio-demographic and media information were already known, the dual questionnaire comprised only the items concerning attitudes, perceptions, behavior and values. The sample breakdown is presented in Table 2.

RESULTS

A. Comparing mother and child's attitudes, behavior and values

A first question concerned the extent of congruence between mother's and child's answers. Do the latter's merely reflect the former's? Two types of statistical analyses were done : a comparison of the answers of each member of mother-child dyad. A positive difference means that the mother adheres more to the item than her child. The second anaylsis is merely correlational. Table 3 presents the results of these analyses.

The major picture emerging from the data is the high level of mother-child correlations, ranging from 0.13 to 0.48, with an average of .28. Since these correlations were computed on single items, subject therefore to unreliability, it can be considered that these correlations reflect a strong convergence between mothers' and their own child's attitudes, behavior and values, at least indicated by their paper and pencil answers. It is also noticeable that materialism is the item where the correlation is highest.

Looking now at difference figures, children like advertising more than their mothers, understand television manufacturers relationships less, are more materialistic and self indulgent, are less prone to self restriction. As to their perception of advertising, children are more likely to see a mere formal difference (shortness), to find that, as in fairy tales, the bad are always punished. Curiously, mothers seem to perceive more than their child that advertising shows things which are almost magical. Finally as expected from the literature, mothers perceive more that some advertisments are especially designed for children and look more for information before purchasing.

On all other items the differences are insignificant. Mother and child share the same perception of the selling purpose of advertising, of its informative role, build the same expectations concerning products actual performance, pay as much attention to price, evaluate similarly TV news violence and going to school.

Now a major question arises : do the observed differences vary accordingly to the child's age? Since age is a major developmental variable, one would expect so. Table 4 presents the mother-child differences within three age brackets (8-10, 11-12, 13-15) and the significance of the "differences between differences". Six items only show a significant variation along the child's age :

The younger the child the more he/she believes (more than the mother) that it is television itself which asks manufacturers to present their products, that possession of goods and things brings happiness, and that advertising differs only by its shortness (a concrete formal difference).

The older the child, the more the mother declares (more than the child) to be looking for information before purchasing, looking at price differences, and finding that advertising is a bit like

132

magic.

A possible explanation of this latter result is that mothers know the reality of most products effectiveness. Therefore presenting, for example, the instant effect of a laundry detergent is akin to magic and has little relationship with the known process and its length, taking place in the washing machine. Since children have been repeatedly shown to express critical opinions about advertising as they grow older, they are also less likely to say that "it's like magic" since this sentence may mean to their eyes a positive evaluation.

TABLE 2

SAMPLE BREAKDOWN

MOTHER'AGE	%	CHILD'S AGE	%	CHILD'S SEX	%
Less than 30	7.4	8	4.7	Female	49
31-35	33.4	9	15.4	Male	51
36-40	26.2	10	16.8		
41-45	21.5	11	17.9		
46-50	8.3	12	15.9		
51 and above	3.0	13	12.8		
		14	9.2		
		15	7.3		

MOTHERS EDUCATION	%
Primary School	23.3
Primary Superior	17.4
Technical/Commercial	23.0
Secondary	20.0
University	14.9
None	1.4

TABLE 3

A COMPARISON OF MOTHER'S AND CHILD'S ATTITUDES
AND OPINIONS VIS A VIS ADVERTISING CONSUMPTION AND TELEVISION

ITEMS	CHILD	MOTHER	DIFFERENCE [1]		
			M - C	T.VALUE	R
I like advertising	3.52	2.65	- 0.87	+++	0.31
TV ask manufacturing	2.32	1.89	- 0.43	+++	0.31
Happier if you buy a lot	3.18	2.88	- 0.30	+++	0.48
May be a bit naughty	2.49	2.25	- 0.24	+++	0.28
Advertising is only shorter	2.15	1.97	- 0.18	++	0.33
In advtg. the bad are punished	3.30	3.14	0.16	+	0.26
I look for information	3.44	3.68	0.24	+++	0.22
There are advertisements espec. made for children	4.25	4.48	0.23	+++	0.13
Advertising like magic	3.21	3.37	0.16	+	0.38
One may not get all	4.53	4.64	0.11	++	0.17
TV news scares me	2.21	2.34	0.13	NS	0.29
I pay attention to price	4.06	4.16	0.10	NS	0.17
Advertising develops knowledge of products	3.60	3.67	0.07	NS	0.27
Advertising tries to sell	4.28	4.29	0.01	NS	0.32
One is often disappointed after purchasing	2.98	3.06	0.08	NS	0.22
Going to school is fun	2.83	2.80	- 0.03	NS	0.30
In advertising, people are sympathetic	3.36	3.37	0.01	NS	0.32

+++   p   0.01

++   p   0.05   LIKERT ITEMS = Fully disagree (1) to Fully

+   p   0.10   Agree (5) Mid-Point (3).

NS   Non Significant

(1) Difference between each dyad (mother and her own child)

A. Do heavy viewers differ in terms of attitudes, behavior and values

On the basis of the multiple questions concerning television exposure, a summative index of exposure was created, and trichotomized, leading to three groups (light, average and high viewing level). When one controls for age and sex differences in each exposure sub-group (by means of a statistical weighting procedure that provides homogeneized samples), are there differences in children's attitudes, behaviour and values? Table 5 presents the results of seventeen analyses of variance.

A significant difference appears for only one item : materialism. Believing that possession of goods brings happiness increases with television viewing ($p < 0.6\%$). None of the other values were affected by differences in TV exposure.

Table 5 reveals five items showing marginally significant differences ($1.62 < F < 2.10$). Interestingly all three's perception of advertising as a fairy tale are present, although their pattern is not similar. Heavy viewers declare less than average and light viewers that advertising shows things which are magic. However they perceive more than others the fact that actually in advertising, people are sympathetic and the bad are always punished. Interestingly, they tend to attribute more than other viewers a mere formal difference between advertising and the other programs, and admit more the knowledge function of advertising.

These results call for a comment. At first, one may consider that finding a single significant item is just what one would expect on a probability basis of 5%. The fact that the materialism item shows a significant Snedecor F at a probability level inferior to 0.6% leads us to consider that chance alone does not explain the result. Furthermore, the five marginally significant items are homegeneous in terms of underlying conceptual variable. We shall not consider that their emergence is due to mere probability factors.

TABLE 4

DO MOTHER AND CHILD DIFFERENCES OF ATTITUDES AND OPINIONS

VARY ACCORDING TO THE CHILD'S AGE?

ITEMS	M-C DIFFERENCES			
	8-10 YEARS (N= 130)	11-12 YEARS (N=120)	13-15 YEARS (N=100)	F
TV asks manufacturers to show their products	- 0.70	- 0.52	- 0.03	+++
Happier if you buy a lot	- 0.58	- 0.20	- 0.02	++
I look for information	0.23	- 0.02	0.62	++
I pay attention to price	0.10	- 0.14	0.46	++
Shortness apart, advertising is like the other programs	- 0.23	- 0.27	0.16	+
Advertising is like magic	- 0.07	- 0.13	0.41	+

LIKERT Fully Disagree (1) to Fully Agree (5)

+++ p < 0.01
++ p < 0.05
+ p < 0.10

137

TABLE 5

HOW CHILDREN'S ATTITUDES AND OPINIONS
VARY ACCORDING TO TV EXPOSURE

(CONTROLLING FOR AGE AND SEX)

ITEM	EXPOSURE LEVEL			F	P
	LOW	AVERAGE	HIGH		
	(130)	(100)	(120)		
Happier if you buy a lot	2.90	3.24	3.49	5.20	0.006
Advertising...Magic	3.41	3.30	3.05	2.10	0.12
Always punished	3.12	3.38	3.48	2.00	0.13
Advtg like other programs shorter	1.98	2.18	2.31	1.96	0.14
Advtg develops knowledge of the products	3.46	3.75	3.67	1.83	0.16
In advtg, people are sympathetic	3.28	3.27	3.52	1.62	0.20
Disappointed with advertised products	3.08	2.97	2.86	0.94	0.40
TV news scare me	2.07	2.29	2.19	0.81	0.45
Price sensitivity	3.97	4.12	4.15	0.74	0.48
We may not get all	4.57	4.58	4.45	0.67	0.51
Advtg tries to sell	4.24	4.37	4.36	0.54	0.59
There are adv for children	4.24	4.38	4.28	0.46	0.63
School is fun	2.80	2.82	2.90	0.17	0.84
TV asks manufacturers	2.31	2.39	2.36	0.07	0.93
One may be naughty	2.47	2.50	2.49	0.02	0.97
Pre-purchase information service	3.44	3.44	3.47	0.02	0.98

C. **Do the differences between light average and heavy viewer hold
when one controls for the mother's attitudes?**

   As indicated in the first section of the paper, covariation does
not mean causality.   It may simply reflect the dual effect of a
third variation (mother's own value and attitude system). Analyses
of co-variance were therefore undertaken to control for this
important likely source of observed differences between viewing
groups.   Table 6 presents the results of these analyses (still
controlling for the child's sex and age) :

- The differences in materialism are still significant (although
   now only at p <.056)

- The perception of advertising as magic is related to TV viewing
   (p < 0.52), and decreases with heavy viewing.

- The perception of mere formal differences (shortness) increase
   with heavier viewing (p <0.10).

- The perception of an informative role of advertising
   increases too with heavier viewing (p <0.12).

- Perception of advertising showing mostly a happy ending (the bad
   being punished)increase with heavy viewing (p <0.112).

The above results show that a major part of the observed differences
in children's materialism was due to their mother's own values. One
should recall that the mother-child correlation on this materialism
item was extremely high (r = .48). Materialistically oriented
families are likely to be more permissive to their child's exposure
level to television (maybe because they do not much control what
their child does, or because they are themselves heavy viewers).
Hence covariation between exposure level and child materialism is
largely due to the hidden persuaders : the parents themselves.

TABLE 6

HOW CHILDREN'S ATTITUDES AND OPINIONS VARIES
ACCORDING TO TV EXPOSURE, CONTROLLING FOR
MOTHER'S ATTITUDES AND OPINIONS (AND CHILDREN'S AGE AND SEX)

| ITEM | EXPOSURE LEVEL | | | | |
	LOW	AVERAGE	HIGH	F	P
Advertising...magic	3.48	3.25	3.05	2.98	0.052
Happier if.. buy a lot	2.97	3.21	3.41	2.89	0.056
Advtg like other programs, shorter	1.92	2.13	2.27	2.31	0.101
In adtvg, bad people are always punished	3.12	3.36	3.51	2.20	0.112
Advtg..knowledge of products	3.46	3.77	3.70	2.15	0.118
Disappointed with advertised products	3.12	2.98	2.82	1.68	0.19
In advtg, people...sympathetic	3.31	3.31	3.52	1.22	0.29
One may not get all	4.60	4.62	4.45	1.07	0.35
Liking advertising	3.47	3.68	3.47	0.95	0.38
There are adv. for children	4.24	4.38	4.33	0.47	0.62
Adv. tries to sell	4.26	4.39	4.34	0.43	0.65
School is fun	2.73	2.81	2.90	0.40	0.67
TV news scare me	2.14	2.27	2.19	0.25	0.78
Price sensitivity	3.98	4.07	4.08	0.25	0.78
Pre-purchase information seeking	3.44	3.50	3.44	0.06	0.94
One may be a bit naughty	2.53	2.48	2.51	0.05	0.95
TV asks manufacturers	2.33	2.35	2.34	0.01	0.99

DISCUSSION

Now, unless one is an orthodox statistician, refusing to consider any result having an alpha superior to 5%, it is noticable that some covariation remains between television amount of exposure and materialism, perception of advertising as magic, perception of mere formal differences and information value, even after controlling for mother's answers and children's age and sex.

Why should perception of advertising as magic decrease with heavy viewing? A possible explanation involves an habituation process. As exposure to violence leads to habituation to violence and to decrease the rating of the programs as being violent (Liebert et al. 1973), the heavy viewers might not see any more how unreal is the presentation of the effects of the products in advertising. For them, it would be almost credible. A second explanation involves a learning process. Heavy viewers would be more realistic and aware of how advertisements are made : they have demystified them. A third explanation would be that by seeing more spots heavy viewers see a lot of poor spots, which shadow the impressions created by the good ones. The second explanation seems more likely : although the differences are not significant (p< .19) light viewers seem more disappointed by advertised products than average and heavy viewers (Table 6). It seems that they build unrealistic expectations from seeing heavy advertising. They are struck by the magic-like products. Heavy viewers know it's not magic but visualization techniques, hence are less disappointed if they purchase an advertised product.

How can the remaining positive covariation between TV viewing and materialism be explained? Influence might work both ways : materialistic children tend to expose themselves more to television or television programs may reinforce if not heighten materialistic values among children. Now it is an open question whether advertising alone conveys most of the materialistic message. Content analyses of typical programs attracting a large young audience show that they also convey materialistic values (Chambart de Lauwe and Bellan, 1981).

Finally, it is extremely interesting to notice that perception of a mere shortness difference between advertising and the remainder of the program increases with heavier viewing. Similarly, recognition of an informative role of advertising increases with exposure, although recognition of its selling purpose is not affected. Confronting similar results, previous researchers (Crioc, 1983) called for an habituation explanation : permanent contact with advertising makes people forget about its fundamental objective.

Our results support partly this explanation : exposure does not affect the perception of the selling goal. However, heavy viewers tend to say more than others that advertising differs mostly in terms of length, as if the selling objective was less salient. Future research will have to explain this paradox.

141

CONCLUSION

Worried by the amount of television exposure of children, many critics have expressed fears that heavy viewing might lead to negative effects. In the context of advertising, consumption and values, the present research has shown that many of these fears were not grounded.

Heavy viewers do not differ from light viewers on a very small number of items. Furthermore, when differences exist, they are mostly attributable to the parents' own attitude values. In fact, although not included in most of the research on advertising and children, the parents act as a potent hidden influencer. What seems a priori to be the effects of television exposure is largely due to the parent's influence.

Our research confirms Atkin (1975) results : television viewing heightens materialistic values among children. But most of the materialistic values of children are inherited from their parents. Also, it seems that heavy viewing leads to recognition of the informative role of advertising and to less obsession about its selling objective.

Our results do not support Rossiter and Robertson's (1976) finding that heavy viewing leads to disappointment with the products purchased after seeing an advertisement. No difference between viewing levels was observed : on the contrary, a non significant negative trend emerged, heavy viewers declaring being less disappointed. Also, heavy viewers did not differ in terms of liking advertising.

In terms of public policy, on the basis of the present results, demands expressed by consumerist groups concerning the reduction of the amount of advertising seemed unwarranted. One may wonder if attributions to television of many of the discrepancies between the child as he/she is and the child-as-their-parents-would-like-he/she-to-be do not serve the purpose of hiding the truth. Television might play the role of a scapegoat : children play back more what their parents believe than what TV says.

(1) The author wishes to thank l'Institut de Recherches et d'Etudes Publicitaires (I.R.E.P.) for its financial support and for agreeing to this partial disclosure of the results.

Intra-family processes —
the American experience

PROFESSOR TOM ROBERTSON

An issue of some importance is the interaction between children's exposure to television advertising and intra-family processes of communication. Indeed, considerable concern has been voiced by consumer advocates and policy-makers about the effects of advertising on family relations, both in the United States (Adler, et al, 1980) and in Europe. (See the papers in this volume by Graham, Grunert, and Kapferer). The concerns are that advertising is a potential source of conflict between parents and children and that advertising may interfere with parental teaching concerning appropriate consumer practices.

Research on parent-child relations may be rather culture-bound due to differences in family structures and socialization processes. Nevertheless, a reasonable body of research has been conducted in the United States, which offers some initial conclusions and hypotheses for further testing in the international environment.

Mediation processes while viewing

An initial question is how much parental mediation of television content occurs while viewing. Greenberg, et al (1972) found limited family interaction about television programming. Ward, Wackman, and Wartella (1977) found a very low incidence of discussion about television commercials. Similarly, Robertson, Rossiter, and Gleason (1979) reported only moderate parent-child interaction in their examination of proprietary medicine advertising and children.

143

The later study also shows that parent-child interaction about medicines and medicine advertising is positively related to the child's beliefs in the efficacy of medicines and his or her requests to parents for medicines. The authors conclude that "mediation does not act in such a way as to build critical insight but rather to accentuate acceptance and usage of medicines" (p. 58). This is a similar finding to that of an earlier study with adolescents by Ward and Robertson (1972), which showed that adolescents from families with high levels of communication about consumption held more materialistic orientations and were more accepting of advertising.

In other research however, Reid (1979) suggested that the nature of the viewing environment and the role which the parents assume strongly influences the child's television advertising experiences. Similarly, Wiman (1983) reported that parents who exert stronger efforts to control their children's viewing succeed in communicating a better understanding of the nature and purpose of advertising. Such control is exercised by more highly educated parents. In yet another study, Corder-Bolz and O'Bryant (1978) demonstrated experimentally that intervention by a significant adult "can greatly influence what a young child learns from programs..."

The ability to achieve a positive interaction between television advertising and children's consumer learning would seem to depend on parent-child co-viewing, the exercise of viewing control, and the level of discussion which results. Experimental research which documents the opportunity for a positive effect generally has not taken into account the levels of co-viewing, control and discussion which actually occur.

Co-viewing

Nielsen data for the United States (1975) reveal considerable diff-erences in adult-child co-viewing levels by time segment. Such co-viewing reaches a high of 70 percent for prime-time programming (7:30-11:00 p.m.) and a low of 20 percent for Saturday morning. Nielsen data further reveal that co-viewing varies by specific program and is most pronounced when younger children are involved. However, viewing without parents is more common than viewing with parents.

A problem in evaluating research on viewing is that television use is often accompanied by a variety of other activities, such as eating, reading and studying. If the term "viewing" can take on a variety of different interpretations, consensus as to what constitutes parent-child co-viewing becomes somewhat problematic. For example, does joint viewing occur if a parent is in the same room but engaged in another activity?

Control

The extent of parental control over television is found by Bower (1973) to vary by parental educational level. Bower reports definite rules in effect about children's viewing among 46 percent of college-educated parents but only 25 percent of parents with a grade-school education. In these latter households, television use is found to be encouraged more as a means to occupy the child's time—the "pacifier" role. Bower also concludes that children from households with a higher educational level have some input in deciding which programs the family is to watch, but less than in households of a lower educational level. Wiman (1983) has found that the level of viewing control is strongly negatively associated with parental attitudes toward television. As would be expected, negative attitudes are most pronounced at higher education levels.

Another methodological consideration is the discrepancy in reporting between parents and their children. Greenberg, et al (1972) found a lack of significant agreement between reporting by mothers and children on rules associated with television viewing. Concerning viewing patterns agreement was highest on the frequency of parents being present. There was good consensus on frequency of viewing with friends, but a relative lack of consensus as to the amount of viewing children do alone.

Rossiter and Robertson (1975) examined 253 mother-child pairs regarding commercial influence and television control. Parents claimed less viewing, more co-viewing, stricter control, and greater parent-child interaction than their children reported. The study found that upper-class parents consistently gave the most "socially desirable" answers. Therefore, actual parental control may be as low among better-educated parents as among the more poorly educated.

Parent-child discussions

Unfortunately, it may be that parent-child discussions about television programming and advertising are limited. Greenberg, et al (1972), for example, found that television viewing is generally not accompanied by any significant family interaction directed toward the medium or its content. Research by Mohr (1978), concerning parental guidance of children's Saturday morning viewing behavior, shows a similarly low incidence of advice -- either positive or negative -- about programs. In fact, only 8 percent of parents reported offering advice to the children in the sample (9 to 15 years old). Also of interest is the fact that about 70 percent of parents reported never having seen the programs aired on Saturday mornings.

The overall conclusion would seem to be that, although parents have the ability to positively affect the child's television viewing experiences, the actual mediation level may be somewhat limited. Co-viewing may be a necessary prerequisite combined with an active parent-child discussion process. The amount of such discussion indicated by the research to date is not particularly high.

Request/yielding behavior

Potential conflict between parent and child arises in the process of the child's making purchase requests and the parent's response in yielding or denying. Given limited discretionary spending by children, this is the main means by which they are involved in consumer behavior.

Requesting behavior

In general, evidence indicates that children's purchase requests within their families vary with the age of the child and the product

145

category. Social class has not shown a consistent relationship.

Age of child. On balance the evidence indicates that requests decrease somewhat among older children (Adler, et al, 1980; Ward, Wackman and Wartella, 1977). This may be due to a number of factors, including the child's increasing sophistication in dealing with his or her parents in more indirect ways. The relationship between age and requests is not particularly strong, however, and is mediated by the product category involved. Furthermore, the relationship may even be curvilinear with fewer requests from very young children and among older children.

Product category. Children are more likely to make requests for products which are frequently consumed by them, such as breakfast cereals, or of particular interest to them, such as toys. This intuitively obvious observation has been substantiated in a number of studies (Galst and White, 1976; Adler et al, 1980; Wells, 1965).

Television advertising is an important information source for child-oriented products, and even for products not oriented toward children, such as medicines (Robertson, Rossiter and Gleason, 1979). Such advertising encourages requests to parents and the strength of the advertising-request relationship is reasonably well documented in research (Adler, et al, 1980). However, the actual frequency of requests is not as high as the controversy surrounding children's advertising might suggest. In a diary study within homes, Isler, Popper and Ward (1979) found an average of 13.5 requests per child over the four-week period of the study.

Yielding/denial

In general, yielding by parents to their children varies by product category and increases with the age of the child. The relationship between social class and yielding is again inconsistent across studies. There is some preliminary evidence that parental attitudes toward television and advertising may be related to their tendency to yield to their children's requests.

Product category. Yielding depends on the product category and whether the product requested is primarily for the child's consumption. For example, Ward and Wackman (1977), report yielding levels as high as 87 percent for cereals, 63 percent for snack foods, 54 percent for games and toys, 42 percent for candy, 39 percent for toothpaste, 16 percent for shampoo, and 7 percent for pet food (p.317).

In an observational study, Atkin (1975) found that 62 percent of parents yield to the child's cereal "request" or "demand". Based on a similar study in supermarkets, Wells and Lo Sciuto (1966) report that parents acquiesce to the child in 69 percent of requests for cereal and 57 percent of requests for candy. Galst and White (1976), in another supermarket observation study, found that parents yield to 45 percent of children's requests. Robertson, Rossiter and Ward (1984) found that parents yield to 43 percent of children's Christmas gift requests. These results show that yielding levels can be fairly high for child-relevant products.

Age of child. Positive associations between the child's age and his or her parents' yielding levels have been found in a number of research studies, whereas other research has shown a lack of a relationship (Adler, et al, 1980). Accepting the general age-related findings, Wells (1965) offers an interesting hypothesis: "Older children are more selective and more circumspect...especially when the product is one they are going to consume themselves" (p. 9). The strength of the age relationship may be correlated to as-yet unspecified variables, such as social class and family structure.

Parental knowledge and attitudes. Research by Ward and Robertson (1972) with adolescents suggests that television advertising may complement communication about product consumption within the family. Commercials sometimes provide a basis for family communication and their impact seems to be related to family values and consumer goals. Adolescents from homes characterized by high levels of family communication about consumption hold more favourable attitudes toward advertising and are more materialistic in orientation than are adolescents from homes characterized by limited amounts of family communication about consumption. Similarly, Robertson, et al (1979) found that children from families who hold more discussions about medicine have more positive attitudes toward medicine.

Preliminary research by Clancy-Hepburn provides further evidence of an interaction between parents' and children's attitudes, in this case toward food advertising (1974). Mothers who are well-informed about the validity of nutritional claims have children who express significantly fewer preferences and fewer requests for advertised foods and report less consumption of these products. Furthermore, mothers well informed about advertising claims tend to yield less to children's requests for snack foods.

Evidence is offered, therefore, that yielding may be a function of product category, age of child, and parental knowledge and attitudes. These factors alone certainly do not fully explain yielding behavior; other variables, expecially family interaction style, are undoubtedly involved and multivariate analysis is needed in order to understand the relative impact of these variables.

Mediation outcomes

Given that most research on children and advertising is geared to hypotheses of negative effects, the prevalent findings generally focus on conflict and disappointment rather than on positive learning and socialization outcomes. Robertson, Rossiter, and Ward (1985) have studied children's disappointment when they do not receive the Christmas present they requested. Disappointment, measured some two weeks after non-receipt, was not as high as anticipated. Parents refused 57 percent of children's requests, but only 35 percent of the children indicated disappointment when their requests were denied. It might be expected that children's disappointment would be higher immediately after denial and that the two-week lapse before the measurement was taken was responsible for the low level of reported disappointment.

Disappointment was most pronounced among younger children, children with high television exposure and, contrary to expectation, children from homes with a high degree of parent-child interaction. Hindsight analysis by the authors suggests that children from these homes may feel more "let down" if they have discussed presents and do not receive them. The children handled refusal in a number of ways -- external blame, 41 percent (e.g. "my parents couldn't afford it") internal denial, 36 percent (e.g. I didn't really want it); no explanation, 14 percent; and self-blame, 9 percent (e.g., "I was a bad boy").

Research by Atkin (1975) has focused on arguments and anger versus Robertson, Rossiter and Ward's focus on disappointment. After they are denied toys, Atkin finds that one-sixth of the children argue with their mothers "a lot" and another one-third argue "sometimes". One-fifth of the children become angry "a lot" about toy denials, and two-fifths become angry "sometimes". Argument and anger over cereal denials follows a basically similar but somewhat less pronounced pattern. Atkin reports a tendency for arguments and anger to increase as children grow older.

In another study, Atkin (1975) recorded conflict and disappointment resulting from cereal requests based on an in-store unobtrusive observation method. In cases involving denial by the parent of the child's request, conflict occurred 65 percent of the time, and unhappiness resulted 48 percent of the time (p. 7). There was some tendency for conflict and unhappiness to be highest in the middle age group (6 to 8 years old). As noted by Atkin, "...conflict is seldom intense or persistent. Displays of child anger or sadness are also short-lived in most cases". (p. 10). Exposure to television advertising was not examined in this study.

Isler, Popper and Ward (1979), however, in an in-home diary study completed by parents, found conflict to be infrequent. When requests were denied, some 50 percent of the children were disappointed, but only in 5 percent of the cases did conflict occur (p. 18).

Children's requests provide an opportunity for parental socialization and training regarding consumption, but this focus has not been pursued in the literature. It would seem, for example, that parents' verbal responses to children's requests would help to teach the child about the realities of the marketplace -- whether explicitly or implicitly. In Atkin's research (1975), for instance, the most frequent parental response regarding denial of toys was "expense" followed by "poor value"; very few parents simply said "no" without further explanation.

CONCLUSION

Parents occupy the pivotal position in mediating the effects of advertising on children. One such opportunity for mediation occurs in the viewing situation; the other opportunity occurs in responding to children's requests for purchases. Although it has been demonstrated that parents can positively affect children's understanding of advertising during viewing, the incidence of direct mediation is limited in the U.S. family. Co-viewing of television with children, for example, is considerably less prevalent than children viewing alone. Viewing rules for children may be common only among college-educated parents. Most importantly, only limited intra-family discussion occurs about television and television advertising. Thus, a major opportunity for parents to influence children's attitudes toward television may not be directly exercised as much as possible. Alternatively, of course, the mediation process may be much more subtle and it may be that role modeling is the more important socialization medium, rather than direct discussions.

The process of children's requesting products provides the other important opportunity for mediation, but also for conflict within the family. Purchase requests generally decrease among older children. They vary by product and are highest for products frequently consumed by children (such as cereals), or of particular interest to them (such as toys). Exposure to television advertising is found to be associated with children's requests for both toys and cereal. Parental yielding to children's purchase requests varies by product category and seems to increase with the age of the child.

Parent-child conflict is sometimes realized. Disappointment and even anger may occur when parents deny requests and television exposure seems to be linked to these outcomes. How much conflict occurs is open to interpretation. Perhaps as relevant is how quickly the conflict is dissipated; yet research on this is generally lacking. What meagre evidence is available suggests that conflict is short-lived.

These results, based primarily on U.S. research, suggest some tentative conclusions and hypotheses for additional cross-cultural research. The existing findings also suggest the opportunity for positive parental intervention and teaching about consumption. It may be that the television medium could also assume greater obligations to teach children about the realities of the consumer marketplace.

The author wishes to thank the Wharton Centre for International Studies for financial support.

Relevance of parent-child interactions

PROFESSOR P. GRAHAM

The television commercial is clearly a potential source of conflict between parents and children. If children, stimulated by a commercial, request their parents to purchase goods which are thought by their parents to be unnecessary, too expensive, or perhaps simply undesirable, then conflict which otherwise would not have occurred may ensue. There are, of course, good reasons why there should be a ban on advertisements which the majority of parents regard as undesirable, because they might have adverse consequences on a child's physical or mental health, such as alcohol, health damaging foods, or toys that might stimulate anti-social, sexually precocious or deviant behaviour. There are also good reasons why children should not be exposed to such advertisements even when they are directed at adults. For example, although cigarette advertisements do not depict children smoking, they do depict the sort of adults with whom children might well wish to identify - and not wait until adulthood before attempting imitation. Advertisements with such obvious harmful content will not be considered further in this paper.

There are other advertisements whose message is so weak or ineffectual that it is improbable that they would ever stimulate children to make unwanted requests, and others (probably very few) where the message really is limited to the communication of information without encouragement to purchase. There are also, doubtless, situations (probably more numerous) in which advertisements that do encourage purchase merely serve to remind parents of something they intended to buy or are quite happy to buy anyway. None of these situations is likely to induce conflict, and again I shall not consider them further.

151

I shall therefore be restricting my remarks to the possible adverse consequences of powerful advertisements for non-harmful products, directed towards children, where there is encouragement to purchase articles that parents do not want to buy. It is everyday experience that this is a common phenomenon, but how important is it likely to be?

The "commercial" as a potential stress

The reception of a "dissonant" message that stimulates the child to request something his parents do not wish to give him can be seen both as a reason for conflict and as a stress on the parent-child relationship. Now the resolution of conflict is a process necessary for development, and therefore conflict is necessary for development. Children who do not have disagreements both with authority figures, such as their parents, and with children their own age, cannot be regarded as prepared for adult life. Nevertheless, some conflict is seriously negative in its effect. When disagreement is intense and painful it can lead to adverse emotional and behavioural outcomes that I shall mention in more detail below. Further, some conflict is either not resolved or is resolved in a manner that is maladaptive for the healthy development of the child and the family. In relation to our subject today, such a resolution might be the purchase of something the family cannot really afford or something which means that a more important purchase cannot be made. What are the sources of conflict that might be regarded as maladaptive?

Sources of parent-child conflict

There is a certain amount of evidence from total population studies carried out in the U.K. that bears on this question. In the pre-school period, the main battlegrounds over which parent-child conflicts are fought relate to feeding and sleeping - what to eat, how much to eat, when to go to bed, how long to stay in bed (Newson and Newson 1968). In middle childhood, from say five to twelve years, conflicts again occur mainly over issues relating to bedtime, but matters concerning the child's autonomy, such as playing out in the street, riding a bicycle etc. predominate. In adolescence, (Fogelman 1976) conflicts over dress, hair length, choosing friends, staying out late, are the main overt issues. Throughout childhood and adolescence there are frequent disagreements over purchases which the child wants to make but the parents do not, but there is no evidence, of which I am aware, that suggests these are major sources of conflict. Unfortunately, this does not mean that such issues are unimportant, merely that, in the major surveys, they have not been the focus of systematic enquiry. Further, it is quite likely that there are marked cross-national and cross-cultural differences in the foci of conflict.

Prevalence of parent-child conflict

There is evidence to suggest that conflict between parents and children is a relatively common phenomenon, but most parents of young children do not report this aspect of their children's behaviour as problematic. Thus, in one general population study of three year olds (Richman et al 1982), 9% of girls and 12% of boys were said by their parents to be definitely difficult to control. When the same population was followed to 8 years, 10% of the children were said to be definitely difficult to control. In a study of 10-11 year old children carried out on the Isle of Wight however, problematic disobedience was found to be more common, and there was a bigger sex difference - 31% of boys and 20% of girls were said to be definitely disobedient (Rutter et al 1970). Such problems are more common in city children of this age. They may decrease in adolescence, for only 1 in 6 (17%) of parents of 14 to 15 year olds reported altercations with their children, though twice as many actually disapproved of their son's or daughter's hairstyle, clothing etc. (Graham and Rutter 1976).

The significance of conflict in relation to the child's adjustment

The existence of parent-child conflict, even to a degree that parents regard as problematic, need not necessarily be regarded as a significant handicapping disability. After all, if, as I have suggested, conflict is necessary for development, perhaps it is not too surprising or too worrying that many parents find such conflict painful. There is however evidence to suggest that parent-child conflict is an indicator of more widespread disturbance in children's behavioural and emotional development.

Advances in questionnaire and interview methodology have enabled psychologists and psychiatrists to identify in a reliable and valid fashion children who must be regarded as showing significant emotional and behavioural disorders. Such children are not, in general, suffering from mental illnesses, but they are showing severe and persistent psychological problems that are disabling in their own right and that may result in psychiatric disturbances in adult life. Such psychological problems are mainly characterised either by seriously agressive or antisocial behaviour, or by the presence of significant anxiety, withdrawal or depression. Such disorders occur in about 5-10% of children living in rural or semi-rural areas and in about 10-15% of children living in cities. These prevalance rates have been found not only in the UK, but also in a large number of developed countries throughout the world, including other European countries.

Now there is evidence that children showing such significant behaviour and emotional problems are those in whom parent-child conflict is particularly likely to occur. For example, in the study of three year olds already mentioned, 34% of children with disorders were difficult to control, compared to 2% in the non-disturbed control group. In the 10 and 11 year old study, 20% of girls in the general population were rated as disobedient, but 54% of the generally disturbed group. In 14 year olds only 13% of non-disturbed children had frequent marked altercations with their parents, but 32% of those with significant widespread psychological problems. It is not surprising that many psychiatrists, who, of course, only see disturbed children, take a bleak view of parent-child relationships!

Factors associated with behavioural and emotional disorders

Psychological disorders in childhood are therefore rather common. For those involved in making television commercials, the factors associated with such disorders are of relevance if they wish to ensure that, as far as possible, they want to avoid the precipitation of such problems. Let me therefore briefly list those factors known to be related to their presence (Graham 1979).

First, the sex of the child. From school entry onwards, boys are more likely to show disturbance than girls, and indeed there is evidence that boys are more vulnerable to stress situations. Second, socio-economic factors. Parental occupation is of little importance, but disadvantageous social conditions - financial stress, over-crowded housing, are of greater significance. Third, the quality of family relationships. Parents whose marriages have broken down or are disharmonious, and who are cold, critical and rejecting of their children, are much more likely to have disturbed offspring. Fourth, the physical and, more especially the mental health of parents. Fifth, parents whose child rearing practices are characterised by inconsistency and punitiveness. Sixth, one must consider the temperament of the child. It has been reasonably well demonstrated that some children are more vulnerable to stress than others by virtue of their genetic constitution. Seventh, the presence of a physical disability in the child. Eighth, the presence of educational retardation, such as disability in reading. Ninth, peer, school and neighbourhood influences have all been demonstrated to be relevant.

Now I have suggested that "commercial" producers might bear these in mind when considering the adverse effects of their products. It will be readily apparent that this might not be an easy task.

Relevant mechanisms in the production of childhood disturbance

Numerous theories have been put forward to explain the development of psychological problems in childhood, and I shall not attempt to summarise these. Instead I thought it might be of value if I considered a number of processes which might be particularly relevant to the issue of conflict induced by the communication of "dissonant" messages.

First, let me consider the cumulative nature of stresses acting upon the child. Each of the factors I have listed above is linked to the presence of emotional disturbance, and indeed is probably causally related. However the presence of a single adverse factor often hardly makes any difference at all to the likelihood that the child will show a disorder. Thus, most children whose parents have a broken marriage are not disturbed. Nor are most with physical disabilities or most with severe retardation in reading. There is however a substantial rise once factors become multiple. A child living in a financially stretched, one-parent family, whose mother is depressed and inconsistent in her discipline is therefore at great risk. Repetition of the same stress is also more harmful than a single dose. For example, adverse effects of repeated hospitalisation of a young child can be detected several years later: a single hospitalisation seems to cause no adverse effect (Douglas 1975). If such exist, "commercials" that aim to induce their effect by repetition of dissonant messages might therefore be more stressful.

The mechanisms whereby child-rearing practices relate to disturbance, are probably also of relevance to the impact of the television commercial. As I have indicated, there is evidence that parents who are inconsistent in their disciplinary procedures are more likely to have disturbed children. Let me consider this in a little more detail. Such parents might accede to a child's request and then change their mind, or convey a double message by saying "no" in a manner that implies that, with a bit of further pressure, they might give in. Further, when fathers and mothers disagree over child-rearing practices, psychological problems are more likely to follow. In the study of three year olds mentioned earlier, in 28% of the disturbed group, parents said they frequently disagreed over punishing the child, whereas this was the case in only 11% of the comparison group. Parental inconsistency in relation to television commercials is likely to be particularly marked where material possessions contain an unusually heavily laden significance, perhaps for both parent and child, as symbols or substitutes for parental warmth, positive feelings and emotional commitment. Thus, a mother feeling guilty perhaps because of feelings of inadequacy towards her child, or a father who habitually returns home later from work than he might because he cannot resist a drink with his colleagues, might well be especially vulnerable to the purchase of a superfluity of toys. Christmas is, of course, a time of year when guilt and lavish expenditure are particularly closely associated. Some problem families spend January to November clearing up debts for rent, gas and electricity they have incurred because of gross overspending on their children at Christmastime.

A research strategy

The points that I have been making so far have, it seems to me been reasonably well grounded in factual information in relation to the development of disturbed children in general, but highly speculative as far as the impact of advertising is concerned. This may be because of the fact that I am ignorant of the work that has been carried out. If the former is the case, it might perhaps be helpful it I suggested one research strategy that might take knowledge further in this area.

It would first seem necessary to establish, on representative samples, the frequency with which parent-child conflict occurs in relation to television commercial viewing. Interview methods to establish frequency in children of different ages could fairly readily be devised. However conflict, in itself, is not of much significance, and it would be helpful to establish criteria for painful, distressing conflict based on the length of disagreement, the manner of resolution etc. It would also be important to establish the proportion of conflicts at this level arising from commercial advertising and from other potential sources of disagreement.

Once such information had been obtained, it might be at once apparent that "commercials" are of little relevance to serious parent-child difficulties. If this were the case, one might suspect that this was due to the present weak capacity of television advertising to influence children's behaviour rather than to the fact that powerful messages could be absorbed and acted upon without producing conflict.

155

Assuming however that it was demonstrated that conflict was induced to a degree that was worrying, a number of further important questions would need to be addressed. These would relate to the nature of the commercial message - what type of commercial, defined by product advertised, content, length, time of day shown, time of year shown etc. How are affected children characterised, by age, sex, family structure, disciplinary procedures - indeed the entire list of vulnerability factors outlined earlier, would become relevant at this point.

Factors within the child and family can certainly be considered in isolation, but in the case of commercial advertising, it would seem necessary also to examine the problem in social context. The degree to which other children already possess the product in question is of importance. Many parents would find it difficult to know whether, when a child says "All my friends have got one", this is the truth or an exaggeration. Further, even it most other children do possess the product, its popularity may already be on the wane. The position of the product in the hierarachy of values held by children and whether this is increasing or decreasing in "social" value is of relevance.

Studies examining the relevance of these factors to the impact of TV commercials are, given existing social science methodology, feasible, though very expensive to conduct properly using interview methods. Whether they are worthwhile would depend on preliminary studies establishing the frequency of the problem. It needs also to be stated that the induction of parent-child conflict, with the possible outcome of the development of psychological problems in the child need not necessarily be seen as the priority issue for those concerned with the possibility that television commercials interfere with the healthy promotion of child development.

Possibly more important might be the following:-

i) Commercial advertising may encourage the purchase of expensive, superficially attractive goods, which the child might well find boring after a few hours, in place of an item of more durable interest.

ii) Commercial advertising may appeal to and reinforce the impulsive rather than the more thoughtful elements of the child's psychological make-up.

iii) TV advertising interrupts programmes and may thus reduce a child's opportunities to develop powers of concentration.

iv) The content of advertising commercials may reinforce undesirable sex stereotypes of kitchen-bound women and pub-bound men.

v) Advertisements that emphasise the importance of possessing products owned by others may encourage children to adhere mindlessly to group norms rather than consider their own personal needs.

vi) Children may be persuaded by advertising that possession of the material product in itself produces happiness and satisfaction.

They may thus be led to undervalue sources of satisfaction such as creative activities that are not, in general, advertised.

vii) Children and parents may be led to believe that not to buy an advertised product represents a significant deprivation for the child when, in fact, this is rarely the case.

These and doubtless other matters might well deserve at least as much attention.

REFERENCES: JEAN NOEL KAPFERER

Adler, R.P. et al. (1980) The Effects of Television Advertising on Children, Lexington : Lexington Books

Atkin, C. (1975), 'Effects of Television Advertising on Children – Survey of Children's and Mother's Responses to Television Commercial", Report n° 8, Michigan State University , December.

Chalvon, M., P. Corset, M.Souchen (1981), L'Enfant devant la Television; Paris : Casterman ed.

Chambart de Lauwe, M.J., and C. Bellan (1981) Enfants de l'Image, Paris, Payot.

Crioc (1983), les Enfants et la Publicite Televisee, Brussels, La Vie Ouvriere. Liebert, RM., J.M. neale and E.S. Davidson (1973), The Early Window : Effects of Television on Children and Youth, New-York : Pergamon Press Inc.

Rossiter, J.R. and T.S. Robertson (1974) "Children TV Commercials : Testing the Defenses". Journal of Communication, 24 (Autumn), 137–145.

Rossiter, J.R. and T.S. Robertson (1976), " Canonical Analysis of Developmental, Social, and Experimental Factors in Children's Comprehension of Television Advertising".Journal of Genetic Psychology, 129 : 317–327.

Sounchon, M. (1978), La Television et son Public, Paris, La Documentation Francaise

Ward, S., D.B. Wackman and E Wartella (1977), How Children Learn to Buy. Beverly Hills : Sage Publications

REFERENCES: THOMAS S ROBERTSON

Adler, R.P., et al. The Effects of Television Advertising on Children. Lexington, MA: Lexington Books 1980.

Atkin, C., "Parent–Child Communication in Supermarket Breakfast Cereal Selection". In Effects of Television Advertising on Children, Report 7, East Lansing: Michigan State University, October 1975.

Atkin, C., "Survey of Children's and Mothers' Responses to Television Commercials". InEffects of Television Advertising on Children, Report 8, East Lansing: Michigan State University, December 1975.

Bower,R.T., Television and the Public. New York: Holt, Rinehart and Winston, 1973.

Caron, A., and S. Ward, "Gift Decisions by Kids and Parents". Journal of Advertising Research 15, August 1975, pp. 15–20.

Clancy-Hepburn, K., et al. "Children's Behaviour Responses to TV Food Advertisements". Journal of Nutrition Education 6, September 1974, pp. 93–96.

Corder-Bolz, C.R. and S. O'Bryant, "Teacher vs. Program". Journal of Communication 28, Winter 1978, pp.97–103.

Galst, J.P. and M.A. White, "The Unhealthy Persuader: The Reinforcing Value of Television and Children's Purchase-influence Attempts at the Supermarket". Child Development 47, 1976, pp.1089–1096.

Goldberg, M.E. and G.J. Gorn, "Some Unintended Consequences of TV Advertising to Children". Journal of Consumer Research 5, June 1978, pp.22–29.

Greenberg, B.S., P.M. Ericson, and M. Vlahos, "Children's Television Behaviours as Perceived by Mother and Child". In E.A. Rubinstein et al. (Ed) Television and Social Behaviour. Volume IV. Washington D.C.: U.S. Government Printing Office, 1972, pp.395-409.

Isler, L., E. Popper and S. Ward, "Children's Purchase Requests and Parental Responses: Results from a Diary Study". A working paper, Marketing Science Institute, 1979.

Mohr, P.J., "Television, Children and Parents". Unpublished report, Department of Speech Communication. Wichita State University, 1978.

Nielsen, A.C. The Television Audience 1975. Chicago, III A.C. Nielsen Company, 1975.

Ratner, E. et al. FTC Report on Television Advertising to Children. Washington, D.C. Federal Trade Commission 1978.

Reid, Leonard N., "Viewing Rules as Mediating Factors of Children's Responses to Commercials:. Journal of Broadcasting 23, Winter 1979, pp. 15-26.

Robertson, T.S. and J.R. Rossiter, "Children's Responsiveness to Commercials". Journal of Communication 27. Winter 1977, pp.101-106.

Robertson, T.S., and J.R. Rossiter, and T. Gleason, Televised Medicine Advertising and Children. New York: Praeger Publishers, 1979.

Robertson, T.S., and J.R. Rossiter and S. Ward, "Children's Product Satisfaction". Advances in Consumer Research, in press 1985.

Rossiter, J.R. and T.S. Robertson, "Children's Television Viewing: An Examination of Parent-Child Concensus". Sociometry 38, 1975, pp. 308-326.

Wackman, D.B., E. Wartella, and S. Ward, "Learning to be Consumers: The Role of the Family". Journal of Communication 27, Winter 1977, p.138-151.

Ward, S. and T.S. Robertson, "Adolescent Attitudes Toward Television Advertising: Preliminary Findings". In E.A. Rubinstein et al. (Ed) Television and Social Behavior. Volume IV Washington, D.C.: US Government Printing Office, 1972, pp.526-542.

Ward, S. and D. Wackman, "Television Advertising and Intra-Family Influence: Washington D.C. Office of Child Development, Dept. of Health, Education & Welfare, September 1973.

Ward, S.,D.B. Wackman, and E. Wartella, How Children Learn to Buy. Beverly Hills, California: Sage Publications, 1977.

Wells, W.D., "Communicating with Children". Journal of Advertising Research 5, June 1965, pp.2-14.

Wells, W.D. and L.A. Lo Sciuto, "Direct Observation of Purchasing Behaviour". Journal of Marketing Research 3, August 1966, pp. 227-233.

Wiman, Alan R., "Parental Influence and Children's Responses to Television Advertising". Journal of Advertising, 12   1, pp. 12-18.

REFERENCES: PHILIP GRAHAM

Douglas J.W.B., (175) "Early hospital admissions and later disturbance of behaviour and learning". Dev. Med. Child Neurol. 17 456-480

Fogelman K. (ed) (1976) Britain's Sixteen Year Olds National Children's Bureau, London

Graham P. (1979) Epidemiological Studies. In: H. Quay and J.S. Werry (eds) Psychopathological Disorders of Childhood Wiley, New York, pp 185-209

Graham P. & Rutter M. (1977) Adolescent disorders. In: M. Rutter & L. Hersov (eds) <u>Child Psychiatry: Modern Approaches</u> Blackwells Scientific Publications, Oxford. pp 407-427.
Newson J. & Newson E. (1970) <u>Four Years Old In An Urban Community</u> Penguin Press, Harmondsworth
Richman N., Stevenson J. & Graham P. (1982) <u>Pre-school to School: a behavioural study</u>. Academic Press, London
Rutter M. (1975) <u>Changing Youth in a Changing Society</u> Nuffield Provincial Hospitals Trust, London
Rutter M., Tizard J. & Whitmore K. (1970) <u>Health, Education and Behaviour</u> Longmans, London

PART VI
CONSUMER
SOCIALIZATION

Session summary

Children are consumers in their own right, gathering information and making purchases, asking their parents to buy things for them, and, presumably, accumulating experiences through consumption which form patterns for purchase decision-making in adult life. In a more formal sense, these processes constitute "consumer socialization, "defined as processes by which a person's dispositions are formed which are relatively consistent over time, and which determine basic structures of consumption-related behaviour. In other words, what are the sets of knowledge, skills and attitudes that relate to consumption behaviour, and how are they acquired?

Papers in this session focus on this question from markedly different perspectives. Sander takes a sociological view, tracing the development of communications media and television in particular in industrialized societies. He notes that television has come to integrate heterogeneous groups in societies - a notion akin to McLuhan's characterization of television as contributing the "global village". The nature of children's play has been redefined with increasing urbanization and smaller living spaces, and television has provided a means for different kinds of play among children. Sander argues that the family plays a powerful role in shaping how children use television, and that the television contributes to children's cognitive organization abilities. These notions are related to Uusitalo's ideas, discussed earlier, of the uses and gratifications children obtain from television. Moreover, Sander's notion of television's role in contributing to children's abilities to organize what they see is related to the findings of Sturm and Grewe-

Partsch regarding the "half-second" in properly-paced television during which children categorise and label what they see.

Grunert takes a totally different perspective to the question of television advertising's role in consumer socialization: that of the information processing psychologist. This approach means that he is concerned with how individuals select information from their environment, store it in memory, and retrieve it for use in certain tasks. Grunert proposes the SNPS model, for Semantic Network/Production System. This is essentially a model of cognitive structure: reference to interconnected concepts and associations in memory which store factual knowledge; "production systems" refers to how the information is retrieved and used for specific tasks. For different types of stored knowledge, individuals use different criteria to link products to their needs, to select products and attributes, and to deal with different preference strengths. Grunert relates these information storage and retrieval processes to two outcomes: consumer behaviour which strengthens the functioning of markets, and outcomes which increase an individual's autonomy in consumer behaviour.

Grunert presents empirical data which suggest that television advertising encourages knowledge of brands and participation in market economies, and so enhances market functioning; however, television advertising may not encourage autonomous consumer behaviour, since children do not learn normative guidelines for consumption behaviour.

Finally, Asle Dahl speculates about the socialization function which may occur as Norway considers the introduction of a commercial television network. He broadens the concept of consumer socialization to include other socialization outcomes of television: educational outcomes, and changes in "media consciousness". Dahl poses several hypotheses which could guide research which traces the effects of commercial advertising in Norway. He speculates that children will initially acquire scattered pieces of information about products, until they develop abilities to integrate product information from advertising; Dahl believes that advertising does not represent any stronger influence on children than other types of television content, and that advertising will strengthen teaching in consumer education and media awareness.

In total, these papers indicate that consumer socialization is an important area for study. However, it is also important to study concomitant socialization processes which occur as children experience television advertising, as Dahl suggests. Moreover, the perspective one can take in studying socialization processes varies from the macro-level perspective of Sander, to the microscopic perspective of Grunert. In any case, the issues are not whether consumer socialization occurs. The issues concern the mechanisms of consumer socialization, and the relative influence of television, the culture, the child's social environment and family influences, and children's cognitive functioning as determinants of socialization outcomes.

The role of mass media in modern society

DR. R. A. SANDER

Approaches

If we wish to study television as a phenomenon of social life in industrial societies, we have two possibilities: One is to consider relations between the "stimulus" (television programs of any type) and the "response" (reactions of the recipient). Here we try to learn about the persistence in or change of attitudes, values and behavior, about the diffusion of innovations, about social learning and about the "uses and gratifications" of television in daily life. Unfortunately, it seems that the complexity of the subject and the difficulties in operationalization of relevant variables lead to inconsistent results in many aspects: "The science of communication is characterized by its contradictions", as LECHLEITNER (1983) laments, "the findings cancel each other out".

If we decide on the second possibility, macro-analysis, we certainly avoid getting involved with the obvious problems of empirical research. Yet climbing to that level means to leave the relatively safe ground of data-proven evidence, restricted as it may be in fact. The delicate walk on the fence may often tumble into ideology or, at best, into cultural criticism. Encouraged by Lazarfield's statement on the theorist who always has the empiricist against him - "He cannot win, but we would be lost without him" - I will try to outline some rudiments of what could become a general hypothesis of the functional interdependencies between the stage of civilization and the structure of communication.

Aspects of Writing

Fieldwork among tribes with different expressions of culture led LEVI-STRAUSS (1981, p.292-295) to assumptions about the social significance of writing. He sees the purpose of writing to be the manifestation of authority, prestige and mastery rather than aesthetic or intellectual pleasure. In building and ruling empires such as Egypt, Rome or China, writing became an indispensible part of the political system in establishing a social hierarchy, administering huge metropolitan agglomerations and integrating heterogeneous populations within the imperial boundaries.

As we know from ancient Greece and China, the art of writing not only discriminated between different social strata but also had the function of stimulating ethnicity as well as ethnocentrism. Both cultures defined those who did not write (Greek or Chinese) as "illiterate" and "rough" (barbaros = "to stammer" in Greek) or to be "primitive" (chi = "uncivilized" in Chinese).

Besides its political aspects, writing developed into the most important medium for expansion of commerce in the respective cultures. The merchants used writing, "the most rational form of documentation" (JURGENS 1983, p.12), for orders, shipping documents and contracts, as well as for their accounting. In feudal medieval society, contemporary knowledge was systemized (and controlled) by the experts in interpretating the world in those times, the literate clergy.

That the use of a medium communication affects the structure of consciousness was already reflected upon by Socrates (and written down by PLATO): "he who has learned to write, will at the same time learn forgetfulness, for he will neglect his memory. In relying upon writing for remembering, people will depend on strange symbols and not upon their own mental powers".

Aspects of Printing

While writing remained a medium of the elite until printing was invented, the printed media rather quickly familiarized great sections of society with the art of writing and reading. In this way, printed media functioned as media of socialization from the beginning.

The low percentage of literacy in the 15th century (JURGENS, 1983, p.15, speaks of only three to four percent of the total population) had an important impact. Due to the industrial mode of producing printed media as books, pamphlets, etc. printers and publishers had to distribute their products over an extended area to get rid of the relatively large editions. Therefore, it was useless to publish in local dialects. Under this techno-economic compulsion, the development of national languages was certainly supported, if not initiated.

From the viewpoint of the exercise of power, mass education, based on a schooling system employing printed media, provided a more intensive control of the population on the one hand, as knowledge of laws and sanctions became common. On the other hand, printed media and the growing know-how for producing and using them as sources of information and agitation, became a valuable vehicle for oppositional movements against the establishment. The most significant example was the schisma in the Christian church. No doubt, the Lutheran Reformation is inconceivable without the printed media. Now the Bible, the "holy book", became available in the vernacular and could be used and understood without the professional guardians of dogma who had until then monopolized its interpretation.

Together with the common use of calendar and chronometer, literacy is one of the functional prerequisites for the mode of production in modern societies. The technological innovations of the late 18th and 19th centuries needed an appropriate communications system for their introduction and implementation. Besides the effect of accumulating and distributing scientific knowledge and increasing the number of people able to translate the printed word into action and to reflect upon it, the printed media favored the development of a certain kind of reasoning required for increasingly sophisticated technology. Reading and, in particular, writing follow rules which are comparable to those necessary to scientific research and industrial production. The "ABDED-mindedness", as James Joyce called it, of modern man includes linearity in thinking, proceeding in logically connected sequences, adapting expression to a formal order (grammar, orthography), common to producers and the consumers of the message.

Moreover, the introduction of printed media, especially books, can be regarded as the materialization of the humanistic ideal of the individual. Aside from the fact that books bear a particular message, transmitting it from the study of the philospher to the growing number of students and lay-scholars, both writing and reading a book are clearly individualistic acts, even antisocial acts, as writing and reading isolate the writer or reader from his social environment.

Another implication of Gutenberg's invention has been discussed recently by POSTMAN (1983). According to Neil Postman, literacy, the condition for and the result of printed media, even created a new social category, childhood. Referring to ARIES (1975) and ELIAS (1976), Postman shows quite convincingly that childhood is far more a social product than a biological necessity or a natural category. In the Middle Ages, before the letterpress was introduced, the difference between the child and the adult was only manifest in size and physical abilities. When reading became popular, adults and children were separated into the categories of readers and non-readers, which later became connected with concepts of maturity. In the view, theories in developmental psychology, as given by Freud, Piaget or Ericson, are of diminished validity, due to their historic perspective.

Aspects of Television

Not long after electricity was introduced into the industrial production of goods, it was also employed for transmitting messages. Telegraphy, the telephone and radio broadcasting, as well as television, originated in the technological progress of the late 19th century. During a period of enormous expansion of industrial production and worldwide trade, but also a time of growing tension between colonial claims and hegemonial aims of chauvanist states with powerful but unwieldy military forces, the relevance of new instruments of communication was apparent.

While the success of the telegraph and the telephone can easily be explained by those arguments, more is needed to describe the function of radio and television broadcasting in society.

Of course, radio and television can and do serve as instruments of mass mobilization in the hands of political leaders. Not without reason are broadcasting networks and their technical installations a major target in any form of coup d'etat. Even in the case of modest political shake-ups, the new elite tries to replace the network personnel with its own confidants, while the management of the industrial sector usually remains untouched.

Yet the undeniable political relevance of the networks is only one aspect, and nothing could be more misleading than to adhere to theories of conspiracy against the manipulated masses, or - hardly any better - not to see beyond the fact, that networks are used for political indoctrination. At least until today, mass media, of whatever type, never were a perfect tool of oppression and indoctrination. As the existence of the underground press, dissident, literature, illegal transmitter etc. prove, mass media can also work against dominating political powers.

The integration of heterogeneous population groups is accomplished by the mass media in general, and television in particular, through means not to be confused with covert political agitation. It should be kept in mind that the division of labor, a major characteristic of industrial life, encourages segmentation of society into innumerable specialized roles linked through their complementary function in the production process. Television addresses the total population with a rather homogeneous progam received by all, regardless of the individual role and position in society.

In this sense, television surely unifies a most diverse population. Although Marshall McLuhan's vision of the "global village" is too idyllic for my taste, it is a fact that millions share the same experience every evening in watching television. Not only because the "medium is the message", to use one of McLuhan's better aphorisms, but also due to the fact that the usual social differences in the choice of media by age, sex and strata are vanishing in the case of television (see WILENSKI 1973, p.145), we face a social paradox: Due to the effects of extensive consumption of the products of the mass media, reinforced by mass entertainment, mass education and a centralized government, cultural uniformity grows simultaneously with structural differences in society (WILENSKI 1973, p.144). Through a common context of amusement and information, as transmitted by mass media, above all television, a pluralist society with subpopulation of all kinds achieves integration, whatever its range and permanence may be.

Although it costs me quite some effort to use the term, one can ascribe integrative qualitites to television also in the case of the modern family. My general thesis, that television has to be considered as an integral part of industrial society, is supported by lots of evidence, particularly with regard to family life. As we know, with the development of an agricultural type of society with subsistence economy into an industrial society with a market economy (or a planned distribution economy) the family loses many functions. From an entity of production, consumption and mutual dependence, the family has shrunk to a partnership between man and woman, based on the myth of never-ending love. Neither economic dependency nor unlimited obligation to each other usually exist in a society which believes in the equality of gender. Kinship is not an important category any longer, even children and grandparents are not necessary components of the modern type of family. Living in an extended family is deviant in tendency.

As empirical studies from different countries show, and as summarised by LANG (1982, pp.37-40), television substitutes for family relations in many respects. Besides serving as a "baby-sitter" to achieve controlled passivity in place of the unpredictable activity of children, television quite often takes over the role of story-teller and enlightener. This has to do with overburdened mothers, but it is also an expression of the overall conditions of production. Due to overspecialization, typical of advanced industrial societies, it seems to have become more difficult than ever to act self-confidently in unfamiliar areas without the direction of a professional. Thus many parents have little confidence in their own ability to educate and enlighten their children. This is why they consult the "objective" advice of the specialist, who is nowadays omnipresent on television, either in person or in the form of "recommended" educational programs. Through this "loss of authority" (WINN 1979, p.238), created by the intrusion of experts and specialized institutions into the family, commitment and loyalty of family members to each other, as well as intimacy, are losing ground (see POSTMAN 1983, p.168/169).

Another point concerning the family in modern society is (horizontal) mobility as an effect of a nationwide labormarket and the aspiration toward professional achievement and the material rewards attached to it. Many of us have personally experienced the problems of social integration in new settlements. Here, television again fills the gap until new social contacts are established or, at worst, substitutes for satisfying friendships and acquaintances. This problem, by the way, exists not only for adults, but also for children.

Television integrates - I hesitate again to use the term - the aged, the sick, the handicapped and other deprived individuals. The elderly have lost their role in the working world, and, with it, prestige and function. The sick are kept in hospitals with insufficient personnel and a lack of human attention. And the handicapped, mainly victims of the violent nature of traffic in modern society - RATZKE (175, p.134) mentions 100,000 per year, among them 50,000 children - are threatened by isolation. For them all, and for the poor and other marginal groups, television seems to be a means of contact to the "healthy" world.

The fascination of television lies to a great extent in the poss-ibility of participating in an unlimited number and variety of events. Critics call it vicarious experience, the "expropriation of experience" (MANDER) even. FORSTHOFF (1964) express the circumstances more subtly by explaining that modern means of communication compensates for the

169

loss of mastered living space by an extension of the effective living space (p.112). It is of importance for our discussion to be aware that this loss does not necessarily mean deprivation but adaption to a changing reality (p.113).

Television appears to be a symbol of alienation to many, and there is enough evidence to support this viewpoint. One example would be the "mood channel", transmitted by a private network in California. It presents no films, no news, no sports, but only pictures scarcely found in an urban agglomeration, such as sunsets on the beach, rustling trees in primeval forests, crackling campfires and so on. In this case the lack of "real" experience and the substituting role of television is clear. Yet we should not overlook with examples like that, the fact that even before television was introduced as a medium to transform "reality" into consumable bits, nature, history, culture, religion and many other components of human existence were mediated by experts to users, either through a technical medium, such as books, or through institutions, such as the school or church. This means that total experience (ganzheitliche Erfahrung) is a myth. It has rarely been accessible to the ordinary person.

Accordingly, not only television-viewing, but also the reading of books involves "second hand experience", maybe even "tertiary experience", as FELDMANN (1972, p.159) puts it, due to the multiple filtering through process of writing and reading. The difference lies mainly in the apparent factuality of a film, representing seemingly direct "reality", while a book must be interpreted by the reader, who has to reconstruct a "reality" with the symbols (letters) the author has put in a specific order. This requires, no question about it, far more than watching television, certain intellectual achievements, to be able to "read between the lines", which is what intelligence (inter legere) literally means.

We may be alarmed by the fact that in the EEC Countries more than 15 million adults can neither read nor write, and that in the United States even 40% of minors must be regarded as "practically illiterate" (see JURGENS 1983, p.28). At the same time, an average of four to six hours TV-consumption per day is reported in this age group, depending on the source. We should be careful in drawing conclusions about the correspondence between these two facts; the risk of false correlations is rather great. With regard to integration, we may understand the situation to be that television provides programs in a common language (even on a simplified level), demonstrating nationwide values and a common style of living and, therefore, filling a gap apparently not bridged by traditional school education.

In my opinion, a certain percentage of illiteracy is not necessarily dysfunctional even in, or especially in an advanced industrial society. As history teaches, the media change with the means and mode of production. To register a purchase, to use an illustration, literacy is no longer required. The reading of the selling price, the statistical information on the goods and the typing of the bill is not executed by a trained clerk, but by an electronic "reading pen", more quickly and reliably than a very well-educated person could do it.

Definitely, traditional education is losing relevance as the gap between humanistic education and job qualification widens year by year. Coping with modern techniques requires top qualifications on the part of the designers and rather low qualifications for most of the consumers. The middle level seems to be vanishing slowly, as studies on the problem of de-qualification of jobs show. From the point of effective productivity, education as defined by the humanistic ideal has become of minor importance. Instead, pragmatic training in simple skills or particular qualifications take the place of "superfluous" abilities. The filling out of (computerised) forms, use of the telephone and the reception of information from television leads to neglect of writing and reading skills by a growing part of the population.

From the point of view of an intellectual with a humanistic background, my statements may sound cynical. The facts may be taken as signs of the dawn of Western civilization. "How many injuries can our society bear?", Karl Markus MICHEL (1984, p.149) asks. He refers to the "central myth" of Occidental culture, the myth of the completely developed and autonomous individual – which has alwasy been "an illusion or a privilege". MICHEL reminds us to learn from the history of evolution how innovations are taken up in the repertory of man, "as if governed by an entelechy" (p.150). So it may be possible that another type of reasoning will develop in the process of technological progress and its social and cultural effects.

Television plays a prominent part in this regard, not only because it seemingly takes over the integrative function of formal education. In addition, television actively teaches skills required in the advanced stages of an industrial society. As we see in the case of video games or interactive channels, television has an educative function in forcing users to "think in digits", a type of reasoning required by the omnipresent computer. In a certain sense, video games do not differ greatly from work with the computer screen as involved in many jobs nowadays.

Use of the alphabet not only provided access to knowledge, but also brought about the discipline necessary for industrial production. The same may be said about television. Although television is watched normally in what we call leisure time, it requires behavior structurally similar to working behavior , i.e. planning of time, rational organization of time and, perhaps, specialization in programs (sports, films, entertainment). In this way, and due to the similarities in the technical systems, the spheres of work and leisure time are becoming more and more alike.

The function of television in connecting the spheres of production and recreation can also be seen in the fact that children show less "marginal disorganized behavior" when they watch television regularly (see LANG 1982, p.37). Their early life, too, is structured and given order by the inherent "hidden curriculum" of television, preparing them for a productive life. As we know, children play less than usual when watching television (see LANG 1982, P.35). This fact may be regarded as appropriate socialization in an achievement-orientated society also, but other perspectives have to be considered. One point is the urban life of the majority of the population, which usually offers little chance for outdoor games, as WINN 1979, p.287) mentions. This thesis is backed up by survey results, showing that television is more often in the lower strata of society than in the upper classes, where living space is generally greater. And the small family, which is the product, as well as one of the conditions for industrial labor, normally cannot provide as much stimulus for games and entertainment as a big family potentially can.

We may regret the decrease in children's play, but we can as well share SAINT-GEOURS' opinion "... the inability to play, which many critics of our civilization bewail, seems to be founded on a narrow and obsolete concept of playing. The objects of play have indeed changed. Play consists today in all forms of watching - especially watching television and films. Play is found where one seeks relaxation ..." (1973, pp.318-319). In fact, one of the basic functions of television is to provide relaxation and to reduce tensions. EURICH (1980, p.26) stresses the necessity for distraction from daily troubles and disappointments, caused by the restrictions of industrial work and the conditions of an achievement-based society. And television is the ideal medium to "switch off", as opponents and proponents of television acknowledge in rare agreement.

Considering the demands made on children, as they are dramatically described by ELKIND (1981) recently, their need to relax from the early competition in preschool programs and similar forms of "career"-training is plausible. "The hurried child", additionally burdened by its difficult role in the modern family, sits in front of the TV-screen because he may really need diversion after a day full of duties and because his parents believe in the educational effects of the programs. Emotional problems in children, being normal rather than exceptional, as studies on pupils show, should not be equated with abusive television-viewing, although the two correspond. According to THAILMANN (1978, pp.30-32), the fact that four out of five children show symptoms of emotional disturbance, and that half of the psychotherapy, is actually not the fault of television but of their families who are not able to provide the internal and external conditions for raising reasonably healthy children. That they spend many hours watching television is a symptom of their situation, but not the cause - and certainly not a source of therapy, since television cannot really compensate for emotional deficiencies. By the way, poor school performance is often erroneously correlated with television-viewing too. Yet, also in this case, "low achievement in learning as well as the excessive consumption of television are an expression of a complex life situation, that cannot be reduced to simple causalities" (HUNZIKER 1980, p.22). In other words, when 40% of American children prefer the TV-set to their own fathers, this does not confirm the demonic power of television, but rather the severely disturbed situation in those families . This, of course, is not due merely to individual problems, but to the general pattern of family life in an industrial society.

Aspects of Advertising

As explained, complex societies with a high degree of diversified labor, frequent innovations, bureaucracy, urbanization and social differentiation, need, create and use adequate means of communication.

172

Yet mass communication is not only the "glue" that holds the particles of society together, as SILBERMANN and KRUGER (1973, p.9) put it, "... but at the same time the aim and the means for processes of investment, production and distribution." For quite a few authors (HOLZER 1975, 1981, is a typical representative), mass media, especially television networks, are a most powerful exponent and instrument of the capitalist drive for profit. According to this view, advertisements are the crass expression of the imminent greed of the system itself.

There is no question, I believe, that television and commercial interests are closely linked, not only, but most obviously in countries with private networks. As a matter of fact, television is extraordinarily useful in introducing goods as well as patterns of consumption. Nevertheless, a purely economistic approach is certainly not sufficient for comprehension of the polyvalent meaning of television.

In some respects, advertising has similarities with television, being a medium in itself. Therefore, we first inquire as to the relation between "stimulus" (advertisement) and "response" (consumer's behavior). We have symptoms, such as "gimmes" which are blamed on advertising, especially in television. And we have data (as summarized by GRUNERT and STUPENING 1981 or by HAASE 1981) from international studies, that do not confirm simple monocausalities between the exposure to television advertising and particular acts of consumption. Comparably to the influence of television on attitudes, values and behavior in general, it seems that, between the tempting presentation of goods and personal patterns of buying, "gate-keepers", such as parents or peers, play significant roles. The influence of (television) advertising is indeniable, yet in a less specific way, and strongly dependent on the social context of the recipient, i.e. age, social stratum, family etc. As HERMANNS (1979) found, the effect of advertising is strongly dependent on "pre-communication" attitudes and behavioral dispositions. Actually, the same conclusion can be drawn from most of the studies evaluating the effect of television as such.

From a macro-sociological perspective, the exposure of children to commercials is a part of their confrontation with a given environment and, therefore, a particular field of social learning. Advertising is an "ephi-phenomenon", as LINDNER (1977, p.123) quite correctly names it, of the conditions of life in an industrial society with a market economy. LINDNER (1977) explains that advertising is an "ideal-imaginative and aesthetic phenomenon", evoked through a specific structure of economy (p.14) which requires a value-transformation of products into wares (pp.28-29). Simplified, that means that products are of no value until they find a buyer. Advertising functions in this process of transformation and the mass media are the vehicles which carry the producer's message to the (potential) consumer.

At the same time, we should not forget that mass media are wares in themselves and that the material they present (films, news, enter-tainment) are wares as well. Strictly interpreted, the differences between the "regular" programs and commercials are only of an aesthetic nature. ADORNO (1976, p.348), an acid critic of the "culture industry", remarks bitingly, "Cultural wares follow the principle of commercial-

173

ization.   Intellectual products are no longer also wares, but they are wares through and through." Against the conservative on the one side and the Marxist on the other, both lamenting the commercial character of the mass media, ENZENSBERGER (1962, p.12) says, "it is hardly less moral to earn money by broadcasting symphonies or news than by selling tyres."

No doubt our lives are commercialized in many, some say in every aspect. And, of course, television is a major exponent of life in our society by presenting views of it. Films, news, sport, family series, quiz shows etc. reflect our own reality in an oversimplified and disproportional way. Commercials do just the same, containing concepts of everyday life which are transformed into fragmentary messages, headlines and slogans, colorful and simple structures - not much different from the "normal" programs.   Consumption is part of behavior in everyday life (Alltagshandeln), as HUNZIKER (1972, pp.79-99) classifies it, taking the symbolic aspects of wares and consumption into consideration. Therefore, it is more realistic than ironic when MANDER (1981, p.141) calls television "the nursery of commercial life". If, as LANG (1982, p.72) writes, television advertisements teach children to reduce tensions and to compensate for unfilled desires by buying, not the "obscene ideology of the autonomous customer" (DAHL MULLER u.a. 1973, p224) is at fault, but the circumstances that create the situation.

Synopsis

It is legitimate and valuable to study the relation between TV ads and children with the focus on the socialization of consumers' patterns etc. Yet remaining on this phenomenological level does not account for the general meaning of mass media in an industrial society.

As did the implementation of the alphabet and the printing of books and newspapers, electronic mass media became a basic prerequisite of everyday life in our contemporary western societies. Each mode of production needs, creates and uses adequate forms of communication. Therefore, media such as television are primarily to be seen in their functional quality as integral parts of the social, cultural, political and economic structure of modern societies.

In this wider context an analysis of television advertising and children will lead from the isolated relations normally in the research of effects (evaluations studies) to a profile of the general life-style of the majority of the population. Accordingly, our topic is to be seen not as an isolated phenomenon, but as a segment of life in a society based on the division of labor. In this given set of conditions, mass media may and certainly do compensate for some of the deficiencies resulting from the fragmentation of society into (highly) specialized sections.

Television provides not only information and entertainment, but also takes over, for example, traditional functions of the family to a certain extent. Consequently, TV connects isolated individuals and particular groups (especially the aged, handicapped, hospitalized etc.) with the outside world, even "cares" for children. In a sense, TV provides a source of shared experience which is perceived as "real" by

174

the viewers, partly due to the nature of the medium, which gives the illusion of participation in events projected on the screen.

Advertising, as presented in television, is in no way less realistic than news, films or entertainment. No matter how "true" it is, it actually is a representation of the "reality" with which our children are instilled. As the world into which our children are born highly commercialized, TV ads only reflect this world in a somewhat caricatured way.

To understand television as a social phenomenum, we should reformulate Harold D. Lasswell's famous heuristic question ("Who Says What In Which Channel To Whom With What Effect?") maybe to "Why Does Someone say Something in Some Channel to Someone?" or, "Why Do Millions Watch and Listen to What Someone Says in Some Channel?" The answer will be, I believe, that we cannot actually blame television for undesirable developments. To express it with a metaphor VIVELO (1981, p.141), "If we want to use an electric toothbrush, we should not mourn about the state of social relations in our society." In other words, the price we have to pay for the productivity and technical progress we usually enjoy.

TV advertising, product preferences and consumer socialization: A German perspective

DR. K. GRUNERT

CONSUMER SOCIALISATION : PREVALENT CONCEPTS

While definitions of the concept of socialisation and the process that leads to it abound (Ward, 1974), most researchers would probably agree that the process of socialisation refers to the formation of intrapersonal dispositions which are relatively constant over time, and which determine basic structures of human behavior in a socially desirable way (Kuhlmann, 1983). In breaking down this very broad phenomenon into investigable problems, various socialisation agents and effects are usually distinguished. This paper is concerned with television advertising as a social agent, and it is restricted to socialisation effects with regard to consumption-related behavior. Thus, neither general socialisation effects of TV advertising will be dealt with (cp. Meyer & Koller, 1971), nor effects of television or mass media in general on consumer socialisation. While socialisation is assumed to be a life-long process, it is mainly associated with children, because childhood is basically where enduring dispositions are formed which change only gradually later.

The effects of television advertising on consumer socialisation of children have been discussed heatedly both in the United States and in Germany (for reviews compare Adler et al., 1980; Bergler & Six, 1979; Haase, 1981; also Grunert & Stupening, 1981; Stupening, 1982) within the broader context of the effects of television advertising on children. While the main thrust of the arguments has been different – more orien-

177

tated towards a general critique of consumer culture in Germany in contrast to an emphasis on consumer skills at the micro level in the United States - there has been a certain convergence in the theoretical approaches used: Social learning theory, cognitive development theory, and attitude theory have been the main lines of theoretical reasoning. In this paper, I will first briefly review these three approaches, before developing an information processing perspective of consumer socialisation based on modern cognitive psychology, which can be regarded as an extension of the information processing model of consumer socialisation proposed by Ward (Ward, Wackman & Wartella, 1977). The approach will be illustrated with empirical results from studies conducted in Germany and in the United States. The paper closes with suggestions for future research.

Social learning theory

The process of socialisation can be viewed as a learning process, and hence social learning theories have traditionally been used to explain socialisation. According to these theories, there are three basic mechanisms that govern learning in a social environment (Hermanns, 1972; Kuhlmann, 1983; Stupening, 1981): interaction, imitation, and reinforcement.

Interaction between the social agent and the social learner is assumed to be a prerequisite for learning, and frequency of interactions determines likelihood and intensity of the learning process. This is probably one of the reasons why many people believe television to be an important socialisation agent simply because children spend a lot of time viewing television: Two estimates are three and a half hours per day for children aged six to eleven years in the United States (Adler & Faber, 1980), one hour and a half for children aged eight to thirteen in West Germany (Infratest, 1981). It is estimated that this includes an average of about 50 commercials per day in the United States. In West Germany this figure must be assumed to be lower, because television advertising is legally restricted to twenty minutes per day. In spite of this, frequency of interaction between children and television in general and commercials in particular leads some to hypothesize that television is an important social agent.

Interaction says nothing about what is actually learned. The main process here is assumed to be imitation: The social agent serves as a model whose behaviour is imitated by the social learner. An implication is that television advertising can lead to social learning only if commercials show people which can serve as a model for viewers. It is known that modelling is a technique that is widely advocated in advertising textbooks, and content analyses of both German and American TV spots indeed show that models abound in commercials (Atkin, 1976; Kratzer & Silberer, 1976).

The degree to which learned behavior becomes an enduring disposition is assumed to depend on the reinforcement of this behavior by the social agent. It is not immediately clear how a mass medium like television could reinforce individual behavior; the argument advanced is that perception of mass media is selective and governed by dissonance avoidance, which implies automatic reinforcing tendencies. In addition,

178

advertisers are assumed to take this process into account and design advertising content accordingly, leading to an essentially conservative picture of society (Meyer & Koller, 1971).

The main argument that can be advanced against the use of social learning theories in socialisation research is that they are derived from simple stimulus-response paradigms and fail to address questions such as when children choose which models, and when and what they may choose to imitate. Children's dispositions are intervening variables which are omitted in S-R approaches, yet questions such as those posed above persist, and require a cognitive approach to socialisation research.

Cognitive development theory

The use of mass media involves the processing of information transmitted via these media, which is contingent on the cognitive capabilities of the receiver. Cognitive capabilities develop over time, especially during childhood, and it appears only natural that Piaget's theory of cognitive development has been applied to analyse the socialising effects of television (e.g., Blatt, Spencer & Ward, 1972; Bockelmann, Huber & Middelmann, 1979; Stupening, 1981; Sturm & Jorg, 1980; Ward et al., 1977). According to Piaget, cognitive development is in four stages (sensorimotor, preoperational, concrete-operational, and formal-operational stage), which differ in how the two basic principles of accommodation and assimilation are used to cope with the environment. It seems natural that the effect of a certain informational input on the receiver will depend on his stage of cognitive development. Applying this to the effects of television advertising on children, two opposing viewpoints have been advanced: on one hand it has been argued that the cognitive ability of children especially in the pre-operational stage, is not sufficient for them to comprehend the meaning of commercials, especially their selling intent, leading to miscomprehensions and false impressions of the consumer world. It is claimed that commercials should be adapted to children's cognitive abilities. On the other hand, it is argued that the simple language and short plots of commercials do indeed conform to the limited cognitive abilities of children, so that advertising to children becomes especially effective as opposed to advertising to adults. A related claim is that frequent viewing of this simple material will retard cognitive development because it supplies no incentive for improving cognitive abilities. The latter argument points to a potential problem with cognitive development theory: It mainly describes a process that is correlated with age, but it does not specify how changes in cognitive development come about and how they can be accelerated or retarded. This is a problem that may be overcome by certain neo-Piagetian theories (e.g., Pascual-Leone, 1980). Another problem is that the level of cognitive development itself says nothing about consumption-related dispositions, unless the concept of cognitive structure is specified in much more detail. A possible extension in this direction will be presented later.

Attitude theory

An enduring disposition to respond favourably or unfavourably towards an object is also called an attitude. If socialisation is defined as the formation of enduring dispositions, then attitude theory should be

179

an obvious source for theoretical arguments (Hermanns, 1972). However, applications of attitude theory in the realm of consumer socialisation have been comparatively few (Kuhlmann, 1983). Attitudes that would be of interest here are not the brand attitudes that form the core of attitude research within consumer research, but attitudes to more general objects like advertising as a source of information, other information sources, information seeking as an activity, or certain product classes. It would be interesting to know how television advertising contributes to the formation of such attitudes. Some of the studies published report on some attitude measurements, usually consisting of either a Likert-type battery of statements (e.g. Haedrich, Adam, Kreilkamp & Kuss, 1984; Rossiter, 1977) or a uni-dimensional assessment of affective reaction. As an example, it was typically found that attitude towards advertising becomes more critical with age (Prisma, 1976; Stupening, 1981; Ward et al., 1977), which, however, says nothing about the effect of TV advertising on this attitude. A German study by Infratest (1981) showed that frequent viewers of TV advertising have a more critical attitude towards advertising than nonfrequent viewers (Infratest, 1981), which is discrepant to American results reported by Ward and Robertson (1972).

Most of these attitude measurements do not explicitly invoke attitude theories. Especially, they do not relate attitude to cognitive structure, in spite of the fact that the concept of cognitive structure is used in cognitive development theory, and that theories relating attitude to cognitive structure have been widely used in marketing research. Multi-dimensional attitude theories like those by Anderson, Fishbein or Rosenberg might be useful tools in consumer socialisation research as well. On the other hand, these theories make very restrictive assumptions about the cognitive structures underlying attitudes and hence may have difficulties in coping with different levels of cognitive development. In this respect, a more general information processing perspective may be more useful.

THE INFORMATION PROCESSING PERSPECTIVE

Before presenting a new approach, it seems appropriate to mention the major attempt to date to bring the information processing perspective of consumer behavior to the question of consumer socialisation.

The Ward Model

The analysis of consumer behavior from the perspective of information processing has gained so much momentum in the past fifteen years that it can today be regarded as the main paradigm governing research (for an excellent review cp. Bettman, 1979). Ward et al. (1977) have incorporated this paradigm into their research model. They regard behavior as being mediated by initial and central information processing. Initial processing encompasses information search, attention, and information selection; central processing consists of interpretation and comprehension, structuring of information, and use of information. In an analysis of the socialisation effects of TV advertising, these concepts can be applied not only to the analysis of television advertising information, but also to the processing of product

180

information in general, since processing skills not only determine how television information is processed, but can themselves be developed and changed under the influence of television advertising. This leads to a complex array of causal relationships some results of which will be taken up later, together with results from a German study by Stupening (1981) which used essentially the same framework. Here it shall be noted that it suggests itself (and has been suggested by the authors themselves, cp. Wartella, Wackman & Ward, 1976) to extend such a model in at least two directions. Firstly, the model does not specify how new stimuli interact with existing structures, i.e. the impact of incoming information, including that emanating from TV advertising, on the development of cognitive structure is not clear. Secondly, there is no clear distinction between knowledge and skills. The way these terms are usually used seems to indicate that they have different meanings, but the exact nature of this distinction and its implications for information processing is not clear.

The following section outlines an extended model that takes these two aspects into account.

The SNPS model

The neglect of these two aspects in consumer research, which has been lamented in other contexts as well (Olson, 1978), is partly due to the fact that it presupposes a well-specified model of long-term memory which cognitive psychology was not able to supply until recently. There has been, however, considerable progress in this area within the past fifteen years, and several ambitious models of long-term memory have been specified (e.g. Anderson,1976; Norman & Rumelhart, 1975; Quillian, 1968; Reitman,1965) and successfully applied to consumer research (Grunert, 1982a, b; Olson, 1978). One such approach will be outlined now and applied to the question of consumer socialisation later. It is built on the basic assumption that factual knowledge (usually simply called "knowledge") and procedural knowledge (usually called "skills") are stored differently in memory. There are various reasons for this:

- Differences in learning: Factual knowledge is preferably learned by being told, while procedural knowledge is preferably learned by doing;

- differences in durability of the memory trace: Procedural know-ledge seems to be more easily adaptable to situational circum-stances, while factual knowledge seems to be very enduring;

- differences in use: Factual knowledge is usually easily verbal-ised, while procedural knowledge is not.

Of the various tools that can be used to model these two different types of cognitive structure, two seem especially promising. Factual know-ledge stored in memory can be regarded as a network of concepts and associations, commonly called a semantic network. Procedural knowledge can be regarded as a system of productions. Both concepts will be elaborated in turn, stressing their interpretation in a consumer socialisation context. Lacking a better name, the model outlined will be called the SNPS-model (Semantic Network/Production System-model).

181

A network model of consumption-related factual knowledge has been proposed by Grunert (1982a). A memory network can be regarded as an
associative net of concepts, where the meaning of each concept is
defined by its associations to other concepts. For example, "beverage"
can stand for a general class of phenomena, like the class of all drinks
or for a subclass of phenomena, like the class of soft or alcoholic
drinks. Finally, "beverage" can mean a single object, like a certain
brand of soft drinks. A network of consumption-related factual knowledge can thus be structured according to the substantial meaning of
concepts, and according to the generality of concepts. A hypothetical
excerpt from such a network is shown in figure 1. The associations
between concepts, which are of varying strengths not only define the
concepts' meaning, but are also crucial for information usage which is
assumed to be based on the concept of spreading activation: Concepts in
a memory network can be activated, where activation can be caused both
by sensory impressions (such as a picture of a bottle) and by
motivation, such as thirst. This activation is assumed to spread along
the associations to other parts of the network, thus opening up
additional relevant stored information.

Of course, such networks change over time, and we can define criteria
by which we can compare networks used by different age groups or
consumer segments. These criteria can serve as useful starting points
for the analysis of socialisation effects. We can distinguish
substantial and formal criteria.

Substantial criteria refer to elements of semantic networks, such as:-

- Which products are associated with which needs;

- which products are prominent in the network and which are not;

- which attributes are prominent in the network and which are not.

Formal criteria refer to structural aspects of networks, including:

- The degree of vertical network differentiation, i.e. the number of
  levels of generality that are distinguished.

- the degree of horizontal differentiation at each level of generality, e.g. the number of brands that are known for a product
  class, the number of attributes that are known for a brand etc.

- the distribution of association strengths, like whether all brands
  associated to a product category are associated with the same
  intensity.

This list of criteria is not meant to be exhaustive, but is a useful
starting point for the ensuing analysis.

Turning to production systems, these refer to the ways behaviours are
produced based upon the nature and structure of knowledge in these
semantic networks (Anderson, 1976, Newell & Simon 1972).

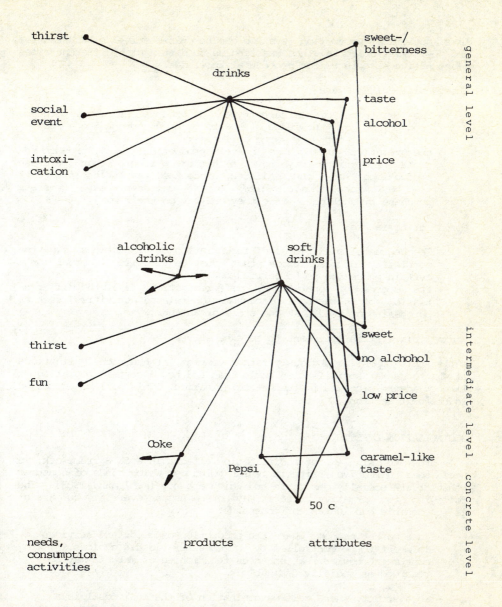

FIGURE 1: EXCERPT FROM A HYPOTHETICAL SEMANTIC NETWORK

Like networks, production systems can be characterised by substantial and by formal criteria, thus enabling us to distinguish different types of cognitive structures for procedural knowledge.

Substantial criteria are:

- The existence of certain types of productions (e.g., purchase productions or knowledge of how to go about purchasing a product may not exist for very young children);
- the relative strength of certain productions (e.g., product request productions may have a higher strength than purchase productions for young children, since they may ask their parents to buy for them, while older children may generate purchase productions, since they can buy on their own).

Formal criteria are:

- The degree of conditional differentiation of productions, i.e. the complexity of conditions that must be fulfilled in order for a certain procedure to be carried out;
- the degree of operational differentiation, i.e. the differentiation of the arsenal of consumption-related activities, such as purchasing or credit at one store or another.

Again, this list is not meant to be exhaustive.

While this model is obviously rather complex, it has rich implications of what consumer socialisation could mean and how a certain social agent like TV advertising can influence socialisation. This will be addressed in the next section.

SOCIALISATION EFFECTS

In order to single out socialisation effects in a SNPS framework, we need some normative criteria which point out which kinds of consumer behavior are socially desirable and which are not (Kuhlmann, 1983). The following two normative criteria may not be uncontroversial, but are at least possible candidates for consensus:

- In a market economy where the production of goods and services is meant to be controlled by the consumer via his choices, consumer behavior that enhances functioning of markets may be regarded as socially desirable;

- in a society where self-determination of the individual is a widely accepted goal, this should hold for consumer behavior as well - a claim for which the concept of "autonomous consumer behavior" has been proposed (Scherhorn, 1981).

If we relate the four types of characteristics of cognitive structures presented in the preceding section to the two normative criteria just presented, this results in the matrix presented in figure 2. In thinking about which characteristics may be important for which normative criteria, it seems that functioning of markets is mainly dependent on formal characteristics of the network and substantial characteristics of the production system, while autonomy of consumer behavior is mainly dependent on substantial characteristics of the network and formal characteristics of the production system.

As for substantial characteristics of the production system, consumer behavior that is adequate to a market economy certainly presupposes the existence of productions for purchase and information search. A child that has only product request productions always needs an additional authority that acts for him on the market. A consumer that has only purchase and no (or only weak) information search productions cannot control supplier behavior because he has no basis for the discrimination of brands. This leads to the formal characteristics of the semantic network. It seems desirable that brands are not considered as unique phenomena, but rather as members of a more general class of products, and that products can be used in different contexts, which calls for at least three vertical levels of differentiation. A certain amount of horizontal differentiation both at the brand and at the attribute level also seems desirable, i.e. brand choice should be based on a minimum number of relevant attributes. Finally, the distribution of association strengths in this part of the semantic network should not be too skewed, because selected extremely strong associations lead to very routinised buying behavior that cannot be broken up by new information, which seems dysfunctional in a competitive market system.

Autonomous consumer behavior can be regarded as the opposite extreme of behavior that is governed by simple stimulus-response relationships (Scherhorn, 1983). Thus, specific behavior based on very specific conditions, as expressed by high conditional and operational differentiation of the production system, is more apt to lead to autonomous behavior than if the behavioral repertoire is very simple and is invoked in simple mechanistic ways. Consumer autonomy is also violated if the consumer acts in a way that is incompatible with goals he himself considers important, like the purchase and consumption of harmful products. Thus, the prominence of harmful products or product attributes within the consumers' semantic network must be regarded as discrepant with the normative goal of autonomous consumer behavior.

We have thus identified states of a consumer's cognitive structure which can be regarded as desirable or undesirable by certain normative criteria. If we find that a certain social agent furthers or inhibits development of these states, then we can say that this social agent has a socialisation effect. This will be taken up for the case of television advertising in the next section.

Some empirical evidence on socialisation effects of TV advertising

In this section, some empirical studies on the effects of television advertising on children will be screened to see whether they contain any results concerning the four types of socialisation effects that have been outlined in figure 2. It should be noted that none of these studies has used the theoretical approach just sketched, so that matching of theory and results requires some additional inference. We will concentrate on results from three major studies that have been conducted in Germany in this area:

characteristics of cognitive structure		normative criteria	
		functioning of markets	autonomy of consumer behaviour
semantic network	formal	at least three vertical levels of differentiation; horizontal differentiation at brand and attribute levels; uniform distribution of association strengths	
	substantial		no prominence of harmful products; no prominence of harmful attributes
production system	formal		high conditional and operational differentiation; uniform distribution of production strengths
	substantial	existence of information search and purchase productions	

FIGURE 2: CHARACTERISTICS OF COGNITIVE STRUCTURE AND NORMATIVE CRITERIA

- The study by Bockelmann, Huber and Middelmann (1979), who interviewed 260 children aged 6-14 from different socioeconomic strata;

- a representative sample of 900 mother/child-pairs (children aged 6-13) interviewed by Infratest Medienforschung in 1979;

- the still unpublished study conducted by Stupening (1981), in which a representative sample of 959 mother/child-pairs (children aged 6-14) were interviewed.

The results from these studies will be compared to results from American research, without claiming comprehensiveness in this respect, especially since excellent reviews of American research are available (Adler et al., 1980).

It should be noted that the topic, effects of TV advertising on social-isation, involves a hypothesis about a causal relationship the invest-igation of which would call for an experimental design. None of the German studies is experimental in design, and it is indeed hard to imagine an experimental study that goes beyond short term effects of TV advertising. Thus, results reported are mostly correlational in nature, where amount of exposure to TV advertising is usually used as the independent variable. It should also be noted that only the study by Stupening uses an explicit information processing approach.

Looking at these studies, it becomes clear that more is known about some of the effects shown in figure 2 than about others. Especially, there is practically no evidence on the effects on formal characteristics of the production system, to be found in any of the German studies. The four cells will be addressed in turn.

Formal characteristics of semantic network and functioning of markets: Both Bockelmann et al and the Infratest study found that increased exposure to TV advertising leads to a higher number of brand names remembered for a given product class. The Infratest study also found that high exposure to TV advertising is correlated with more correct notions about price ranges for certain products, indicating that exposure to TV advertising may enhance horizontal differentiation of the network not only at the brand, but also at the attribute level. A positive relationship between exposure and awareness of brand names is also reported by Ward et al. (1977) for two of their age groups; in addition they found that brand awareness is higher for heavily advertised products. Ward et al. also had data on strength of brand preference, which is related to another formal aspect of the semantic network (distribution of association strength). Inter-estingly enough, increased exposure leads to weaker brand preference for the middle and upper age group, a finding replicated later by Moschis and Moore (1979). Summing up this evidence would lead to the conclusion that TV advertising has a positive socialisation effect here in that it furthers differentiated consumption knowledge.

Substantial characteristics of production system and functioning of markets: Some indirect evidence can be cited here. Infratest and Stupening have both investigated the frequency of product requests by children. However, the results are not consistent. While Stupening (as

187

well as an American study by Galst & White, 1976) found a rather strong positive relationship between TV exposure and frequency of product requests the strength of which seemed to increase with age, the Infratest study found very little covariation. Ward et al. (1977) report mixed results: A significant relationship to exposure to TV advertising seems to exist only for certain products, and seems to decrease with age. Apart from these inconsistent results, the implications from a socialisation viewpoint are not clear. If strengthening of a product request production would inhibit the development of a purchase production, then the effect would have to be considered negative based on the reasoning given above. However, this implication is not clear, especially since children's possibilities to purchase by themselves are limited and they might have to turn to product requests even when a purchase production becomes invoked. Another possible indirect piece of evidence concerning the formation of a purchase production can be seen in the results reported about the awareness of the purpose of TV commercials.

If children say that the purpose of TV commercials is to sell products, to make money, to seduce consumers, or similar answers, then the existence of a purchase production can safely be assumed. While the major explanatory variable here is age (Meringoff & Lesser, 1980a), both Infratest and Stupening report positive relationships between awareness of the purpose of TV commercials and exposure to TV commercials when controlling for age. Ward et al. (1977) found effects that were different for the age groups. Ward et al. also ascertained quite a number of variables that can somehow be linked to the existence of information search productions, with however no consistent relationship to TV advertising exposure. Moschis and Churchill (1978) found that amount of television viewing is negatively related to "economic motivations for consumption", which was essentially defined as a desire-to-search index.

Summarising the little evidence that is available would point to the conclusion that if TV advertising has any socialising effects concerning the functioning of markets, then these effects must rather be regarded as positive in the sense that they further cognitive states which enable the consumer to behave in a way that is in accordance with the principles of market economy. Only the Moschis and Moore study provided distinctly negative evidence, while several other studies hint at possible positive effects.

Substantial characteristics of semantic network and autonomy of consumer behavior: this is concerned with the possible prominence of harmful products or attributes in the semantic network of children which some individuals would feel are dysfunctional for children, at least in the absence of parental supervision e.g. snack foods, tobacco, etc. Stupening (1981) has shown that the degree of recall of spots is related to the number of spots broadcast. Thus, to the extent that such products are heavily advertised, there is indirect support for the existence of a negative socialisation effect here. This is supported by other evidence: There was a clear positive correlation between exposure to TV advertising and consumption of snack foods, which remained stable when controlling for age. The Infratest study showed that there was no relationship between TV advertising exposure and the percentage of

"income" of children that is consumed or saved, emphasising that differences in goods consumed are due to the prominence of certain goods in
the semantic network. American studies also show that exposure to TV
advertising is related to consumption of and purchase requests for
snacks (Meringoff, 1980). Of particular interest is a field experiment
by Gorn & Goldberg (1982) showing that children exposed to snack food
commercials at a summer camp chose significantly more candy instead of
fruits as snacks than children receiving other or no messages. These
results are hardly surprising: we should expect products which children
like to be featured in their semantic networks. However, the extent to
which these liked products are consumed, depends upon their production
systems which, in the case of young children, are heavily influenced by
parents.

Formal characteristics of production system and autonomy of consumer
behavior: The German studies do not include any variables that could be
cited here. Ward et al. (1977) have used the number of types of
prescriptive and proscriptive money norms reported by children as one
dependent variable, which could be regarded as a concept approaching
differentiation of productions. The number of proscriptive norms was
negatively related to exposure to television commercials for two of the
three age groups, whereas the number of types of prescriptive money
norms was positively related to exposure in one age group, with no
significant relationships in the remaining age groups.

It is obvious that much more research is needed before something
definitive could be said about socialisation effects of TV advertising
within the SNPS framework. Some suggestions for this will be presented
later. But if we simply wanted to summarise the little evidence that
exists in a pointed statement, it would be this: TV advertising is a
positive social agent as regards functioning of markets, but a negative social agent as regards autonomy of consumer behavior.

SOME SUGGESTIONS FOR RESEARCH

The categorisation of socialisation effects in figure 2 obviously
points to some lacunae. This refers especially to the question whether
TV advertising furthers or inhibits development of high conditional and
operational differentiation of consumption productions. There is
virtually no research evidence on this question, and it would be highly
interesting to see results here. Another area that has received little
attention is TV advertising's potential with regard to the formation of
productions of purchase and information search. It would be interesting
to see replications and extensions of the result reported by Bockelmann
et al. (1979) that information search and purchase behavior is usually
not demonstrated in commercials.

The information processing orientation of the model outlined, drawing
heavily on the psychology of memory, also suggests certain research
instruments that could fruitfully be employed in socialisation research.
Most research to date has relied heavily on questionnaires and observational methods. The process methodology initiated by Jacoby and his
co-workers to study consumer information processing (Jacoby, 1977) could
be applied when the influence of TV advertising on consumer skills is of
interest. A little-used method (at least in consumer research) with a

high potential is the method of free elicitation in order to ascertain structures of factual knowledge (Grunert & Keller, 1984; Olson & Muderrisoglu, 1979). This method could make it possible to actually compare cognitive structures of, e.g., light and heavy users of TV advertising.

Two more suggestions do not directly follow from the approach presented. With the rapid development of new media like videotex and home computers, the television screen will become increasingly multi-functional. Simply analysing the effects of traditional TV commercials on consumer socialisation may soon become too narrow. Already we have numerous hypotheses and also some limited research evidence on how advertising in videotex will influence consumer behavior (e.g., Grunert, 1984; Kaps, 1983). Future research in consumer socialisation should take into account this additional socialisation potential of the TV screen.

Finally, there are very few international replications in consumer research. The German discussion on consumer socialisation is strongly influenced by the results of American research. Institutional differences in broadcasting systems aside, hardly anyone has investigated the question whether there may be intercultural differences in consumer information processing.

The role for TV advertising in consumer socialization in Norway

DR. ASLE DAHL

Concerning allowing advertising on television, Norway has for a long time been like fallow ground. Advertising on radio and television has been prohibited, and for as long as television has existed, one has never considered advertising as something to be broadcast on the state channel.

However, after realizing that future European satellites will mainly be financed by advertising, the "comet" has literally lit up the media-political sky. This technological development has two sides: 1. It introduces a new phenomenon from abroad, and 2. It makes possible the production of domestic TV advertising. Because of this, TV advertising is now on the agenda of our political parties and will probably stay there till the end of next year's election campaign.

The general public has never really paid attention to the debate about advertising through the media. Like other future phenomena it has been a topic particularly for specialists. However, minor gallup polls show a clear majority in favor of television advertising[1], and in the small group of persons who can receive the ECS broadcasting the attitude towards advertising seems to be positive, especially among the youngest viewers[2]. In spite of this the authorities have been very restrictive. They say that indirect advertising reflecting fashion and style in certain programmes for children has been questionable.

But there is a clear inconsistency here. For years advertising films for special brands of clothes, chewing gum, etc. have been shown in Norwegian cinemas, without any protests. Behind this ambiguity is probably the fear of great changes in communications which has delayed media development for generations. In the recent debate the question of influence has become subordinate to the economic consequences the TV ads are likely to have.

The three main points are: 1) mutual competition between mass media, 2) competition between Norwegian advertisers and foreign ones and 3) financing scheme for a new television channel. A total evaluation of these things show that it will be quite impossible to keep ads off Norwegian screens. More and more politicians have changed their points of view and there is every indication that Parliament will pass a resolution that will enable us to start experimental operation of advertising this very autumn.

In the debate, little attention has been drawn to the question of advertising directed towards children, but when this happens it is always the influence aspects that form the conclusion. Many people seem to be of the opinion that advertising represents the strongest and most direct method of media influence and therefore children should be protected against it. A government committee appointed to look into the development and expansion of cable television proposed to prohibit advertising towards children[3]. But even here the points of view differ and fluctuate. Less than two years later another committee says we must realize that future advertising broadcasts surely will have children among their viewers.[4]

This is the result of weighing the question of influence against the practical problems concerning the enforcement of the advertising ban. It seems that the pragmatic considerations have superceded the fear of a topic about which very little is yet known.

THE INCREASING INFLUENCE OF THE MEDIA ON SOCIALIZATION

The mass media are playing an increasing role as socializing agents in society. Earlier the church and school were the prime relayers of knowledge, culture and values. Today the mass media have taken over these functions, and increasingly represent the cultural life most children come into contact with. They define the areas where children do not yet have the knowledge of direct experience. The media have also helped to make this relaying of values a field abounding in contrasts by focussing on controversial questions in daily life and with their continual flood of idols.

The media have also affected conditions concerning the spreading of role patterns and children's experiences with them. Previously it was family members and the local society who transferred societal roles to the young. Today children mix impressions from direct observation of adult roles with knowledge of contrasting types of roles in the larger society which they have mainly learned from viewing TV. Here, as in other areas of socializing, children's ideas of the variation and degree of values lead to uncertainty concerning selection of values, norms and social intercourse. This is clearly expressed in a study from 1967 concerning the introduction of TV in the northernmost and most sparsely-populated part of Norway. After a period of time it was shown that children in the area desired a change: to move and to obtain a big-city job or dream career.[5] No medium possesses so many and varied means of influence in this connection like TV. While adults have three media they use often enough to be called base media, children often have only one, and that is television. Norwegian children spend 2 - 3 hours daily watching TV.[6] Television has therefore also become the dominating socializing agent among the media.

It is commonly accepted that people are influenced by TV, and children more easily than adults. We see it in role-playing in kindergartens and nurseries, where popular series create the basis for the drama to be enacted. When Robin Hood fills the TV screen, doctors report an increase of children hit in the eye by arrows. We also know that children follow the advice of program leaders to send in letters and drawings, or pester their parents to buy a book which has been presented on a program for younger children. Sometimes, however, television's message produces the opposite effect of what was intended. Thus a program meant to prevent discrimination of foreign laborers can lead to a cementing of prejudices against foreigners. Films which mean to discourage drug use can actually stimulate young people to experiment with dangerous drugs. In exposure to TV it seems that there exists a law of multiple effects, where factors such as message type and content, recipient situation, children's expectations, etc. dictate the result. It is this law we wish to obtain a clearer definition of through our investigations.

PROBLEMS CONCERNING RESEARCH METHODS

The main goal in the study of the influence of TV is to connect as far as possible unambiguous causal relations between TV consumption and differing aspects of children's attitudes and actions. Many obstructions exist during such a survey, the greatest being to isolate TV from other socializing agents in the children's surroundings over a length of time. Children are exposed to a stream of impressions daily, and a cluster of variables is included in the socializing process. There can be no hope of bringing these under control outside actual laboratory experiments. The Finnish researcher V. Pielia stresses that influence has occurred when there is something in the media's surroundings which wouldn't have been there if the communication process hadn't taken place. But can this something be traced back to TV's own qualities, the amount of time children spend watching TV, or to influence from the program's content?

In this connection it is of most interest to observe television's actual content. But even here the same problems occur. One cannot isolate variables. We know that advertising in general influences our purchasing habits, but how much of this influence is caused by ads in brochures, magazines and shop windows - and how much by TV advertising? We also know that TV messages influence children, but how much of this can be traced back to actual commercials, and how much is caused by other types of programs?

193

Investigating how TV influence occurs and how strong it is also leads to a time–span limitation problem. The length of time which often exists between TV use and its consequences means that it is difficult to be completely sure when a medium's message no longer has any effect. So it is difficult to differentiate between short–term and long–term effects. Most researchers are more interested by long–term effects, but because they are so resource–consuming to investigate, researchers usually complete studies of short–term effects. I am a typical example, because my resources are extremely limited – and because research into such a new phenomenon as commercial TV (in the long–term perspective) cannot be completed for 5 – 10 years yet. Research concerning children and TV is very modest in Norway. The same can be said of advertising research in general. Concerning the theme of children and advertising, I have noticed that only one of the 45 members of the Norwegian Union of Media Research has completed investigations in the area. A realization of the project outlined in this paper will therefore require the establishment of a new branch inside Norwegian media research. With the increasing interest the authorities are showing concerning commercial TV, and the increasing importance of producing research results which can improve decision–making in this area, such a development seems natural. But the limited resources, including human resources, will lead to small dimensions in the future research of children and commercial T.V.

Objections can be made, of course: perhaps it's unnecessary to chart all the previously–mentioned variables on a national scope. Many countries already have solid research traditions in this area, and can produce results which Norwegian researchers could build upon. In other words, the doors are open for an extensive transfer of knowledge from the USA for example. But not even this process is free of problems. "American research results" which are often quoted in Norwegian debate are probably not suited for direct comparison and conclusion concerning TV commercials and their effect on children. There is of course little reason to believe that Norwegian children would react perceptually and emotionally differently to commercials than American children. But the structure of the ad, and especially the volume of advertising will in the foreseeable future be different in the USA than in Norway. It is therefore probable that the intellectual and social effects of children will also vary.

As a first step in the research it will be necessary to establish a group which can effect a critical review of foreign research material and evaluate how much of the available results are relevant for Norwegian research. This would be a natural part of a preliminary project with the intention of clarifying variables and forming of suggestions for methodically solving the general problems referred to here. In addition, the group, in its research, must expect a formidable novelty effect which could make it especially difficult to draw unambiguous conclusions concerning the effects of commercial TV.

CHOICE OF PROBLEM STATEMENTS

When one is faced with an extensive research area like television advertising and socialization, and only has a small research potential, it's necessary to make a strict list of priorities. Because there is no traditional ratings system in Norway, it's difficult to know which children watch which types of programs - and what they think of them. Once in a while an advertising company might ask adults that type of question in an inquiry or poll, but this would not be easy to accomplish with children without the risk of it being interpreted as part of a marketing campaign.

What most interests me is an investigation of problem statements with educational relevance. This is in line with the normal public interest in this area and the interest politicians show concerning the media's supposed effects on children. They are afraid that children will be exposed to negative influences and will, through TV, acquire other opinions, attitudes and habits than parents desire, or which are in opposition to the official goals of upbringing which the schools hold. The variables which should first be examined are, in my opinion, TV advertising's importance for consumer socialization and for the creation of media consciousness. This would also correspond well with research tradition in my country.

In the following text I will discuss three hypotheses of central importance to educators, and give my own comments. 1) Concerning the first hypothesis, which has to do with learning, I would say: children gradually acquire scattered, isolated pieces of information about single products from TV commercials. This hypothesis is a result of the understanding that, in general, it is difficult to learn about anything from TV. As a learning situation, TV viewing is doubtfully anything special. Neither children nor adults learn expressly by watching the world being shown on a TV screen. The process of thinking must be activated, children must react and accomplish something. Learning opportunities will probably be proportional to the intensity of the activity. Children can also be relatively passive participants in play and mentally absent in conversations with their peers. But they can be strongly engaged in receiving relevant information through TV. If the program manages to lift the watcher out of his lazy chair, okay. Maybe something will be learned. Television producers know this, and outdo each other in being entertaining. They demand concentration and provide less and less room for pauses which could give the viewer possibilities of complete thought and reflection. There is reason to fear that commercials, with their rapid chain of images and imperative speech, will increase children's stimulation activity but reduce their chances for thought and learning. Studies from TV use in schools in the sixties showed that the medium can be just as effective in teaching as the traditional classroom teaching. But here we are speaking of experimental teaching and clearly-defined educational guidelines regulating its use. A completely different question is whether children are motivated for learning while lying on their stomachs at home in front of the TV. Don't they just want to be entertained? If they're lying there to satisfy their need for information, then the basis for learning is at once better. But it is also possible that commercials will flood them with information - so much so that they will receive answers to questions they've never even asked. This is a barrier to the child's understanding of the message in many TV programs. Learning also assumes the correction of its own activity. But does the TV commercial release any activity which requires correction or feedback? Neither is it only the message, but just as much the social connection where the reception occurs which is important for learning. The mood of the living room does not produce the best conditions for concentration. Others can make comments to the message which can be of a disturbing or governing nature. They can have special expectations for the children's reactions, as well as the children can have expectations for their own way of reacting. It is also important whether one watches commercials together with friends who are opinion-creating leaders. When one watches alone, one doesn't understand - and thereby easily loses the connection.

To the degree ad producers manage successfully to fill the requirements for learning mentioned here, their programs will obtain results. The best method is probably to present a problem which children try to find a solution to. What kind of information is it, then, which will manage to pass the natural or learned filters which are mentioned here? In my opinion it will mainly be information which concerns <u>identification</u> of consumer products: name of product, type, price and certain quality aspects of it. Children also acquire certain information concerning the <u>product's function</u>: what needs it satisfies, how it is used, result of its use and where it can be purchased. Whether an ad gives any deeper insight into these areas is an open question. Learning results will probably show themselves to be primarily concerned with new names, slogans, jokes and characterizing sayings and quotes. Some will perhaps connect a product's name to a person's name and learn, to a degree, how one should act in a store, on the telephone, etc.

Use of television can, in general, be compared with other methods of acquiring knowledge and experience, where the normal rules for acquisition are in effect: children who consume most, learn most (quantitively). Those who know much from before probably get more from what they see. Children who profit most from homes with high socio-economic status and have parents who usually discuss with them what the children watch. It is most probable that the recipients of commercial TV broadcasts will also be subject to these laws.

2.) Learning is the acquisition of concrete experiences, while influencing to a larger degree covers the establishment of abstract attitudes and values. But it is probably correct to maintain that they are based upon each other, and that influencing represents a broader and deeper learning result. My second hypothesis maintains that <u>TV advertising does not represent any stronger influence on children than any other types of program content</u>. The commercial message has the advantage of more easily communicating its message to the audience than other types of program because it is often so unambiguous and is presented in such an easily understood form. Consciously or unconsciously children will more easily understand messages which they know from before or which fit into their existing thought patterns. Like most people in a consumer society, they have many purchasing desires, and commercials on TV will probably only contribute in a minor way to this massive attitude. They can receive impulses to buy or increase the consumption pressure on their parents. In both cases it can lead to increased purchasing frequency and to changes in selection of products. But will these changes last for any length of time? A more interesting question concerning education is whether television ads will also have normative consequences for the young audience. Can they change children's opinions of what is attractive, tough, good to eat, etc? Will commercials be trend-setting when it comes to sports equipment, casual clothes, hairstyles, etc. We don't know. But we have seen that people, patterns of action, and surroundings in differing TV programs seem trend setting. Here it will be important to consider the profile of the program which the commercials will be broadcast with. But there is little reason to believe that advertising will have other effects in the area than the TV series do. The number of repeated messages will hardly be higher in future ads than it is in series and soap operas.

Strong behavioural and attitudinal changes can be manifested in model adaption with what is called pseudosocial interaction. TV advertising's possiblities of starting such an interaction lie primarily in the possibilities for indentification with characters the programs present. Children can put themselves in the place of these characters and share their fates as if they were their own. Through wishful identification they will fantasize themselves into the exciting world which in the ad is connected to certain products and the consumption of them. They can also experience many positive feelings of prestigious people like sports stars - and by purchasing the products being advertised, become more like them. But will this influencing be any different than what they experience while fantasizing about accompanying their hero in a dangerous mission on a TV series?

All such roles can, moreover, occur in such exotic surroundings and be so detached from children's reality that they offer no real model.

Likeness identification is perhaps more common in commercials than in other program categories. Here are often normal children who solve daily problems by purchasing a product. Thereby they became both more satisfied and happier. The nationally-produced commercial will presumably be of the same type, something which in such a case will facilitate identification. But, in short programs, these child figures will possess too few characterizing features for any deeper identif- ication. One can nevertheless not disregard the possibility that norm transfers will occur. One has, however, reason to believe that ordinary children's programs with "daily heroes" in general have a better chance to succeed with their norms - especially since they tell a longer and more consecutive story than commercials. Concerning both categories, it is doubtful that model adaption will be <u>lasting</u>. The identification TV offers is different than that which occurs in families and peer groups, where the children have both emotional connections and can take the initiative and receive feedback on their own identity. Much seems to point to TV actually being perceived of as a new form of play. A part of the media content, perhaps especially within advertising, can probably give wish fulfilment in the same way as physical play in previous children's culture.

Watching TV can be perceived as a thinking game, a psychic-symbol play form which continues as long as the broadcast lasts. With its attractive form, the commercial will probably also stimulate children's imaginations and give them roles and situations which later can be further revised, because they give answers to emotional conflicts

197

children experience. This is true, of course, for many types of programs.

The process of mass communication has many inherent barriers to influencing. Advertising can prove to have little effect because it represents a conscious influence which most people are aware of. Also the communications fellowship - the social surroundings - will be able to limit or advance the further spread of the message within the group. The reason why children watch commercials can be that they have had to accommodate the wishes of others in the primary group - and therefore view broadcasting they otherwise would not have watched had it been up to them. They can also refuse to watch broadcasting for the same reason.

Most children in their everyday lives are exposed to more influencing which supports their previous attitudes rather than challenging them. In this way their earlier attitudes will be exposed to a fairly even current of corroboration, as, for example, the type of consumer attitudes which dominate in an industrialized society.

The majority of TV programs will probably only strengthen this tendency. Otherwise, it seems that Norwegian children's TV-viewing habits are also their best protection against influencing in both attitudes and actions. This lazy indifference will be a difficult wall for the ad producers to surmount. Even if they can manage at the outset, it's likely that the viewers' feelings and reactions with time will become jaded towards commercials as they have with other types of programs.

3.) The last hypothesis concerns the indirect influence commercial TV will exert on parts of the school curriculum. It is more nationally qualified than the previous two, but should also have relevance for research in other countries. I would in fact assert that introduction of commercial broadcasts will strengthen teaching in consumer questions as well as in mass media.

When it comes to the consequences of advertising for the home and the school, consumer socialization and media consciousness constitute two sides of the same question. Each has its own way of meeting advertising phenomenon. But since this will be presented on a newly-established national network channel, interaction between them will be assured.

On a macro level, advertisements will be met with reactions. The phenomenon of advertising will receive wide coverage in the press. It will be discussed and evaluated at work and in the home. Large groups, of children including the youngest age groups who haven't previously been exposed to advertising, will now receive it - at regular intervals, with better conditions for success in attaining its goals than previously. This fact will activate opinion from traditional protectionists and critics who will point out that when authorities increase the total media offering and release such a controversial media category upon the public, they must also provide measures which can strengthen teaching in consumer questions.

For the student, the advertising will be valuable in itself. Through it they will require a mass of information, both about foreign and domestic products. In this way they will extend their product knowledge and get a better basis for comparison when the time comes to choose. They will also notice that some advertisements appeal to their desire to purchase, and that salesmen will convince them of the superiority of their wares.

In the space of a short time they will view advertising as a permanent part of certain milieus which are depicted. This is shown, for example, in the results of a drawing contest for children which a local bank held in connection with the Winter Olympics. A large number of the drawings sent in had brand names as an easily-recognisable background in the different sports arenas.

The student will bring with him to school all his impressions and experiences with advertising, and get them revised in the classroom. This can finally create systematic studies of the role and function of advertising in business and in society as a whole.

Previous use of printed advertising material in teaching shows that students have had difficulties understanding it. They considered the brochures and magazines more as official teaching material than as a biased presentation from identifiable people. The possibility for misunderstanding will be removed during the announcements of forthcoming programs, where it will be stated that advertisements are being broadcast and who is behind them. This can heighten both the curiosity and the consumer consciousness of those watching. In the area of the media we will experience similar reactions, possibly even stronger. The introduction of commercials will occur simultaneously with the general increase in the number of television channels. This will strengthen TV at the expense of other media, and lead to a heightened awareness from the authorities and the public. There is therefore reason to believe that advertising will primarily be viewed as a media phenomenon, not as naked marketing. It will be maintained that the possibilities for influencing increase when a neutral institution (source) such as Norway's National Broadcasting Company stands behind the spread of advertising instead of advertising being distributed through ordinary channels.

All these factors will result in a justifiable demand for the authorities to make an attempt to equip children to be able to withstand advertising. The primary means here will be parent action and campaigns and strengthening of the school's mass media education. In the Norwegian primary school there is already great interest in the subject "media studies", and there is reason to expect an increase of new resources for teaching in this subject. More directly, one can even foresee that advertising programs could provide suitable teaching material. They would create a good collection of examples for analysis of the mass communication process, because commercials are so clear with regard to sender, target group, coding, etc. It will probably be mostly used as material for critical evaluation of messages. Students often have a sharper critical attitude to ads than to other content in the media. Television ads can, through their provocative format and assertions, heighten the students' critical consciousness. They can cause them to investigate means and myths more closely, and by so doing better their understanding of the visual language. There is reason to suppose that advertising will create chain reactions of a positive nature for the schools. It will give schools increased prestige as a factor in media education, and strengthen teaching in two relatively new areas. That is not bad for an effect of television advertising.

PROPOSAL FOR PILOT PROJECT

A pilot project in this area would have several aims. Primarily it would have to inquire into certain relationships which could create a basis for testing the stated hypotheses. Next, it should clarify the problems which could benefit from further research. The classic before-and-after project would in all probability carry with it too many variables for it to be a justifiable project, - since resources are so limited. Here I would like to detail studies of a more limited nature, which primarily would capture spontaneous reactions of children in their first meeting with TV commercials.

Too much space would be required to go into detail concerning frame factors of national nature which could decide the project's plan and scope. The biggest element of uncertainty is that we don't know <u>what kind</u> of commercial we will get on Norwegian screens - and <u>when</u> it will arrive. What do we know is that ads won't occur in breaks but will be collected in permanent and compact sessions. We also know that they will be effected on a new TV channel of which must is expected. The channel will broadcast light entertainment programs in the afternoon and early evening. Advertising will therefore appear together with a series of other programs which occur on a scale somewhere between information and entertainment. <u>What, then, is more natural than to investigate children's reaction to - and evaluation of - commercials as program categories?</u>

Today we know nothing about who will watch the programs, how often they will watch, whether they will become involved in the content or remain indifferent to it.

Such quantitative and qualitative reactions will be useful for advertisers to clarify, so that they might produce a form and style which reaches the youthful audience. For the authorities, such information could provide a basis for producing of a set of guidelines or regulations for broadcasters.

During TV viewing, each child will, have with him his own complicated set of interpretations, expectations and experiences. These predispositions will be important for their evaluation of commercial programs - and the effects the contents will have. One must therefore inquire <u>who</u> receives the media's messages, and what assumptions, they have. The natural target group for investigation here is children at the so-called TV age, of 9 - 14 year olds. Why do they watch TV? What needs are satisfied by television commercials? Does the broadcasting of commercials create new needs for them? How do they edit the information they receive from advertising? With what are impulses and information contrasted & evaluated in contrast? How are they combined with prior experience and results?

Such questions can clarify the knowledge component in the formation of opinions - in other words show what information, conceptions or stereotypes children have towards advertising. But one should also investigate which feelings and evaluations children connect with the programs, and to what extent the content can be said to predict actions, for example, purchasing behavior? Does the media message also work in a stimulating manner on other social processes?

In a pilot such as this it will be natural to involve teachers, not only to administer the surveys, but also to participate in the observations of the children's confrontation with commercial TV. Is knowledge noticeably and negatively affected? To what degree can they register an increase in the understanding of advertising. Does it lead to changes in the children's frame of reference or choice of program? And not least: can they produce evidence that the broadcasts activate teaching in consumer education and media studies?

How precisely such investigations can be carried out will be dependent upon the data collection instruments constructed. But the results will also depend on the novelty effect which blends itself into the studies. It will not be possible to reduce this effect by traditional means. It should probably be included in the interpretation of the results. One will thereby probably be able to draw conclusions about the three hypotheses, which must be modified after time. In this way the project would be an original before-and-after study.

TV ADVERTISING AS A FUTURE SOCIALISATION AGENT IN DANISH CHILDREN'S LIVES.

AN ABSTRACT : Birgitte Tufte

In Denmark we have only got one TV channel and no TV advertising - so far.

However, many Danish children already watch TV ads, as 30% of the population are able to watch TV from Western Germany, and recent research has shown that 95% of the Danish children who are able to watch German TV watch it every day.

Television is a rapidly growing disseminator of <u>culture</u>, and the influence of television advertising on children must be seen in relation to other socialization agents and cultural factors such as family, school, mass media in general, peer group, church etc.

Television is the mass media that children use most. There are differences in their viewing patterns depending on age, sex and socio-economic position. The average for a Danish child is about one and a half hours per day and about two hours for the high-level consumers.

Children, particularly 9-14 year olds who have lots of leisure time, insufficient contact with adults and few meaningful tasks to perform, are the high-level consumers of television. Recent research has shown, however, that another group of high-level consumers are appearing, i.e. 9-14 year olds who are well stimulated in their environment, are active - reading books, newspapers etc. - <u>and</u> watching television and video.

When video enters the family home the average time spent on video is 30 minutes per day (the time spent on TV remains unchanged) and children increase their total time in front of the screen by 40 minutes per day. (15% of Danish families have a videotape-recorder).

Content analysis is an effective measure of the values and norms presented in TV programmes, video films and in TV ads.

We - a group of Danish media researchers - recently made a small study of 11-12 year olds' viewing habits and preferences, combining content analysis with the children's perception of the programmes they prefer.

In the first place children remember situations, peoples etc. which they can use in their attempt to build up personal and cultural identity. They are fascinated by TV fiction and ads, and those they remember relate to family relations, friendship and the future.

Our conclusion is that children are looking for meaning, for some sort of <u>vital coherence</u> and for <u>personal and cultural identity</u>.

Characteristic of our western way of life - and especially perhaps of the European way of life - is that:-

1) **We are living in series** - Jean Paul Sartre compares the modern way of life with a bus queue. You are not in line

then you become ninth etc....
Everybody can be replaced by somebody else.

2) **In a rapidly growing way we get our information about the outer world through the mass media,** a 'second hand experience'. The development of Western society has – among other things – had the consequence that children have become isolated from and alien to adult life and production. Much of what they learn in school has no direct relationship to the world they see around them. And the experience they get through TV is an <u>indirect</u> experience.

3) **European countries are getting a rapidly increasing quantity of cultural influence from foreign countries – through mass media.**

   The culture presented can only to a certain extent be related to the culture of their own country.

   Foreign culture is <u>not</u> by nature a bad thing, but imported TV programmes produced according to the principle of the 'least common denominator' (x) exert a certain influence on minor language areas – such as for instance the Scandinavian countries.

   x) Competition among several commercial TV channels leads to a great quantity of TV production which – in order to reach as many consumers as possible – must integrate the interests of very different groups of people according to the principle of 'the least common denominator'. Being addressed to such a big group TV programmes inevitably become very similar to each other. Accordingly the result is not a differentiation of the total supply of TV but a very easily comprehensible – non-controversial genre of TV.

   Cultural differentiation is a must for the small countries of Europe with a variety of languages, differing cultural back-ground, different senses of humour and so forth.

   In Denmark the main concern among media researchers in TV advertising has been the aspect of '<u>the least common denominator</u>'. The introduction of TV advertising may have an effect on the total profile of the TV programmes leading to more entertainment programmes being produced, following the principle of 'the least common denominator'.

   Finally there follow some quotations from Danish children's written exercises about TV and video.

   The exercises belong to material collected during the past school year in a project about sixty 14-15 year olds. The aim of the project is to create a model for teaching Danish children to analyse and use TV and video as tools – <u>to be active in relation to the TV-screen.</u>

203

"I like TV ads - I think they are great fun .. I could spend a whole day just watching TV-ads".

"No, I don't think we should have TV ads .. Well, in case we do get them I hope they will have a lot of music.."

"I think it would be fun to have TV ads - on the other hand it would be bad for the people who are easily influenced ... Personally I only buy the things I like".

"I don't think that TV ads are a good idea - The only good thing about TV advertising is that it would be possible to find time to go to the toilet then ...

Finally it's only the manufacturers who are really interested in TV advertising - I think it would be much better to use that money for something reasonable like sponsoring an animal in the Copenhagen zoo".

REFERENCES : REINHARD SANDER

ADORNO, Th.W	Resume uber Kulturindustrie: In PROKOP (1984)
ARIES, P.	Geschichte der Kindheit. Muchen: 1975
DAHLMULLER, G HUND, W.D. KOMMER, H.	Kritik des Fernsehens – Handbuch gegen Manipulation. Darmstadt u. Neuwied: 1973
ELIAS, N.	Uber den Proze der Zivilisation. (2 Bande) Frankfurt: 1976.
ELKIND, D.	The Hurried Child – Growing up too fast too soon. New York: 1981
ENZENBERGER, H.M.	Bewusstseins-Industrie. In: Einzelheiten. Frankfurt: 1962
EURICH, C.	Das verkebelte Leben – Wem schden und wem nutzen die Neuen Medien. Reinbek bei Hamburg: 1980.
FORSTHOFF, E.	Rechtsstaat im Wandel – Verfassungsrechtliche Abhandlugen 1950 – 1964. Stuggart: 1964.
FELDMANN, E.	Theorie der Massenmedien – Eine Einfuhrung in ide Medien-und Kommunikationswissenschaft. Muchen/Basel: 1972
GRUNERT, K.G. u STUPENING, E.	Werbung – ihre gesellschaftliche und okonomische Problematik. Frankfurt/New York: 1981
HAASE, H.	Kinder, Jugendliche und Medien – Eine Literatureexpertise Frankfurt: 1981 (Schriftenreihe Media Persoektiven)
HERMANNS, A.	Sozialisation duruch Werbung – Sozialisationswirkungen von Werbeaussagen in Massenmedien. Dusseldorf: 1972
HOLZER, H.	Theorie des Fernsehens – Fernseh-Kommunikation in der Bundesrepublik Deutschland. Hamburg: 1975
HOLZER, H.	Verkabelt und verkauft? Streitpunkt: Kabelfernsehen. Frankfurt: 1981
HUNZIKER, P.	Erziehung zum Uberflub – Soziologie des Konsums. Stuggart/Berlin: 1972
HUNZIKER, P.	Gesellschaftliche Wirkungen der Massenmedien, insbesondere von Radio und Fernsehen. Kreuzlingen: 1980 (unveroffemtlicher Bericht an die Expertenkommission fur eine Medien- Gesamtkonzeption).

JURGENS, E.	Die List der Vernunft und ihre Grenzen in der Geschichte - Zum historischen Verhaltnis von Medienentwicklung und Gesellschaftsfortschritt. In: BETZ u. HOLZER (Hrsg): Totale Bildschirmherrschaft? Staat, Kapital und "Neue Medien". Koln: 1983.
LANG, E.	Kind, Familie und Fernsehen - Untersuchungen fernsehbedingter Storungen bei Kindern. Freiburg/Basel/Wien: 1980
LECHLEITNER, H.	Vor uns die Videotie - Die Gefahren der Neuen Medien in: Suddeutsche Zeitung, 26/27.2.1983
LEVI-STRAUSS, C.	Traurige Tropen. Frankfurt: 1981 (3. Auflage)
LINDNER, R.	Das Gefuhl von Freiheit und Abenteuer - Ideologie und Praxis der Werbung. Frankfurt/New York: 1977.
MANDER, J.	Schafft das Fernsehen ab! Eine Streitschrift gegen das Leben aus zweiter Hand. Reinbek bei Hamburg: 1981 (2. Auflage)
MICHEL, K.M.	Grips und Chips. In: Kursbuch 75 (Marz) 1984
PLATON	Phaidros. In: Gastmahl/Phaidros/Phaidon, Wiesbaden 1978 (zitiert nach JURGENS 1983, S.11)
POSTMAN, N.	Das Verschwinden der Kindheit. Frankfurt: 1983 (2. Auflage)
PROKOP, D. (Hrsg.)	Massenkommunikationsforschung 2: Konsumtion. Frankfurt: 1973.
PROKOP, D. (Hrsg.)	Massenkommunikationsforschung 1: Produktion. Frankfurt 1976 (4. Auflage).
RATZKE, D.	Netzwerke der Macht - Die neuen Medien. Frankfurt: 1975.
SAINT-GEOURS, J.	Es lebe die Konsumgesellschaft - Freiheiten und Zwange von Arbeit und Freizeit. Das Fernsehen. In: PROKOP (1973)
SILBERMANN, A. u. KRUGER U.M.	Soziologie der Massenkommunikation. Stuttgart/Berlin: 1973
THALMANN, H.C.	Verhaltensstorungen bei Kindern im Grundschulalter. Stuggart: 1974 (zitiert nach LANG 1980, S.32)
VIVELO, F.	Handbuch der Kulturanthropologie. Stuttgart: 1981.
WILENSKY, H.	Massengesellschaft und Massenkultur. In: PROKOP (1973)
WINN, M.	Die Droge im Wohnzimmer. Reinbek bei Hamburg: 1979.

REFERENCES : KLAUS GRUNERT

Adler, R.P. & Faber, R.J. (1980). Background: Children's television viewing patterns. In: R.P. Adler et al. (Eds.)., The effects of television advertising on children, pp. 13-28. Lexington, MA: Lexington.

Adler, R.P., Lesser, G.S., Meringoff, L.K., Robertson, T.S., Rossiter, J.R. & Ward, S. (1980) (Eds.) The effects of television advertising on children. Lexington, MA: Lexington.

Anderson, J.R. (1976). Language, memory and thought. Hillsdale, NJ: Erlbaum.

Atkin, C. (1975a). Effects of television advertising on children - second year experimental evidence. Report < 2, TV advertising and children project, Michigan State University, June 1975.

Atkin, C. (1975b). Effects of television advertising on children - survey of pre-adolescent's responses to television commercials. Report 6, TV advertising and children project, Michigan State University, July 1975.

Atkin, C. (1976). Children's social learning from television advertising: Research evidence on observational modeling of product consumption. In: B.B. Anderson (Ed.), Advances in consumer research, Vol. 3, pp. 513-519. Chicago: Association for Consumer Research.

Barcus, F.E. (1975). Weekend commercial children's television. Newton, NA: Action for Children's Television.

Barcus, F.E. (1978). Commercial children's television on weekends and weekday afternoons. Newton, MA: Action for Children's Television.

Bergler, R. & Six, U. (1979). Psychologie des Fernsehens. Bern: Huber.

Bettman, J.R. (1979). An information processing theory of consumer choice. Reading, MA: Addison Wesley.

Blatt, J., Spencer, L. & Ward, S. (1972). A cognitive development study of children's reactions to television advertising. In: E.A. Rubinstein, G.A. Comstock & J.P. Murray (Eds.), Television and social behavior, Vol. 4, pp. 452-467. Rockville, MY: National Institute of Mental Health.

Bockelmann, F., Huber, J. & Middelmann, A. (1979). Werbefernsehkinder. Berlin: Spiess.

Escher, R. (1977). Familiensozialisation durch Fernsehwerbung. Unpublished dissertation, University of Salzburg.

Galst, J. & White, M. (1976). The unhealthy persuader: The reinforcing value of television and children's purchase-influence attempts at the supermarket. Child Development, 17, 1086-1096.

Gorn, G.J. & Goldberg, M.E. (1982). Behavioral evidence of the effects of televised food messages on children. Journal of Consumer Research, 9, 200-205.

Grunert, K.G. (1982a). Linear processing in a semantic network: An alternative view of consumer product evaluation. Journal of Business Research 10, 31-42.

Grunert, K.G. (1982b). Informationsverarbeitungsprozesse bei der kaufentscheidung: Ein gedachtnispsychologischer Ansatz. Frankfurt: Lang.

Grunert, K.G. (1984). Verbraucherinformation in Bildschirmtext - Moglishkeiten und Grenzen. Munchen: R. Fischer.

Grunert, K.G. & Keller, A. (1984). Cognitive determinants of attribute information usage: A pilot study. Paper presented at the 9th Colloquium of the International Association for Research in Economic Psychology, Tilburg, June 26-29, 1984.

Grunert, K.G. & Stupening, E. (1981). Werbung – ihre gesellschaftliche und okonomische Problematik. Frankfurt: Campus.

Haase, H. (1981). Kinder, Jugendliche und Medien. In: Kinder, Medien, Werbung, Schriftenreihe Media Perspektiven, Vol. 1, pp. 9–294. Frankfurt: Metzner.

Haedrich, G., Adam, M., Kreilkamp, E. & Kub, A. (1984). Werbewirkung bei Kindern – Ergebnisse einer experimentellen Untersuchung zue Fernsehwerbung. Jahrbuch der Absatz – und Verbrauchsforschung, 30, 21–39.

Hermanns, A. (1972). Sozialiation durch Werbung. Dusseldorf: Bertelsmann. Infratest Medienforschung (1981). Fernsehen im Alltag von Kindern. In: Kinder, Medien, Werbung, Schriftenreihe Media Perspektiven, Vol. 1, pp. 299–607. Frankfurt: Metzner.

Jacoby, J. (1977). The emerging behavioral process technology in consumer decision-making. In: W.D. Perreault (Ed.), Advances in consumer research Vol.4 , pp. 263–265. Chicago: Association for Consumer Research.

Kaps, R.U. (1983). Die Wirkung von Bildschirmtext auf das Informationsverhalten der Konsumenten. Munchen: R. Fischer.

v. Keitz, B. (1983). Wirksame Fernsehwerbung. Wurzburg: Physica.

Kratzer, V. & Silberer, G. (1976). Imitationsanreize in der Konsumguterwerbung. Working paper, SFB 24, Univeristy of Mannheim.

Kraub, W. (1982). Insertwirkungen im werbefernsehen. Bochum: Brockmeyer.

Kroeber-Riel, W. (1980). Konsumentenverhalten, 2nd ed. Munich: Vahlen.

Kuhlmann, E. (1983). Consumer socialisation of children and adolescents: A review of current approaches. Journey of Consumer Policy, 6, 397–418.

Meringoff, L.K. (1980). The effects of children's television food advertising. In: R.P. Adler et al. (Eds.), The effects of television advertising on children, pp. 123–151. Lexington, MA: Lexington.

Meringoff, L.K. & Lesser, G.S. (1980a). Children's ability to distinguish television commercials from program material. In: R.P. Adler et al. (Eds.), The effects of television advertising on children, pp. 29–42. Lexington, MA: Lexington.

Meringoff, L.K. & Lesser, G.S. (1980b). The influence of format and audiovisual techniques on children's perceptions of commercial messages In: R.P. Adler et al. (Eds.), The effects of television advertising on children, pp. 43–59. Lexington, MA: Lexington.

Meyer-Hentschel, G. (1983). Aktivierungswirkung von Anzeigen. Wurzburg: Physica.

Meyer, P.W. & Koller, B. (1971). Die Rolle der Wirtschaftswerbung bei der Sozialisation. In: F. Ronneberger (Ed.), Sozialisation durch Massenkonnumikation, pp. 378–398. Stuttgart: Enke.

Moschis, G.P. & Churchill, G.A. (1978). Consumer Socialisation: A theoretical and empirical analysis. Journal of Marketing Research, 15, 599–609.

Moschis, G.P. & Moore, R.C. (1979). Decision making among the young: A socialisation perspective. Journal of Consumer Research, 6, 101–112.

Newell, A. & Simon, H.A. (1972). Human problem solving. Englewood Cliffs, NJ: Prentice Hall.

Norman, D.A. & Rumelhart, D.E. (1975). Explorations in cognition. San Francisco: Freeman.

Olson, J.C. (1978). Theories of information encoding and storage. In: A. Mitchell (Ed.), The effect of information on consumer and market behavior, pp. 49–60. Chicago: American Marketing Association.

Olson, J.C. & Muderrisoglu, A. (1979). The stability of responses obtained through free elicitation: Implications for measuring attribute salience and memory structure. In: W.L. Wilkie (Ed.), Advances in consumer research, Vol. 6, pp. 269–275. Chicago: Association for Consumer Research.

Pascual-Leone, J. (1980). Constructive problems for constructive theories. In: R.H. Kluwe & H. Spada (Eds.), Developmental models of thinking, pp. 263–296. New York: Prisma-Institut (1976). Der junge Verbraucher, Hamburg.

Quillian, M.R. (1968). Semantic memory. In: M. Minsky (Ed.), Semantic information processing, pp. 216–270. Cambridge, MA: MIT-Press.

Reitman, W.R. (1965). Cognition and thought. New York: Wiley.

Resnik, A. & Stern, B.L. (1977). An analysis of information content in advertising. Journal of Marketing, 41(1), 33–39.

Rossiter, J.R. (1977). Reliability of a short test measuring children's attitudes toward TV commercials. Journal of Consume Research, 3, 179–184.

Scherhorn, G. (1981). Methoden und Chancen einer Beeinflussung der Konsumenten zur rationalen Uberprufung ihrer Praferenzen. In: R. Tietz (Ed.), Wert - und Praferenzprobleme in den Wirtschafts - und Sozialwissenschaften pp. 171–194. Berlin: Duncker & Humblot.

Shimp, T.A. (1979). Social psychological (mis)representations in television advertising. Journal of Consumer Affairs, 13, 28–40.

Stupening, E. (1981). Kind und Werbefernsehen. Unpublished manuscript. Bonn: Abt Associates.

Stupening, E. (1982). Detrimental effects of television advertising on consumer socialisation. Journal of Business Research, 10, 75–84.

Sturm, H., Holzheuer, K. & Helmreich, E. (1978). Emotionale Wirkungen des Fernsehens - Jugendliche als Rezipienten. Munich: Saur.

Sturm, H. & Jorg, S. (1980). Informationsverarbeitung durch Kinder. Munich: Saur.

Ward, S. (1974). Consumer socialisation. Journal of Consumer Research, 1, 1–14.

Ward, S., Levinson, D. & Wackman, D. (1972). Children's attention to television advertising. In: E.A. Rubinstein, G.A. Comstock & J.P. Murray (Eds.), Television and social behavior, Vol. 4, pp. 491–515. Rockville, MY: National Institute of Mental Health.

Ward, S. & Robertson, T.S. (1972). Adolescent attitudes toward television advertising: preliminary findings. In: E.A. Rubinstein, G.A Comstock & J.P. Murray (Eds.), Television and social behavior, pp. 526–542. Rockville, MY: National Institute of Mental Health.

Ward, S., Wackman, D.B. & Wartella, E. (1977). How children learn to buy. Beverly Hills: Sage.

Wartella, E., Wackman, D.B. & Ward, S. (1976). Children's consumer information processing: Representation of information from television advertisements. In: H.K. Hunt (Ed.), Advances in consumer reserch, Vol 5, pp. 535–539. Chicago: Association for Consumer Research.

Weinberg, P. & Gottwald, W. (1982). Impulsive consumer buying as a result of emotions. Journal of Business Research, 10, 43–57.

REFERENCES : ASLE DAHL

1.) The Norwegian magazine "Marketing". No. 2 1982
2.) Lundby, K: Local TV or Satellite Broadcasting? Research News No. 4, 1983
3.) Norwegian Official Publications 1982: Cable Television Oslo, 1982, p.66
4.) Norwegian Official Publications 1984: Five TV Commercials Oslo, 1984, P.151.
5.) Werner, A: Children and Television. Oslo 1972.
6.) Statistical Central Bureau: Listener and Viewer Inquiry 1983. Oslo 1984.

PART VII

The holistic approach

The world does not consist of disciplines, academic or otherwise. Let us assume (and we must, I think assume) that there is an external, objective reality – that trees do exist when there is no-one observing them, that mountains had a reality before anyone came along to worship, admire, climb, or study them. This reality, from single cells to continents, from joy to misery (for we and our experiences are part of it), from light to poverty, is a huge buzzing, tacky, messy system which is, apparently, reduceable to order.

Disciplines, whether they be academic, religious, aesthetic, or of any other type, attempt to explain reality by making it orderly. The nature of the process is debatable. Does science, for example, create, explore, discover, observe or manufacture truth, knowledge, or reality? In the present context we can leave that as an open question, perhaps agreeing to disagree. But we can agree that the same chunk of reality can be studied by different disciplines and, between and within these disciplines, be reduced to different orderly statements.

For example the family of ball, table, and cue games such as snooker, pool and billiards can be studied by mathematicians, physicists, psychologists, sociologists, economists, not to mention colour chemists, anthropologists and computor scientists. Furthermore, each discipline, successfully applied, will suggest a different set of statements in its orderly definition of the reality or nature of pool. The findings of these disciplines will be more or less helpful to the novice player, the equipment manufacturer, the invester in the leisure business, and so on.

213

For any particular person or interest group a clear and useful understanding arises from the application of an appropriate discipline, or,
more likely, combination of disciplines. Such combinations often, over a
period of time, cross fertilise and produce a distinctive discipline in
its own right. For example, in the last twenty or more years a science
of the study of communications has emerged, or is emerging, from the
collaboration of sociologists, psychologists, economists, cultural
analysts, and others.

Within most disciplines there exist different approaches, for few are
unified. Take the study of audiences for television programmes. On the
one hand the Law of Duplicated Viewing (Ehrenberg, 1973) suggests that
personal preference plays a minor role in deciding what people view. On
the other hand, the uses and gratifications approach (Blumler & Katz,
1974) indicates that people are active and creative in how they use
television. Even a cursory reading of the literature reveals apparently
well founded statements which are contradictory. The point is that for a
particular problem or chunk of reality, we must consider not only the
appropriate approach, but also the appropriate level of entry. The
novice player would gain little from studying what the subatomic phys-
icist or the economist had to say about pool. She or he might, however,
gain from studying the work of the psychologist, or indeed Newton.

So for any particular area of study, we must decide upon appropriate
disciplines, and appropriate levels of entry to the focus. We must also
decide upon appropriate approaches or methodologies. Communications
research is dominated by sociology, psychology, and cultural analysis.
Each has different methodologies to offer. Psychology for instance may
be empirical or non-empirical, experimental or observational (and, of
course, it can be concerned with social or educational behaviour, with
analysis of the self or of others, and so on). And psychological experiments can be of at least three major distinctive types; laboratory,
field, or natural.

The ideal laboratory experiment, (like all ideals it is never achieved),
features a controlled environment, and the control of all relevant
variables except one which is observed and measured. When successful it
allows us to say that under certain defined conditions A causes B (2).

The field experiment attempts to approximate to the control of the
laboratory experiment whilst using a natural setting. Reduced control
leads to greater uncertainty and greater generalisability of results.

The natural experiment records an event, or sequence of events, which
are entirely outside the control of the scientist but, by observation,
prediction and measurement, the scientist treats the 'natural' event as
if it was a scientifically designed experiment. Until the advent of
space travel astronomy was a science based entirely upon theory,
observation, and natural experiments.

In practice, particularly in our field of study, a research programme
may blurr these definitions, featuring more than one type of approach.
In her seminal study of children and television Professor Himmelweit
utilised survey techniques and the field and natural experiment
approaches (Himmelweit et al, 1958); and Professor Halloran, in his

study of the interaction between media and those involved in a political demonstration (perhaps the most underestimated study in our field) also made use of several different methods and approaches (Halloran et al, 1972).

Each approach has its distinctive strengths and weaknesses; the obvious challenge to a researcher is to seek a combination of approaches with capitalises on the strengths and obviates the weaknesses of each individual approach. Such a strategy is complex and usually costly, the results do not lend themselves easily to publication. But the strategy has pay-off in terms of advancing understanding and knowledge.

An example might be as follows; large scale survey, preceeeded by wide-ranging qualitative investigation and piloting of survey instruments generated from the qualitative work; a field experiment conducted in parallel with the survey, using the survey respondents as subjects from the same pool, on the basis of performance in survey and field experiment. Is there need to press the point? The outcome of such a study is far more valuable than the separate outcomes of three separate studies (and there are some economies in data collection). The data file on individual people, or defined groups, would be rich to say the least. This brings us rapidly towards the crux of an holistic approach to the study of young people and media. It is time to introduce a detour.

It is time to introduce a detour to address the question: why so much emphasis on methods and approaches? The responsible social scientist has good reason to be interested to the point of obsession with methodology. She or he is beset by two insidious problems. First, social scientific research expects to get answers. Second, it is generally difficult to assess the "truth" of those answers. The builders of bridges, boats, and aircraft have inbuilt, powerful tests of fallibility - the outcomes of their work float or sink, stand or fall, fly or crash. The same cannot be said for social science. In applying the scientific method for example, as in an opinion survey, tests for validity and for whether theory "predicts" can be applied but such surveys measure reactions to opinion statements. No matter how designed, or how administered, analysed and reported, the results will show certain proportions or respondents reacting in specified ways to those opinion statements.

This is not to say that predicting events based on surveys does not constitute a valid scientific method but there is no infallible test of adequacy; surveys may often be right, such as the polls which accurately predict voter patterns, or which accurately predict the success or failure of new consumer products. But it must be remembered that times change, minds change, opinions change and markets change. And we do not know in advance of further evidence, which surveys will prove to be accurate. If the purpose of a study is to characterize behaviour, trends or opinions at a specific point in time then this is indisputably a valid use of research but, with the proviso that the utility of a study is dependent on a careful and critical analysis of how the study is to be conducted - its methodology.

Social science can in many ways offer less than careful practitioners an open invitation to fool themselves. Hence the <u>responsible</u> social scientist's strong commitment to methodology. A couple of examples of how we can fool ourselves will synthesize the argument. Take the rational or imposed approach to the construction of questionnaires or measuring instruments. The scientist makes up a set of statements or a measurement of, say, aggression and, say, children's attitudes to war films. The technology of attitude scale development tells us to select individual statements from the universe of relevant statements. Sometimes, it may happen that an irresponsible researcher will make up statements which simply reflect his or her personal prejudices:

I like watching war films because...they are exciting...the good guys always win...soldiers are tough...and so on. When analysed, the child's responses and the study as a whole will reflect those prejudices. How could it be otherwise? Studies which use rational scaling techniques are particularly prone to reinforcing researcher's prior assumptions. It is perhaps cruel but not inaccurate to suggest that such studies tell us more about the researcher than the focus of research. For this reason it came as a surprise to many when Grant Noble (Noble, 1975) revealed that a particularly strong motivation for children's viewing of war films was that they appreciated the portrayal of altruism and friendship. Noble was not sitting at his desk when he stumbled across this idea - he was giving a tolerant and sympathetic ear to the actual views of young children (3).

The emergent approach can also easily slip into a sequence of self-reinforcing practices. Take, for example, a study, the author of which I will not name, which after talking with children, featured a twelve item inventory of "things I get out of television". In effect the twelve items were actually three restatements of the same four items, along the lines of: TV sure is exciting; I like exciting things on TV; when they fight it excites me; the things I like best are fights and car chases. After children had endorsed their degree of agreement with these and the other two sets of four statements, the researcher conducted factor analysis and cluster analysis on his data. Naturally enough he found four strong factors, each with high internal consistency. How could it be otherwise?

I emphasize that these are extreme examples, but unless we take great care to be responsible researchers, the process can infiltrate all our work. It is very difficult to debug our instruments and questionnaires, but it is essential that we strive continually to do so. And we can institute for ourselves levels of good practice. We can ensure that our wording, and the range of experience it covers, comes from the children we study, rather than memory, unquestioned assumption or unfamiliar studies. We can pilot our instruments exhaustively, including debriefing children after they have concluded the study and asking them, in an open-ended way, what they thought the study was about, what they thought particular questions and statements meant, and so on. We can guard against designs which cause subjects to respond to the serial position of items, rather than their meanings (response set). And we can probe, probe, probe, to ensure that the full range of experience of the subjects is incorporated in our work.

One further point on language. It is not enough that we know exactly what we mean by a phrase or item in a measuring instrument. It is not enough that the item is apparently responded to in a meaningful or revealing fashion. It is not enough that the item is smoothly stated in idiomatic language. We really do need to explore the meaning of the item to our subjects. Some years ago, to my shame, I was responsible for asking children which of a set of graphically presented media was'.. so interesting that you sometimes get lost in it?' This and other questions appeared to work well in extensive piloting. But analysis revealed a group of very young (five to seven year old) children who responded by pointing to the drawing of a newspaper. Since some at least of these children were illiterate the finding seemed questionable. We questioned it. Yes, the newspaper was interesting - grown-ups spent a lot of time with it. Yes the kids got lost in it - they couldn't find their way through it, they couldn't handle it, the pages flopped all over them.

How often are apparently meaningful and clear-cut results (upon which we base theories and generalisations) the result of such errors? We only tend to question them when they fail to be consistent with our adult assumptions about children. Again we are close to the crux of the holistic, child-centred approach to research and theory.

If we return to the recommended integrative research approach in which different research techniques are applied to the same subjects or respondents, it will be recalled that such an approach leaves us with a wealth of data about a pool of individuals. What is the best method of dealing with the vast amount of information gathered to ensure that its magnitude alone does not "block out the light"?

A traditional method is to apply what can be termed the tyranny of the average. Tyranny because the average is often crude, harsh and oppressive. And worse, the average can also lead to perversely contorted images of reality. It is, as ever, a question of applicability. Few would disagree that the question, "What is the average colour of a European's eyes?" is an example of an inappropriate use of the statistical average. It can be answered. The scientist can go through the motions. But the answer would tell us little about eye colour in Europe. It is possible, I suppose, that no single European would be found who had "average" eyes.

Using the average, especially when we are dealing with, for example, patterns of behaviour, can be very misleading. A society with high infant mortality tends to give an average age for dying at round about thirty years - the great majority of persons in that society either never reach their thirties, or survive them. There are regularities to human behaviour, but if average is piled on average it is possible to provide evidence for patterns of behaviour which are quite typical. Furthermore, multiple use of the average can obliterate evidence of diverse and distinct patterns of behaviour.

But then we researchers, naturally enough, regard ourselves as unique individuals with special insights, experiences and awareness.

All people are unique individuals with special insights, experiences and awareness.

An holistic approach is one which studies a whole organic unit and the functional relationships between the elements which constitute that

217

unit. As we shall see it is an approach which can take qualitative or quantitative forms, be "hard" or "soft". It tends to carry with it respect for the individual and a recognition of the rich complexity of individuals; for some this is an unimportant consequence of applying a useful set of techniques, for others it is the primary and essential benefit.

In social sciences there is always the danger that theory can create reality. Just as the client under analysis may learn how to dream in Freudian images, so people can be brutalised by theories which regard them as brutes, made passive by television programming based upon the theory that viewing is a passive, soporific activity, the content is "chewing gum for the mind" or moving wallpaper. The risk is caught in old aphorism: give a dog a bad name.

In this approach then, the individual is the unit of study, a unit which, by the very nature of its existence, incorporates the range and complexity of the data generated by the researcher. The unit which is the source of that data.

The fundamental reason for this conference was to explore the area of young people and television advertising. I believe that in order to make a useful and responsible contribution to this area we must be prepared to tackle the complexity of young people and the complexity of television advertising. More than this, I believe that we must also place the focus of study in its broader context. Those existing studies, in their thousands, published and unpublished, which reveal, for example, that a blue and red wrapper sells more product than a white and green one (or vice versa) contribute little or nothing to our knowledge. In fact such studies contribute little or nothing (save temporary confidence and folk lore) to the product manufacturer. Generalization from such investigation is as likely to produce poor sales as good sales.

In order to argue that case for complexity and context, it is worth beginning at the beginning. A new born baby has nothing more than enormous potential and an environment. The environment is, at base, located in time and geographical space; it is this time and space location which ensures that the child born in Rome today will learn to speak Italian, probably with a Roman accent, rather than Latin or English. The child is born into a culture shaped by environment and history, informed by a selective and usually distorted knowledge and understanding of history and contemporary world affairs. He or she receives and learns the culture through a number of channels of influence; first hand experience, family, media, education, other social agencies (churches, youth groups, and so on). (4).

In other words, we all exist in three environments; geographical/ physical, social, and a communications environment. The three environments are interrelated; the environments themselves, taken in isolation are immensely complicated, the interactions between them even more so. Any individual and every individual sits squarely at the locus of interaction between these environments. Every individual is a locus of interaction; it is this fact, plus the fact of individual human potential, which creates human individuality rather than endless and indiscriminable conformity. We are nothing without sensory information and the ability to process it – without environments.

What is the communications environment? What is its nature and how can we, as social scientists, begin to come to terms with it, incorporate an awareness of it, into our work? Some years ago I commented on this question in a brief and impressionistic fashion:

> ...it is tempting for empirical research to be conducted 'as if' the communications environment was a static, firmly structured, and externally objectifiable entity, a little thought and intro-spection highlights a different reality. Of course, we can list elements in the environment – radio, press, canteen chit chat, etc., but that tells us little about the experiential reality of our communications environment. What does it feel like? If the reader will now, as it were, experience his or her location in the communications environment, we might reach an agreement that 'complexity' is almost inadequate as a descriptive label. We are rather dealing with a busy, fluid disjointed 'system'; bits and pieces of the mass media, half remembered documentaries, half finished novels, a crumpled Sunday newspaper by the bed, Warhol's Marilyn on the lavatory door, Granny upstairs singing Marie Lloyd and our offspring downstairs listening to Pink Floyd. And that, of course, is not all; the experienced reality of the communications environment transcends time and space – memory and association ensure that. And, in yet another sense, media allow us to transcend time and space, for they not only take us back to our childhood and earlier, they also transport us to meetings we cannot attend and to countries we cannot visit; they are extensions of our senses...' (Brown 1978)

Certainly the 'externally objectifiable' reality requires study, and, equally clearly it is not random but orderly. It is, if you wish, like a lengthy verbal statement or essay; paragraphs take their particular meanings from preceeding paragraphs, sentences from preceeding sentences, words from the words about them. To study the effect or meaning of a word without seeing it in interaction with the words about it would usually be a futile occupation. To study the meaning or effects of a small segment of television programming without awareness of context is similarly futile – it creates misleading generalisations; the literature is littered with them.

And yet how are we, as social scientists, to tackle the problem of rendering meaningful to analysis and understanding, the impact of the interaction between social and communications environment upon people? Studies of two, three, 5,000, or 50,000 variables cannot hope to capture the reality of this experience. Studies which attempt to accept the complexity faced by the individual are immediately hit by our own limitations, limitations of culture, thought, finance, imagination, experience, and time. Hence the holistic emphasis on the individual as the unit of study. The individual has his or her personal experience, and personal understanding. The individual has personal statements, beliefs, actions, which, in a sense, summarise, for this one person, all the elements of all the environments within which the person exists.

In our daily lives we are pattern making creatures, we strive to understand, to extract meaning, from our senses. Psychologist George Kelley, in his theory of personal constructs, argues that the best available model of the individual is that provided by science itself. In daily life, ordinary people (as well as scientists) are forever classifying, hypothesising, testing, analysing, theorising, and generalising.

In brief, then, a child-centered approach can accept the complexity of the child and his or her environment by exploring the meaning read, experienced, or created by the child, in interaction with the environment. Exploring these extracted or negotiated meanings requires that we enter a rich and fruitful field of study. But such riches are not easily achieved. Not only must we be prepared to discard some of our cruder practices - the three point scales which purport to measure experience, the inappropriate average, the refusal to admit context and other influential variables - we must also be prepared to change our standpoint as researchers. In particular the holistic, child-centered approach demands that we rid ourselves of many of our adult prejudgements (and question those we maintain), and that we treat the subjects of our studies with considerable respect.

Having said all this, and to avoid a reductio ad absurdum counterblow, it is worth emphasising what is not being argued. We have seen that the holistic approach accepts the challenge of complexity and that a method of coping with this complexity is to explore the child's understanding of this or her location in it. This does not mean that each and every study must be based upon exhaustive autobiographical explorations of individual children. Nor does it mean that existing approaches must be shunned. Rather, we should accept a changed emphasis such that studies of effects, or whatever, place the child firmly at the centre of the stage.

What we require is some initial articulated formulation which will allow different studies to be interrelated, and which will allow and encourage an organic growth of knowledge and understanding. In other words, a system or framework which will allow the most trite of experiments to not only contribute to an integrated corpus of knowledge, but also be informed (and inevitably improved) by that same corpus. And it is essential that the initial framework is itself flexible and capable of growth.

Figure I, faulty and clumsy as it is, is offered as a possible initial formulation.

The first things to note about this formulation are that it is in no sense definitive, complete, nor yet rippling with fresh insights. It is a slightly expanded and graphically presented version of the 'who said what to whom and with what consequences' formulation, and many other derivatives. It is particularly important to note that in the real world, which is where our work should be conducted, there are many more arrows floating about. For example, 'parents', peers', 'significant adults', 'other media use', and 'opportunities for use' (5) are, in reality, all interconnected.

FIGURE I. POSSIBLE INITIAL FRAMEWORK FOR A HOLISTIC APPROACH TO CHILDREN AND TELEVISION

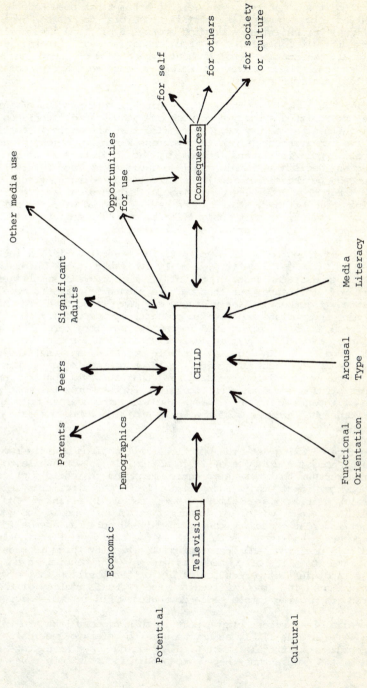

Note also that, at this stage, no attempt has been made to arrange variables into hierarchies. It is possible to argue the case for 'functional orientation subsuming arousal type', and 'media literacy'. But it is also possible to argue cases for media literacy subsuming functional orientation and arousal type and so on. What can be agreed upon is that those three variables (or more accurately, complexes of variables) are interrelated.

What we are dealing with, then, is not a linear process of influence, but a reticulated system, a network of pathways and interfaces through which influences may flow. Note also that the whole is carried by a pervasive environment (indicated by cross-hatching) which is, at least, cultural, political, and economic. The climate of opinion which influences decisions within media organisations (and is, reflexively, influenced by those decisions) has direct and indirect effects upon the child, and the more immediate social and physical environment which contains him or her. And, in an easily ignored way, the child has a reflexive effect, albeit insignificant, on the immediate environments, and the encapsulating, pervasive environment.

It is not my intention to analyse here the several variables included in Figure 1. Each is, I believe, readily available in the literature. Nor need I demonstrate that, not only is the figure a simplication of a network of influence, but that certain elements in it are more readily associated together. Clearly there are many ways of making this basic tool more appropriate to specific concerns or approaches: consequences, or effects, can be categorised in many ways - long term, intermediate, immediate; delayed, physiological, psychological, social; pro or anti-social, and so on. In fact any variable or arrow can itself be (and has itself been) the focus of study. It is enough to indicate that we work in an area which is interrelated, and that it would appear appropriate for our studies to be interrelated also. Furthermore, the most suitable devise of interrelating our diverse studies and concerns would appear to be a constant awareness of the child and his or her understanding and experience.

But before looking at the practical implications of this recommended approach, and some examples of it in action, it is worthwhile to analyse a little further that pervasive environment and the child's place within it. We know that media and politics (both party politics and ongoing cultural politics) are almost inextricably interlinked and mutually influential, that within a country as a whole, media and government interact in order to define the political and cultural agenda for debate and concern, and that both are in the business of legitimising and excluding, praising and denigrating. The reality which is presented by media, the totality of content, is not only influential in shaping the child's (and adult's) perception of his or her position in the world but by doing so, it also influences the actual reality of the world. Children are growing into a media-dominated world in two senses then.

Even media researchers play a part in this process (and are influenced by it). We are as likely as anyone else to refer to America's invasion of Grenada, or Britain's war with Argentina - but such statements owe more to the media than they do to actual fact. In both cases powerful governments, with minority support in their countries (i.e., less than a third of the adult population), made use of military power. Britain and America did not go to war - the media lead us to believe this was the case (6). But this is in passing, the point to be made is that both governments had learned from experience and the work of media researchers in the seventies. As the media explored and reported American involvement in South East Asia, the media researchers explored the consequences of media coverage, those in power (and expecting to be) took note. This time around the public was not given film from the front unless it suited the governments concerned; everything was done in order to ensure that the British and American publics could not mess up their government's military actions. Later of course, the people were given sequences of actuality film edited into "war films".

This is not an irrelevant diversion, it is a relatively simple example of the complexity and organic nature of the context of children's viewing. The orchestration of media output by government, establishment, system, call it what you will, can, must, and does, shape the child's understanding and behaviour. We may endlessly research the effect of a three minute fight sequence, on the behaviour of whatever age group we choose, and never reach a definitive conclusion. But as Professor Halloran has so graphically demonstrated, if the questions asked are the "right" ones, if the complexity of the subject is recognised a critical eclectic research approach is adopted, then the answers come thick and fast. In a study of young teenagers in Hungary, Britain, Denmark and Canada, Halloran and his co-workers explored images of foreign countries and foreign citizens and the role of TV in this. Here is a brief summary of his findings for British youngsters:

The USA received a postitive reaction, it was seen as non-political and fun (even though political information on the USA was available) and the source was the media.

The USSR received a negative reaction, seen as political. The source was the media.

West Germany, by upper class children, received a positive reaction, the source being information from fathers, business contacts, trips, etc. The working class children had a negative reaction, arising from comics, films, etc.

...children adapt to the world they live in and today that world is largely carried to them by media and media play a part in shaping its objective reality.

But how, as researchers with a particular interest in children and television advertising, are we to enter this tangled web of influence and counter-influence? The short answer is - with caution, imagination, awareness, and respect. My own experience with young people shaped this assertion. Those of us who are prepared to learn the language of the young, to be tolerant and listen, to avoid imposing answers, even on occasions, to avoid posing questions, find that the pay-off is

impressive. For example, some years ago I had the opportunity of studying British children who were about to get television in their locality
for the first time. Impressive studies, national studies, of the onset
of television have been conducted in Britain, North America, and
elsewhere (Himmelweit et al 1959, Schramm et al 1961), to my amazement I
found that rural primary school children, in general conversation, were
able to tell me the results of those studies. The principles promulgated
by earlier researchers were stated by children in simple language. (7).

And more besides. War films, I was told by one young boy, are good
because they give rules to the game of war. Prior to becoming a viewer
this boy often played war with his friends, but the game sometimes went
wrong. An ambush never came to fruition because 'the enemy' stalked off
down the wrong lane. Arguments sprang up about who had shot first, or
should be dead or injured. But television allowed these boys to re-enact
sequences of war film - the game became rule-governed, it allowed the
allocation of agreed roles.

Given the chance young people reveal a critical and creative awareness
of their own lives, and the parts played in them by media and other
agencies. They are capable of stunning objective/innocent assessments of
media content, rapidly learning formats and storylines of series and
categories of television content. And, an obvious truism, this is
evidenced not when children are responding to precoded response
categories, but in open-ended response to our questions:

> "It comes in two parts. The first part, one group gets into
> trouble and the other group bails them out. The other part, he
> goes somewhere with the family."

These are the words of a seven year old (Winnick and Winnick
1979).

> "They are movie stars, we aren't. They fight every day, I don't
> fight every day. They're older than me, fatter."

Fifth grader (Klapper, 1981)

And, if further evidence is necessary, we have heard from Cedric
Cullingford of his commitment to active listening. It is worth reitera-
ting some of Cullingford's arguments since he is, as it were, just back
from the front.

As a result of his awareness of the literature, and his contact with
children, Dr.Cullingford has rightly drawn our attention to the lack of
investigations into the '...world of gossip, rumour and conversation in
which advertisements are embedded" - in other words, the child's social
context, the arena in which the individual often comes to terms with the
messages and directives of media. Another white space in the map of our
studies is, he suggests, "...the nature of the response and the means by
which children learn, not just about advertised products, but about all
parts of their environment. And, again, he refers to the "...unexplored
complex mass of change images and personal associations, relations and

distinctions..." which form the child's (and adults) picture of the world. He points out that research often falls into the macro-level approach (the study of television in children's lives), or the micro-level approach (how children process information on television adver- tising), but his experiences with children given the opportunity to talk freely have convinced him that "..the two are inextricably mixed, for to understand either you really need to understand both". Children, of course, are aware of this.

Children know, and are quite capable of telling us - if we, the researchers, adopt the right attitude, ask the right questions in their language and use the right measures, that their reactions to a part- icular sequence of content, commercial or play, or news, is related to their assessments of television as a whole, to its serial position in a viewing session, to its relevance to family and peers. They are aware of the complexity of the outside world. And in learning about the adult world they know better than to approach parent or teacher with the question: "please explain the nature of your interest in ..politics, sex, football.. using one of the three statements on this card". Children learn about adults by questioning in an open-ended way, by listening, observing, testing hypotheses. As Cedric Cullingford has so clearly shown, applying the same approach to children creates a wealth of fascinating and useful data and insights. His work is a testament to the utility of a child-centred methodology (Cullingford 1984).

Before concluding this paper a further comment on the preceeding figure is warranted. It would be a peculiar study of, say, snooker players which ignored the rules and requirements of snooker; a strange investi- gation of vegetarians which had nothing to say about the whole-food business. And a study of advertising and children which ignores those who finance and create advertising is equally one-sided. To the left of the figure, then, are various missing foci: television and advertising content, advertisers, creative departments, media organisations, and so on. We need to explore the intentions, practices, myths and folklore of these institutions, and to relate them to the cross-hatched environments which they share with the television audience. And, furthermore, as responsible social scientists we must recognise that we and our institu- tions and funding bodies are also encapsulated by a wider environment - our theories and practices are based upon assumed objectivity, a constructed objectivity. Our work is conducted within the limitations of a value system, those of our peers who cling onto the notion of 'value free' research are simply accepting a specific value position. All too often it is a value position which is left unquestioned.

In conclusion, then, this excellent conference has revealed wide-ranging approaches to the study of young people and television advertising, it has shown itself to be a potential basis for the development of a sus- tained and integrated approach to the whole field. It is my contention that the holistic, child-centred approach outlined in the preceeding pages allows greater cross-fertilisation and enrichment of our researches and awareness, than would a piece-meal continuance of our individual interests.

225

NOTES

1. Although all errors, lapses in good taste, and faults of any kind
    are entirely my own, I must acknowledge the considerable influence
    of Professors Halloran and Himmelweit, and also Cedric Cullingford.
    More than this, whilst other contributors to this conference have
    influenced my thinking (an advantage gained by the last speaker), I
    have attempted to take on board some of the ideas and arguments of
    the three named participants.

2. The very notion of causality has been under attack throughout this
    century. This is not the place to review arguments for and against
    the concept, but those social scientists who desire a 'tough'
    approach based on the 'hard' sciences might present a more
    convincing case if they showed a greater familiarity with the
    theories and practices of physics in this century.

3. By exploring the child's experience of television Grant Noble is
    able to report some remarkable findings. Children in Front of the
    Small Screen (1975) is a stimulating and often delightful book which
    does much to highlight the peculiar logic of young viewers.

4. Obviously it is this which makes us French, Irish, or whatever,
    which gives us our regional accents, and our peculiar tastes. In a
    real sense a child who experienced no cultural context would, if a
    survivor, not be human.

5. Opportunities for use here refers to both 'use' as understood in the
    uses and gratifications tradition, and also consequences or effects.
    The realisation or acting out of a learned sequence of behaviour may
    be delayed some time simply due to the absence of a suitable social
    or physical situation in which to 'bring out' the behaviour.

6. The assumption which equates democracy and free media is, of course,
    at best a gross simplification. The less support a democratically
    elected government has, then the more that government will attempt,
    one way or another, to control the media. In Britain at the time of
    writing we have the paradox of a Prime Minister who gained less than
    a third of the country's support castigating as undemocratic a Union
    leader who gained over 80% support from his Union membership.
    Interestingly, children are often more capable of seeing carefully
    concealed simple truths than are adults – parents know this to their
    cost.

7. These children were aware of the displacement effects of television
    because they experienced them, however their language was both more
    immediately accessible and less elegant: marginal disorganised
    behaviour became, in their words 'mucking about'. In fact 'mucking
    about' included such acts as throwing stones in the sea, sitting on
    fences, watching animals. It became clear in the course of this
    study that most 'marginal' activity could be accompanied by day-
    dreaming. Whether television has reduced the duration of daydreaming
    and fantasising is an open but perhaps important question which
    awaits study. (Brown R. (1976) "Children and Television", Sage,
    Beverly Hills.

REFERENCES: RAY BROWN

BLUMLER, JG and KATZ, E (Eds) (1974), "The Uses of Mass Communications: Current Perspectives on Gratification Reasearch", Sage. Beverly Hills.

BROWN, R. (1978), "Characteristics of Local Media Audiences", Saxon House, London.

CULLINGFORD, C. (1984), "Children and Television", Gower, London.

EHRENBERG. ASC., "The Law of Duplicated Viewing", Saxon House, London.

HALLORAN, JD, et al (1970), "Demonstrations and Communications: A case study, Penguin Books, London.

HIMMELWEIT et al (1958), "Television and the Child: An Empirical Study of the Effect of Television on the Young", Oxford University Press, London.

KLAPPER, HL (1981), in "Television Advertising and Children", Ed. Esserman CRS., New York.

NOBLE G (1975), "Children in Front of the Small Screen", Constable, London.

SCHRAMM, W et al., (1960), "Television in the Lives of our Children", Stanford University Press, Stanford.

WINICK, MP and WINICK C, (1979), "The Television Experience", Sage, Beverley Hills.

PART VIII

Conclusions

Extracting conclusions from such a wealth of fact, opinion, and debate is an invidious task. In one sense it is a task best left to the individual reader. The conference, and this publication, will of be interest to advertisers, researchers, teachers, parents and many others in both the media industry and government - each will bring his or her own interests and values, each will reach her or his own individual conclusions. Nevertheless the contributors to this volume found themselves in agreement on numerous occasions. It is these areas of consensus which are here presented as conclusions.

Perhaps the first conclusion should in fact be drawn from the fact that twenty academics, from nine countries, were able to find so many areas of agreement. In and of itself, this is a statement of considerable importance. The area of children and television is, as it were, 'wide-open' in Europe. When specialists from different disciplines and different countries are able to meet, discuss and find consensus, then there is a basis for the hope that this is an area in which exploration and development will be both rapid and fruitful.

It was agreed that the notion of the child as a passive unit in an audience consisting of identical passive units had no place in this area of study. Young viewers, even very young viewers, are sophisiticated individuals who should be neither underestimated nor idealised. To gain a realistic understanding of the area, we must accept a realistic image of the child. By the years seven to nine children have come to terms with the nature of television, understanding as well as most adults that television content is a mixture of fact and fantasy, documentary and drama, actors and presenters, and so on. They also know by this stage that a television advertisement has 'selling intent' and that this makes such a sequence of content not quite the same as its televised context. On the other hand children often judge commercials as if they were mini-programmes - short dramas or comic acts. In other words, on one level at least, children can actively choose what they regard as an appropriate way of 'using' the television commercial.

The child is an active viewer who contributes to his or her own under-standing and experience of television commercials. This is not to say that commercials have no effect upon children, nor that they do not have the effect desired by advertisers. Rather it is a pointer to the complexity of the process in which commercials influence young people. To understand this process, to assess the influences, it is necessary to accept complexity.

Studies which have begun to accept the complexity of the process reveal that commercials as such do not have the simple, one directional (and perhaps desired) effects some people have feared. The child is open to a world of experience and influence, one segment of which is provided by media. Advertising forms one part of media. The sources of influence interact and studies (or theories) which do not acknowledge the context of advertising are likely to produce misleading conclusions.

Needless to say, particularly in the light of the above, students in this area are exercised by the problem of finding appropriate method-ologies and conceptual frameworks. The emphasis is on conceptualisation since different methodological approaches can make valid or invalid contributions to the field according to how and why they are applied. The researchers see little advance coming from the application of the now outdated, simple, stimulus-response model of effects and, as a body, lean towards a child-centred approach with an emphasis on both context and process.

The majority of viewing, and therefore exposure to television advert-ising, takes place in the family home, often as an activity accompanied by other family members. The family becomes a filter (or, part of a broader filter) through which commercials pass. Thus the social and family context of viewing is influential in the process by which advert-ising works. Furthermore the consequences of advertising for family life and consumer behaviour are worthy of detailed study. However, it was generally accepted that advertising as such is unlikely to create significant discordance within the family. To the extent to which tele-vision advertising might cause intra-family conflict, then this need not necessarily be an ill-effect; a degree of conflict is unavoidable, and often essential, in the process of socialisation and, in this case, can afford the opportunity for rudimentary consumer education.

But it would be incorrect to assume that television plays a significant positive or negative part in the development of consumer skills. (Although advertising could be used in programmes of education designed to enhance consumer decision taking and awareness). Once again it is important to recognise that children are active and creative in their use of television, like adults the extent to which they take seriously the intentions of those who make television content (of any kind) is greatly influenced by their orientation to the content, which is itself only partly influenced by producer intentions.

It was generally felt that research evidence to date provided little reason for advertisers to be over-defensive about their practices, and whilst some felt that it would be inappropriate for researchers to make value judgements about recorded influences, none could point to adequately recorded negative effects of viewing commercials. Indeed, to the extent that the majority of commercials carry values which are consistent with the majority of televised content, it would be foolish to single out television advertising as a major focus of opprobrium.

Several intriguing and tantalising ideas and predictions are to be found in the body of this volume, many occurred in informal conference discussion (some of which has been incorporated in rewritten contributions). Two areas of ignorance were recognised as being of signal importance. Research with young children poses special problems of communication. The younger the child, the less accessible to study are his or her verbal and preverbal thought processes and levels of understanding and experience. As computers, and computer based games, become more freely available to the very young it becomes yet more obvious that even the most liberal and humane (and generous) of researchers and theoreticians have tended to underestimate the sophistication and complexity of the young child's inner experience. And, furthermore, as we recognise the 'increasing complexity' of children, we must also accept the increasing complexity of media. New media and media forms now proliferate, increasingly these new forms turn to advertising for financial support. Exactly what effect this will have is unclear, although some felt that the result would be a decline in resistance to advertising. But one opinion was held by all, with the expansion of media and advertising into new forms and areas, the capacity of children (and adults) to make individual choices will become increasingly important.

Finally, inevitably, conference agreed on the desirability of further research. It is however to the credit of those who organised this conference that this familiar tailpiece has greater substance and promise than is usually the case. With foresight the organisers timed the conference to coincide with an increasing awareness of one implication of the spread of satellite broadcasting in Europe. For the first time children in certain Nordic countries will soon become exposed to television advertising; this development provides an opportunity for a significant multi-disciplinary, multi-national study of the part played by television advertising in the lives of children. Conference was unanimous in emphasising that this opportunity should not be missed. With funding, and the interest and expertise evidenced by this volume, the Nordic study will, without doubt, make an invaluable contribution to the studies of advertising, media, and children.

Appendix
Biographies of Conference Participants

BIOGRAPHIES OF CONFERENCE PARTICIPANTS

Dr. Ray Brown (United Kingdom)

Ray Brown was trained as a psychologist. After several years as a Research Fellow at the Centre for Television Research, Leeds University, United Kingdom, he became a freelance researcher and writer. His academic publications include books and papers on young people and media, local media, and the social functions of media. He has held consultancies with the BBC, IBA, Gulbenkian Foundation and CSV. His major publications include: Children and Television (1976) and Characteristic of Local Media Influences (1979).

Current activities include participation in a multinational study of music and youth culture.

Mr. Cedric Cullingford (United Kingdom)

Cedric Cullingford taught literature at Oxford University, Toronto, and in schools before becoming involved in education. His research interests changed from the influence of the mass media on literature to the area of children's response to television. He was the assistant director of studies, Charlotte Mason College and an external examiner for Cambridge, Leicester and London University. His major publications include: Children and Television, Gower, (1984), and Parents, Teachers and Schools, Robert Royce, London (1985). Gower is shortly to publish Children and Learning, Cullingford's latest work.

Presently he is Dean of the Faculty of Educational Studies at Oxford Polytechnic.

Mr. Asle Gire Dahl (Norway)

Asle Dahl's background lies chiefly in media education as a lecturer, researcher and writer. During the seventies he worked at the Bergen College of Education and since 1980 Dahl has been a scholar in Norway's state bureau of research.

His publications include Media Education in Norway, (1981) and Media Education – on the establishment of a new subject in school – published in Norwegian in 1984.

Currently Asle Dahl is senior lecturer and associate professor at the Norwegian Council of Research in Tyristrand.

Professor Philip Graham, FRCP, FRCPsych (United Kingdom)

Professor Graham practices as consultant child psychiatrist at the Hospital for Sick Children, Great Ormond Street, London and is involved in teaching and research at the Institute of Child Health, London. He has published papers on a wide variety of subjects including studies of the prevalence of childhood behaviour and emotional disorders, management techniques and ethical issues in child psychiatry.

His major publications include: Epidemiological Approaches in Child Psychiatry, Academic Press, (1977) and Pre-School to School: a behavioural study (jointly) Academic Press, (1982).

Professor Graham is currently Walker Professor of Child Psychiatry at the Institute of Child Health, London.

Dr. Marianne Grewe-Partsch (Federal Republic of Germany)

Dr.Grewe-Partsch's background is as a consultant in adult education. She is a director on the editorial staff of the International Institute for Youth and Educational Television at the Bavarian broadcasting station and a director of the Department of Adult Education and Women at Radio Hessen.

Her publications (joint) include Grundlagen einer Medienpadagogik (1979) and Women, Communication and Careers (1980).

Dr. Grewe-Partsch is currently senior lecturer in the Department of Communication Psychology, Educational University Rheinland-Pfalz.

Dr. Klaus G. Grunert (Federal Republic of Germany)

Klaus Grunert's main research interests are in consumer behaviour, marketing and public policy and survey methods in market research. He has recently completed a five-year research programme on consumer information sponsored by the German Federal Department for Research and Technology. He is the author of four books and 28 articles in the areas of consumer information and advertising.

Dr. Grunert is currently assistant professor of consumer economics at the University of Hohenheim.

Professor James D. Halloran BSc (Econ), BSc. (United Kingdom)

Professor Halloran has been Director of the Centre for Mass Communications Research at the University of Leicester since 1966 and President of the International Association for Mass Communication Research, also headquartered at Leicester, since 1972. It now numbers over one thousand members from 63 countries.

Amongst other interests Professor Halloran is a regional director of Central Independent Television and a research consultant to UNESCO.

Profesor Halloran's publications include: Attitude Formation and Change, (1966), The Effects of Television (1970) and the Context of Mass Communication Research (International Commission for the study of Communication Problems, No. 78, Unesco, Paris 1980).

Professor Hilde T. Himmelweit (United Kingdom)

Trained as a clinical psychologist, Professor Himmelweit occupied the first chair in Social Psychology at the London School of Economics (LSE). In her long and distinguished career, her reponsibilities have included being Director of the Nuffield Foundation Enquiry into Television and the Child, a member of the Annan Committee on the future of Broadcasting, and Chairman of the Academic Advisory Committee of the Open University.

Professor Himmelweit's publications in the field of children and television include: Television and the Child (jointly) Oxford Univ. Press (1958), The Audience as Critic: An Approach to the Study of Entertainment (jointly) New York (1979) and Social Influence and Television (in Television and Social Behaviour: Beyond Violence and Children) New York, (1980).

Professor Himmelweit is now Professor Emeritus of Social Psychology at the London School of Economics.

Mr. Jean-Noel M. Kapferer (France)

Jean-Noel Kapferer is Professor of Marketing at the French business school, L'Ecole des Hautes Etudes Commerciales (HEC); he also works as a consultant in advertising and as a scientific advisor for an international advertising agency.

His most recent books include: Les Chemins de la Persuasion, Dunod, (1983) and La Sensibilite aux Marques (jointly).

Madame Dominique Lassarre (France)

Dominique Lassarre has been lecturing in social psychology since 1972 and is now Assistant Professor of Social Psychology at Paris University. She participated in the CNRS '(The French national research council's) study into the effects of TV advertising on children's purchase requests.

Madame Lassarre's latest publication is Le Choix Preferentiel des Objects Domestiques, (1982).

Dr. Theo Poiesz (The Netherlands)

Theo Poiesz graduated in 1972 from the Dutch Scientific Institute for Tourism in Breda (Netherlands) and from Tilburg University (Department of Psychology) in 1977. He then worked with Dr. Milton Friedman, Eastern Michigan University on the psychology of consumer behaviour. Since 1978 he has worked at Tilburg University as associate professor in the Economic psychology department.

For his doctorate Dr. Poiesz undertook an investigation into the relationship between exposure frequency and consumer affect.

Professor Thomas S. Robertson (United States)

Tom Robertson is an associate dean and professor of marketing at The Wharton School, University of Pennsylvania. He holds a Ph.D. in marketing and an M.A. in sociology from Northwestern University. He has taught at Harvard Business School and UCLA.

His current research interests are in marketing strategy, deregulation strategy and consumer behaviour. He is active in a number of professional associations including the American Marketing Association, the Association for Consumer Research and the American Psychological Association.

His major publications include: Consumer Behaviour; Advertising and Children; and Innovative Behaviour and Communication.

Dr. Reinhard A.M. Sander (Federal Republic of Germany)

Reinhard Sander is a lecturer in sociology at the Institut fur Socialwissenschaften at Munich's technical university. His studies have led him to research industrial leadership (the impact of management training) and "new" media. He is presently working on "The Change of Values in Industrial Societies" and on "Patterns of Leadership in China".

Author of several books in German and English, Sander has just published Management Andragogik Jahrbuch (1983).

Professor Dr. Hertha Sturm (Federal Republic of Germany)

Hertha Sturm is the director of the Department of Communication Psychology at the educational University of Rheinland-Pfalz.

Her work experience includes being Professor of Psychology at Freiburg University and Professor of Communications at Munich University. She is also Director of Youth and Education Broadcasting for ZDF, Germany's second television station and Director of the International Institute for Youth and Educational TV at the Bavarian broadcasting station.

Until 1982 Professor Sturm was editor of the international periodical: Fernsehen und Bildung (TV and Pictures). Other published works includes: Information Processing by Young Children - Piaget's Theory of Intellectual Development applied to Radio & TV (1981 jointly with Sabine Jorg).

Dr. Birgitte Tufte (Denmark)

Dr. Tufte is currently working on a research project on media education in Danish secondary schools at the Royal Danish School of Educational Studies in Copenhagen. Her work in mass communication research has covered children's use and perception of TV and video (at Copenhagen University) and TV advertising as a socialisation agent (at the Copenhagen School of Economics and Business Administration).

Her publications include: Born i Blalys (Children under the spotlight) 1983.

Professor Liisa Uusitalo (Finland)

Liisa Uusitalo is associate professor in marketing at the Helsinki School of Economics and senior researcher of the Academy of Finland, Council for Social Sciences.

Mrs. Uusitalo's work experience includes research at the University of California, Berkeley; the International Institute for Environment and Society, Berlin and the Academy of Finland.

Her publications include various articles in the Journal of Macromarketing, the Journal of Consumer Policy and the Journal of Psychology. Her most recent book is: Consumer Behaviour and Environment Quality (Gower) 1983.

Professor W. Fred van Raaij (The Netherlands)

Fred van Raaij has been Professor of Economic Psychology, Department of Economics, Erasmus University, Rotterdam, since 1979 prior to which he was visiting Assistant Professor in business administration at the University of Illinois.

Among his many interests and commitments, van Raaij is a member of the editorial board of the Journal of Consumer Research and of the Journal of Economic Psychology. He is also a member of the board of the Dutch Consumer Association.

Professor van Raaij has written well over 100 articles and reports in Dutch, German and English on consumer behaviour, advertising effects, consumer choice processes, etc. His books include: Consumer Choice Behaviour: An Information-Processing Approach (1977) and Consumer Behaviour and Energy Policy (1984).

Dr. Peter Vitouch (Austria)

Peter Vitouch is Associate Professor at the Insitute for Psychology, the University of Vienna. His major fields of interests are physiological psychology, learning theories, social psychology and mass communication. In 1975 Vitouch was appointed a psychology consultant to the Austrian Broadcasting Company (ORF) on pre-school broadcasts which he continued until 1980 on his appointment as a member of the scientific board of the Northern Germany Broadcasting Company (NDR).

Professor Scott Ward (United States)

Scott Ward is Professor of Marketing at the Wharton school (University of Pennsylvania) and Senior Research Associate at the Marketing Science Institute, a non-profit research center in Cambridge Mass. Prior to

Wharton, Ward taught at Harvard Business School (1970-1980) and the University of Washington. Professor Ward has published over 70 articles and monographs in the area of advertising and children, and testified before the FTC and the FCC on several occasions, incuding the FTC's 1972 Hearings on Modern Advertising Practices. His earlier books include How Children Learn to Buy (with D.B. Wackman and Ellen Wartella), Consumer Behaviour: Theoretical Sources (with T.S. Robertson) and Advances in Consumer Research (with P. Wright). Processor Ward's current research interests are in the area of marketing strategy and customer behaviour. His most recent publication is "Marketing Stragegy Under Deregulation" (with T.S. Robertson), published in Harvard Business Review.

He is a member of several organisations, such as the American Marketing Association and the Association for Consumer Research, and serves on the Editorial Boards of the Journal of Consumer Research, the Journal of Advertising Research, and the Journal of Marketing Research. He is also a member of the Advisory Board for the Children's Review Unit of the Naional Council of Better Business Bureaus, and has sat on the boards of 3 corporations.

Kaj Wickbom (Sweden)

As both a political scientist at Lund University and Director of the mass media education department at Vaxjo Katedralskola, Kaj Wickbom has gained wide experience in critical assessment of mass media techniques. On behalf of the Swedish Naional Board of Education, he is currently working on a nine year pilot project training students to understand mass media and the education process.

His books include: Proposal for a curriculum of Media Knowledge (1980) and Media Knowledge - Changes and Perspectives (1984).

Eric Williams (United Kingdom)

Eric Williams works as an education advisor with the County of Avon (West of England) Education Department. In this capacity, Williams is responsible for the media education in 7-18 age range including examination courses, teacher training programme, materials and collaboration with the local broadcasting agencies.

Dr. Brian M Young (United Kingdom)

Brian Young is lecturer in the Department of Sociological and Anthropological Sciences at the University of Salford. From 1966-1969 he researched into cognitive and linguistic development at the University of Edinburgh and then spent seven years lecturing at Hong Kong University where he developed an interest in cross-cultural psychology.

An initial interest in the psychology of leisure developed into several research programmes in media psychology. Dr. Brown is presently working on a Health Education Council project on children and the television advertising of sugared products. Future research in 1985 will be into the development of advertising literacy and the development psychology of rhetoric.